Yorùbá Art and Aesthetics

Bloomsbury Introductions to World Philosophies

Series Editor:
Monika Kirloskar-Steinbach

Assistant Series Editor:
Leah Kalmanson

Regional Editors:
Nader El-Bizri, James Madaio, Ann A. Pang-White,
Takeshi Morisato, Pascah Mungwini, Mickaella Perina,
Omar Rivera and Georgina Stewart

Bloomsbury Introductions to World Philosophies delivers primers
reflecting exciting new developments in the trajectory of world
philosophies. Instead of privileging a single philosophical approach
as the basis of comparison, the series provides a platform for diverse
philosophical perspectives to accommodate the different dimensions
of cross-cultural philosophizing. While introducing thinkers, texts
and themes emanating from different world philosophies, each book,
in an imaginative and path-breaking way, makes clear how it departs
from a conventional treatment of the subject matter.

Titles in the Series:
A Practical Guide to World Philosophies,
by Monika Kirloskar-Steinbach and Leah Kalmanson
Daya Krishna and Twentieth-Century Indian Philosophy,
by Daniel Raveh
Māori Philosophy, by Georgina Tuari Stewart
Philosophy of Science and The Kyoto School, by Dean Anthony Brink

Tanabe Hajime and the Kyoto School, by Takeshi Morisato
African Philosophy, by Pascah Mungwini
The Zen Buddhist Philosophy of D. T. Suzuki, by Rossa Ó Muireartaigh
Sikh Philosophy, by Arvind-Pal Singh Mandair
The Philosophy of the Brahma-sūtra, by Aleksandar Uskokov
The Philosophy of the Yogasūtra, by Karen O'Brien-Kop
The Life and Thought of H. Odera Oruka, by Gail M. Presbey
Mexican Philosophy for the 21st Century, by Carlos Alberto Sánchez
Buddhist Ethics and the Bodhisattva Path, by Stephen Harris
Contextualizing Angela Davis, by Joy James

Yorùbá Art and Aesthetics

Methodologies and Their Consequences

Barry Hallen

BLOOMSBURY ACADEMIC

LONDON • NEW YORK • OXFORD • NEW DELHI • SYDNEY

BLOOMSBURY ACADEMIC
Bloomsbury Publishing Plc
50 Bedford Square, London, WC1B 3DP, UK
1385 Broadway, New York, NY 10018, USA
29 Earlsfort Terrace, Dublin 2, Ireland

BLOOMSBURY, BLOOMSBURY ACADEMIC and the Diana logo
are trademarks of Bloomsbury Publishing Plc

First published in Great Britain 2025

ISBN: HB: 978-1-3504-7611-0
          PB: 978-1-3504-7610-3
        ePDF: 978-1-3504-7612-7
       eBook: 978-1-3504-7613-4

Typeset by Integra Software Services Pvt. Ltd.
Printed and bound in Great Britain

Carla

Contents

Illustrations

Colour Plates

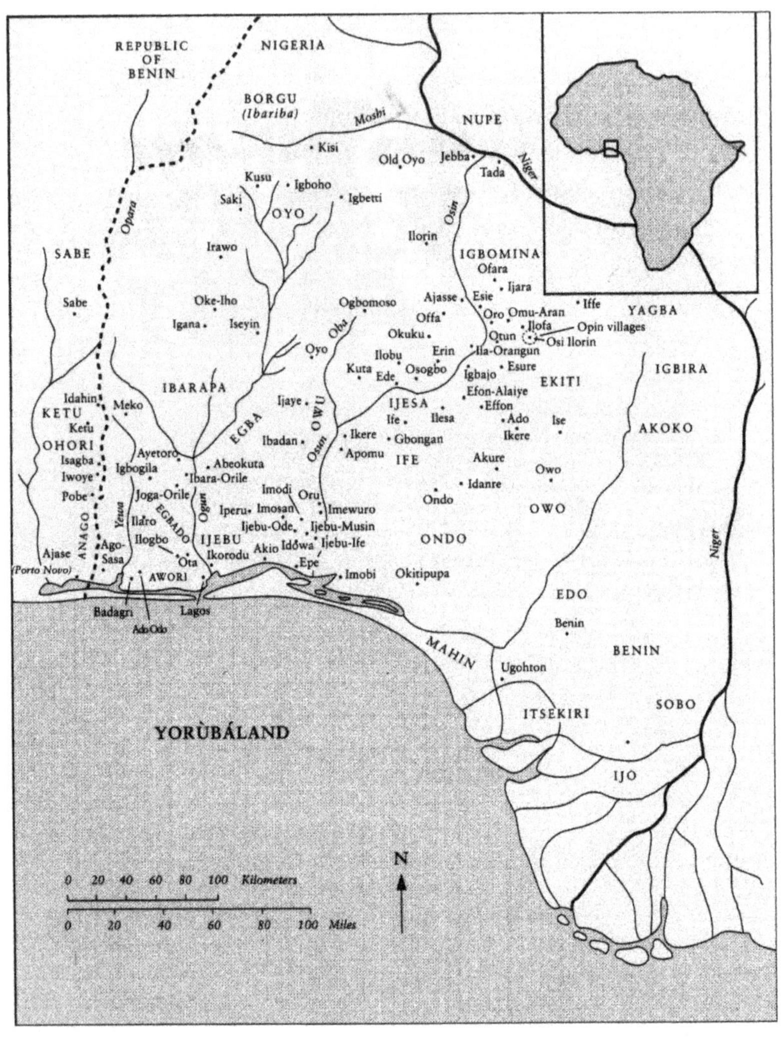

Map of Yorùbáland (Rowland Abiodun, *Yoruba Art and Language*, Cambridge University Press, 2014; Reproduced with permission of the Licensor through PLSclear.)

Series Editor's Preface

The introductions we include in the World Philosophies series take a single thinker, theme or text and provide a close reading of them. What defines the series is that these are likely to be people or traditions that you have not yet encountered in your study of philosophy. By choosing to include them you broaden your understanding of ideas about the self, knowledge and the world around us. Each book presents unexplored pathways into the study of world philosophies. Instead of privileging a single philosophical approach as the basis of comparison, each book accommodates the many different dimensions of cross-cultural philosophizing. While the choice of terms used by the individual volumes may indeed carry a local inflection, they encourage critical thinking about philosophical plurality. Each book strikes a balance between locality and globality.

In *Yorùbá Art and Aesthetics: Methodologies and Their Consequences*, Barry Hallen considers whether the methodologies employed by scholars to study the art and aesthetics of an African culture have facilitated or impeded correct understanding of their subject matter. The resulting methodological recipe's positive ingredients include insights gained from an analysis of work from social anthropology (J.R.O. Ojo), art history (Babatunde Lawal, Robert Farris Thompson and Rowland Abiodun), metaphysics (Lawal, Abiodun and Wole Soyinka) and epistemology (Abiodun, Hallen, Soyinka). All also wrestle with the problems involved in using the English language as a vehicle for expressing the forms and meanings of a non-Eurocentric culture.

If these ingredients are properly digested, the taster-reader will grasp, Hallen hopes, that to experience Yorùbá art practices they should work upon themselves to properly understand the values that inform a Yorùbá community. Only then will they be able to understand how Yorùbá artists lean upon the insights of their culture to create art objects that invite community members to reflect upon the relation of the metaphysical and the physical worlds.

Yorùbá Art and Aesthetics promises to be a vital contribution to Yorùbá philosophy. In many ways, it is a culmination of Barry Hallen's scholarship on the Yorùbá. Hallen has worked tirelessly over decades to illustrate how Eurocentric categories can facilitate or impede a philosophical engagement with African philosophy.

Monika Kirloskar-Steinbach

Acknowledgments

Without the enduring encouragement of Rowland Abiodun, a friend I first made at Great Ifẹ, this little book would not have been written. Another Great Ifẹ veteran, Janet Stanley, now of the Smithsonian Institution, enabled my access to many of the publications that became foundational to telling the stories that follow. Art historian Nancy Neaher-Maas, who visited Great Ifẹ, has also been there as commentator and critic throughout. I am grateful to Susan Meller for her expertise and counsel involving the reproduction of images.

The late Frank Speed, another friend and colleague of Great Ifẹ days, was, even then, famous for his photos of the cultures of Nigeria. Unfortunately, for too many years, they remained inaccessible to scholars and the general public. The absolutely extraordinary efforts of his daughter, Louise, and family resulted in my having access to the collection of 2,500 still photos that now have their place in the archives of The British Library. I found the Speed collection to be stunning and highly recommend it as a source to other researchers. John Picton, distinguished art historian, graciously gave me access to his ideas and photo archives and I thank him, most sincerely, for his contributions.

Then there are the friends and colleagues who in various ways helped with the composition of this text. Among them are Lea Abiodun (Great Ifẹ), Akin Aboderin (Great Ifẹ), Karin Barber (Great Ifẹ), Nicholas Beaulieu, Lanre Bickersteth (Great Ifẹ), Bolaji Campbell (Great Ifẹ), Luis Chu, Min Dahn, Carolyne Dennis (Great Ifẹ), Mary Hamer, Robin Horton (Great Ifẹ), Monika Kirloskar-Steinbach, Roger Makanjuola (Great Ifẹ), D. A. Masolo, Alessandro Morelli, Jill Nicklin, Keith Nicklin, Eric Okoh (Great Ifẹ), Segun Osoba (Great Ifẹ), Darien Pollock, Margaret Renner, 'Femi Taiwo (Great Ifẹ), Rich Wilschke, and www.cdbstudio.com. At Bloomsbury Academic my thanks to Colleen Coalter (Senior Publisher), Aimee Brown (Editorial Assistant) and

Darcy Ahl (Project Manager) for guiding me through the process of transforming manuscript into text.

My time at Great Ifẹ̀ inspired and sustained a remarkable intellectual journey. I hope this text gives some indication of why that was the case.

Finally, appreciation to the institutional sources that have been so kind as to facilitate the inclusion of materials that are under their jurisdiction:

Hallen, Barry. 1979. "The Art Historian as Conceptual Analyst." *Journal of Aesthetics and Art Criticism* 37, no. 3 (Spring): 303–13 [Chapter 4].

Hallen, Barry. 2021. "African Sculpture: Interrelating the Verbal and Visual in Yorùbá Aesthetics." In *Philosophy of Sculpture: Historical Problems, Contemporary Approaches*, 93–110. New York and London: Routledge; reproduced with permission of The Licensor through PLSclear [Chapter 6].

Picton, John. "Art Identity, and Identification: A Commentary on Yorùbá Art Historical Studies, Postscript 2 [excerpt from]." In *The Yoruba Artist: New Theoretical Perspectives on African Art*, edited by R. Abiodun, H. J. Drewal and J. Pemberton III. Washington and London: Smithsonian Institution Press [Addendum].

Thompson, Robert Farris. 1973. "Yorùbá Artistic Criticism." In *The Traditional Artist in African Societies*, edited by Warren d'Azevedo, 19–61. Bloomington: Indiana University Press; reprinted with permission of Indiana University Press [Chapter 3].

Introduction

There is a university in West Africa popularly known as Great Ifẹ̀. It is located in the town of Ilé-Ifẹ̀, Osun State, Nigeria. Today its official title is Obafemi Awolowo University. It attracted the appellation "Great Ifẹ̀" because of a conviction on the part of staff/faculty and students that it was committed to achieving all of the great things that a university community can. The four scholars whose work on Yorùbá art history constitutes the basis for this text were colleagues there and contributed to that greatness. In the opinion of the writer there has been a sin of omission in that they have been treated as independent scholars whose ideas are rarely interrelated. The thesis of this little book is that the writings of the four can be used to complement and supplement one another. When combined they offer a better and higher level of understanding of that remarkable and fascinating form of life associated with the name "Yorùbá."

With reference to African Studies generally, in the early stages Africans found themselves having to contend with foreign scholars who behaved as if they understood their cultures as much or better than Africans themselves. This hinged on these scholars' training in disciplinary methodologies that were said to be foundational to objective inter-cultural understanding. But no matter how insightful the accounts of the foreign scholars proved to be, many Africans who were native to their cultures felt there was still a gap, a distance between foreigners and Africa's cultures, that limited their understanding.

As the Ọọ̀ni, the traditional ruler of Ifẹ̀, once had occasion to remark: "We are the ones who will tell our story by ourselves" (https://www. cnn.com/2017/03/29/africa). The four African scholars whose work is discussed in this text are products of their native Yorùbá culture. In their writings they share a concern to make us understand their culture and the place of art in it better than has been done before. They do not engage in polemics. They go to extraordinary lengths to patiently, painstakingly provide insights and material that will enable us to have a better understanding of Yorùbá culture. Also, as the title of this little book indicates, they want us to understand that the Yorùbá, as Africans, do not represent a different type of human being. They are people with a different culture, but they are not people who evidence differences that make them somehow subordinate or the "Other" to human beings in the rest of the world.

J. R. O. Ojo (Chapter 1) begins by telling us he will use his training in social anthropology, the discipline responsible for labeling Africa's cultures as primitive, to prove that the people of his own culture, the Yorùbá, are not primitive. He is unhappy with objects being removed from the culture for acquisition by international collectors and thereby transformed into "art" that has no role to play apart from being collected and labeled ritualistic or traditional. Relevant Yorùbá-language terminology and oral texts are ignored and the culture that created them is portrayed as incapable of expressing the reasons for their existence. In fact these objects have histories and the society that gave birth to them is constantly undergoing processes of creative innovation.

Babatunde Lawal (Chapter 2), art historian, argues that the way to approach the culture and its art is to understand the Yorùbá cosmos and the metaphysical principles that govern it. He does this by bringing its deities, its masques, its artists and their audiences to life. He illuminates the principle of Selective Realism that Yorùbá artists have worked with from time immemorial that explains why a wide variety of art forms range from the lifelike or natural to the highly stylized.

Robert Farris Thompson (Chapter 3), an American art historian who became famous for his early work on Yorùbá aesthetics, is one of two expatriates whose work is also considered in this text. With hindsight there is something innocent about the way he visits various towns and villages, putting a selection of carvings on display and asking Yorùbá bystanders to comment on them. That helps to explain why the aesthetic criteria he induces from those circumstances are later challenged by Yorùbá scholars who turn to the culture's rich and complex heritage of oral literature as a more informative source.

The other expatriate, Barry Hallen (Chapter 4), was in the Department of Philosophy at Great Ifẹ. He was involved in research relating to the epistemological system underlying Yorùbá discourse that is used to rate the reliability of information. That leads him to undertake an examination of Thompson's findings from a methodological point of view. He finds various assumptions that Thompson makes unwarranted and published this essay detailing those criticisms.

Rowland Abiodun and Babatunde Lawal (Chapter 5), both art historians in the Department of Fine Arts at Great Ifẹ, independently conducted their own research on Yorùbá aesthetic criteria. As "insiders" or native to the culture, their access to a variety of sources enables them to make a compelling case for the aesthetic criteria they present as supplementary and alternative to Thompson's own.

With his work on Yorùbá artists and the qualities that distinguish the exceptional among them, art historian Rowland Abiodun (Chapter 6) offers important insights into the aesthetic foundations of the culture. His work on relationships between the verbal and the visual opens the door to a new appreciation of the epistemology underlying its art. Nobel Prize winner Wole Soyinka (also Chapter 6) is an international figure of literary renown. It is a testament to Great Ifẹ that he too was associated with the university at a time when he was producing important work related to the understanding of Yorùbá art and aesthetics. Soyinka's essay, "The Fourth Stage," provides extraordinary insights into the existential foundations of artistic creation in Yorùbá culture. There seem to be fruitful overlaps between Abiodun and Soyinka on these subjects and that is reason enough to put them in the same chapter so as to explore the interrelations that may enhance understanding of both.

This is a little book and the writer will not be surprised if the colleagues whose writings are discussed are disappointed that their work is not treated at greater length or in greater detail. But the author's background is in philosophy and that is good reason for him to limit his focus to the kinds of argumentation—the methodologies—that distinguish each of the four. That proves to be appropriate because a consistent aim of the scholars concerned is to demonstrate the rational or reasoned basis of Yorùbá art and aesthetics. Each chapter endeavors to provide a methodological "taste" of the person(s) concerned followed by select examples of the consequences of their methodology when applied. The hope is that the "tastes" will motivate readers to then have more serious encounters with the bodies of their work. All of them have produced substantial books and articles that are listed in the individualized and supplementary bibliographies provided.

1

We Are Not Primitive

J. R. O. Ojo[*]

Introduction

On his CV under Professional Accomplishments J. R. O. Ojo lists "Correcting some mistaken notions in the study of African Art and the opening of new vistas." Ojo tells us there was a time when identifying oneself to African colleagues as an anthropologist could be problematic. Because of the continuing outrage at that discipline's use of the category of the "primitive" to characterize the subcontinent's societies and cultures, there were universities there that avoided the subject in their teaching programs. Ojo is well aware of the animosity[1] and it is important to appreciate that his overall aim is to use the methodologies of anthropology to redeem the discipline by proving that both the "primitive" and, later less obviously pejorative, "traditional" labels when applied to Yorùbá culture, in particular, are inaccurate.[2]

Ojo's area of specialization is "art" and, at the outset, some things he has to come to terms with are the problems caused by that English-language term when applied to many of the objects produced by the cultures of Africa. He begins by arguing that "Art is a category word which originated in Western cultural tradition, expressing an

---

[*] J. R. O. Ojo's academic career at Great Ifẹ̀ began in 1966 when he was appointed Research Fellow in Art and Art History. He was awarded the M.Phil. in Social Anthropology from London University in 1974. The title of his thesis was *Ẹpa and Related Masquerades among the Èkìtì Yorùbá of Western Nigeria*. The methodology enunciated and practiced in it would be foundational to the "corrections" and "new vistas" he would proceed to make for the study of African art.

exclusively Western idea" (1982, 200). To understand what he means, consider the definition of "art" that one finds in the *Oxford Dictionary* which is, after all, a dictionary of the *English* language and therefore of the *meanings* of words in *that* language: "the expression or application of human creative skill and imagination, typically in a visual form such as painting or sculpture, producing *works to be appreciated primarily for their beauty or emotional power*" (https://www.oed.com; my emphasis).

African objects have been transformed into "art" after being valued and appropriated by Eurocentric art historians, displayed in Eurocentric art galleries, and sought after by Eurocentric art collectors. In those settings the objects are showcased and applauded for their visual properties—their form, their unfamiliar beauty:

> the [African] objects labeled: "art" are not art by design but by metamorphosis …. African ritual objects have been metamorphosed into art by those who are historically and geographically distant from the users and makers. This transformation was meant originally for Eurocentric eyes, but it carries the assumption that it is also art for the African.
>
> (Ojo 1982, 219)

In fact these objects have been extracted (some would say "torn") from social and cultural contexts where they may serve religious or political ends.

> Consequently, in any consideration of the study of "African art", the European concept is inadequate. Other societies [than the West, including Africa] have concepts determined by their own culture and expressed in linguistic conventions familiar to members of that culture. The translation of these concepts into a foreign language may pose problems which can only be solved by familiarity with the world of thought expressed [by them].
>
> (1982, 202)

There are objects created in the cultures of Africa that are meant to be appreciated purely for their visual properties (1982, 201). But that is not generally the case with those selected, collected and promoted as "art" by Eurocentric interests. The objects that end up in their galleries and collections may have aesthetic properties, but that was not the reason for their creation:[3]

> kings scepters range from shafts shaped like an ordinary rod to elaborately decorated gold objects which raise these objects to the level of aesthetic objects, but not in the sense of art for art's sake.
>
> (1982, 204)

Ẹpa Ceremonies in *Èkítí*

Arriving at correct understandings of these objects will also involve a linguistic exercise: "we must disentangle African art from Eurocentric categories by exploring indigenous concepts" (Ojo 1992, x).

> foreigners often are not willing to learn about African languages and cultures in detail and so end up making the *forms* of the objects the basis for appreciating them as "art."
>
> (Ojo 1982, 203; my emphasis)

In his own work he will begin to do this with the aforementioned *Ẹpa* masks of Yorùbá culture. Ojo is pressing a reset button to indicate he will use social anthropology to return many of the objects Eurocentric interests treat as "African art" to their original social and cultural contexts so we can understand and appreciate them as they were meant to be. "The African art object ... must be examined ... as something deriving its significance and meaning from its place in a living culture" (1982, 204).

In order to make sense of Ojo's fieldwork on the *Ẹpa* masquerades, background information involving a bit of the geography and history of Yorùbáland will be helpful. Among sub-Saharan peoples the Yorùbá are distinguished by the fact theirs has long been a culture that featured cities.

> The flowers of the Yorùbá settlements are their remarkable urban centres, unparalleled anywhere else in tropical Africa. This urbanism is a feature which has characterized Yorùbá culture as far back as knowledge goes.
>
> (Ojo 1966, 104–5)[4]

As Bascom noted in 1955, "the Yorùbá have six cities of more than 100,000" (1955, 446).[5] The Yorùbá themselves are also somewhat culturally and linguistically diverse. They are described as composed of a number of subcultures with their distinctive dialects of the language. The area of southwestern Nigeria where they are principally located is conventionally divided up among the following groups: "the Ọ̀yọ́, Ẹ̀gbà, Ẹ̀gbádò, Ìjẹ̀bú, Ijẹ̀ṣà, Èkítí, Oǹdó, Àkókó, and Ọ̀wọ̀" (Ajayi and Akintoye 1980, 281). *Ẹpa* masquerades are to be found in the Èkítí area of northern Yorùbáland. Their monumental masks are now well known in Eurocentric artistic circles.[6]

Exploring the functions and meanings of these masks internal to the culture is something that a social anthropologist, especially one native to the culture and fluent in the language, should be qualified to do. An immediate complication Ojo must face is that his mother discipline, anthropology, has classified Yorùbá as a *traditional* culture and traditional cultures are defined by an *inability to explain* their *rituals* and *symbols*—in this case *masquerades* and *masks*—in a reasoned or edifying manner. That Eurocentric anthropologists and art historians have said this about "rituals" and "ritual objects" in Yorùbá culture is evidenced by the following:

> The ethnographer has often to face the problem of interpreting symbols or symbolic acts which, within their [Yorùbá] culture, exist without a sanctioning explanation. He must consequently decipher and explain discursively what the native intuitively perceives and responds to. In seeking to discover what significance such a symbol has …. we have interpreted a symbol for which the Yorùbá can offer no explanation … *their meaning is not perceived in rational terms*, and the worshippers were only able to describe its use.
>
> (Wescott and Morton-Williams 1962, 23; my emphasis; paragraphs elided)

Such an attitude legitimizes the foreign observer—be it anthropologist or art historian—to speak on behalf of a "traditional" culture because a defining attribute of such cultures is that, when their members are asked to explain or justify fundamental beliefs and practices, they can only reply along the lines of "This is what we inherited from the forefathers." In other words, such explanations and justifications themselves amount to little more than an appeal to tradition. But this does little or nothing to explain the rationale behind the actual belief or practice. There are therefore three foundational characteristics that are associated with traditional systems of thought when their members are asked to explain or justify their social institutions, social practices, beliefs or attitudes towards beliefs (these latter two also somehow social in scale). The first is that they are *significantly connected with the past.* The second is that there has been a *notable lack of innovation or change* in such practices or beliefs since originally introduced. The third is that beliefs and practices are more clearly and more easily *identified and understood by fieldworkers via observation and analysis of behavior* rather than information provided by informants or direct discourse internal to the culture (Hallen 2006, 293–4).

Ojo will begin his critique of the adjective "traditional" when applied to Yorùbá culture by challenging the generalization that the Yorùbá are unable to express the reasons for *Ẹpa* masks and masquerades. It may be helpful to start by clarifying the meanings of key concepts that will be involved. Eurocentric anthropologists and art historians classify African masquerades as *rituals*. What does use of that English-language term imply? Here is one Eurocentric authority on the subject: "By 'ritual' I mean prescribed formal behavior for occasions ... having reference to beliefs in mystical beings or powers (Turner 1967, 19)."[7] "Formal behavior" means that for a *ritual* to be a ritual the proceedings must follow a prescribed pattern or order. The reference to mystical beings or powers means otherworldly forces are somehow involved with or targeted by those proceedings. One wonders why anthropologists use the English-language word "mystical" when non-Eurocentric cultures are involved. Why not say simply that they are "religious" in inspiration or design?

To make the meaning of "ritual" even more clear, let's involve the term with a ceremony that is familiar to most people. Does a wedding, the event of two people getting married, qualify as ritual? Weddings do seem to involve a certain amount of required or prescribed behavior: there must be two people who want to be legally (and perhaps spiritually) joined and thereby signify their commitment to one another; there must be an agency of some sort (priest, official, family) that officiates and legitimizes the ceremony; there must be some form of witness to the proceedings; the ceremony must therefore proceed in a certain way—it has a beginning, middle and end. Depending upon the families' and individuals' religious affiliations, there may or may not be a spiritual (mystical?) dimension to the proceedings. All of this does seem to indicate there is an essential pattern that must be followed, and that wedding ceremonies can qualify as rituals. But people in Eurocentric cultures don't talk about their wedding *rituals*. They talk about their wedding *ceremonies*. In fact people in Eurocentric cultures hardly ever talk about rituals.

That masquerade ceremonies follow prescribed patterns and thereby qualify as rituals is documented in detail in Olajubu and Ojo (1977): advance notice is given to the community that a masquerade will take place at a point in time; there are special proceedings just before it begins; on the first day the masquerade is welcomed by the community; and on subsequent days (that may become months) different kinds of performances occur; before, finally, the concluding ceremonies in which the masquerade bids the community farewell (1977, 264–8; Ojo 1981, 46). With respect to the role of *ritual* in cultures generally, it is noteworthy that the term occurs much more frequently in literature associated with Africa than it does in literature associated with Eurocentric cultures. One wonders whether that indicates some sort of rhetorical value judgment is involved in its use.

The masks worn by the performers in many forms of African masquerades are treated as *symbols* by Eurocentric anthropologists and art historians. Here is the way the same source defines that term: "The symbol is the *smallest unit of ritual* which still retains the *specific properties* of ritual behavior; it is the *ultimate unit of specific structure* in a ritual context (Turner 1967, 19; my emphasis)." In which case there is something very special about an object, the mask, if it is identified as a symbol or as symbolic in and of a ritual. It is apparently then said to incarnate and manifest the (mystical?) essence, the substance, of the entire ritual or masquerade. When Eurocentric anthropologists and art historians did this to the masks that feature in Yorùbá masquerades, their importance and value dramatically increased. There is no question this contributed to their elevation to objects deserving of gallery and collector status, and to their eventually being assigned monetary values that have become inconceivable to their culture of origin.

Ojo begins his own analysis of all this by refining the English-language terminology he will use to apply to these events. The masks are no longer to be seen as supremely significant components of the so-called masquerades. In fact it might even be better if the proceedings are now described as *ceremonies* (1978, 455) or *festivals* (1998, 444) so that they are no longer immediately associated with an English-language word—"*masquerades*"—that itself involves the word "mask." Rather than the objects involved, what is and should be most important for the communities where these events take place are the *overall ceremonies* themselves. Ojo therefore at points does appear to prefer avoiding the words "mask" and "masquerade" altogether, and replacing them with English-language alternatives like "headpieces"[8] and "ceremonies."[9] Rhetorical deconstruction is further enhanced when it turns out that in Yorùbá discourse the bases of *Epa* headpieces are described as "inverted cooking pots ... referred to as *kokò*, pot, in some towns" (1978, 456; quoting Carroll 1956, 5).

Yorùbá-language articulations of the meanings of the headpieces become particularly relevant when he tells us that on top of the "cooking pots" are the carved superstructures that make these objects of interest to Eurocentric art. They involve "three sets of sculptural motifs (Ojo 1978, 458)" that the Yorùbá *use their language to name*. "The individual names of the headpieces are based on the motifs" on the superstructures (1978, 456; quoting Carroll 1956, 7). These *names* and many more occur in *songs* and *other verbal utterances* during the ceremonies in which the headpieces are used. This *discourse* provides "invaluable clues to the *elucidation* of the *symbolism* and *significance* of the headpieces" (1978, 456; my emphasis). This indicates a level of indigenous conceptualization that one would not expect to find in a culture that is typed as "traditional."

Furthermore, citing the work of Erwin Panofsky (1970), Ojo argues that each of the three forms is associated by the Yorùbá with *specific social concerns* that can also be documented:

> I will now discuss three sets of sculptural motifs from the superstructures of *Ẹpa* masquerade headpieces. These are: mother-with-child or children motifs which can be linked with *the desire among the Yorùbá for plentiful issue*; equestrian motifs which I will link with the *turbulent history of Èkítí and Igbómìnà in the nineteenth century*; and thirdly, motifs based on Ọ̀sanyìn, the deity *associated with medicine*.
>
> (1978, 458; my emphasis)

The mother-with-child *named* headpieces (Ọlọmọyeye, Ọlọmọyọyọ)[10] articulate the importance the society attaches to the bearing of children. Let's take a closer look at the evidence and argumentation Ojo presents for this: names and other forms of verbal expression in the Yorùbá language associated with the mother-with-child motifs (1978, 460); associated songs and dances of women involved with the ceremony in the Yorùbá language that can amount to prayers asking for children (1978, 460–1); the social status and behavior of women who are unable to bear children (1978, 461); positive social responses to the birth of twins (1978, 459); the shrines of deities relevant to the bearing of children in Yorùbáland (1978, 460); studies of family structures and values in the society (1978, 459).

The equestrian motifs (Ológun, Jagunjagun)[11] reflect the possibility that armed conflict can become a concern and that there will be a need for combatants to engage in defense of a community. That these motifs relate to armed conflict is indicated by their association with Ògún, the god of war; by "the participation of the warrior age grade carrying weapons of war; by the names of the headpieces; by the singing of war songs; the beating of war drums and the playing of piccolos (ọyẹ) and deer horn trumpets (ekutu). The last two instruments and the war drums were played in times past during battles" (1978, 462). In addition he provides a historical summary of armed conflicts involving the Èkítí that helps to explain why this became an important concern for the region.

The Ọ̀sanyìn (deity associated with medicine) motif articulates "*Ẹpa* as a giver of physical and spiritual health and welfare" (1978, 467; Ojo 1981, 46). That these headpieces are associated with health is indicated by the fact that they depict a priest of that deity[12] "holding an iron staff ornamented with birds and bells in one hand; and in the other, an antelope horn stuffed with *oògùn*, medicine" (Ojo 1978, 466). These priests are known as *oníṣẹ̀gùn*, masters of medicine, and participate in the ceremony while music and songs associated with the deity and good health are performed (1978, 467).

That the headpieces involved are explicitly identified with specific social concerns indicates these are not situations where the communities involved have continued to perform the ceremonies simply because "this is what we inherited from the forefathers." They continue to perform them because *the social concerns they involve and express are current*, are things that matter in the present day. If this is the case, describing them as *ceremonies* rather than *rituals* seems appropriate. This is not to deny there may be elements of their culture that the Yorùbá are unable to express or explain in a reasoned manner. That can be true of human beings in any culture in the world. The point is that it not be taken as typical or definitive of Yorùbá culture.

The methodologies Ojo uses to argue for this revised understanding of *Ẹpa* are complex. He employs several forms of language analysis, supplemented by observation in the sense in which it is conventional for fieldwork studies and, finally, more generalized in-depth sociological studies of Yorùbáland and its history. One false Eurocentric impression of African masquerades is that they are not verbal in a significant manner. But most Yorùbá masquerades do involve more than non-verbal behavior. Masqueraders talk and sing, their accompanying ensembles of musicians do so as well, and the people of the community often become verbally involved in the performance. One level of language analysis is therefore devoted to detailing the explicitly articulated names, songs, and poetry associated with *Ẹpa*.

At this point some might ask, if this is or was a substantially oral culture, what effect does that have on the form as well as the content of this orature? "Orature" is a much needed term, comparable to "literature," that can be used to describe the variety of texts found in a significantly oral culture. If it is the case that an oral culture preserves its texts in people's memories, does this affect the manner in which they are recorded and expressed? In literate cultures the process of writing a text down does seem to transform it so that it acquires certain attributes. Texts become spatially bounded, with relatively fixed content, beginnings and ends (Derrida 1976).

Olabiyi Yai, a scholar of Yorùbá orature, characterizes "the oral text as a result of uninterrupted production" (1989: 63). What he means is that it would be misleading to characterize the oral texts involved with these ceremonies as fixed and unchanging. Each performance or occurrence is also in part an ongoing process of creation.[13] Ojo as well tells us again and again that "patterns of performance vary from township to township" (Olajubu and Ojo 1977, 265).[14] The social concerns expressed by these ceremonies/masquerades are made clear, but the precise manner in which those meanings are elaborated can vary.

On another level Ojo experiments with a view of language that involves treating the objects and behavior associated with the *Ẹpa* ceremonies as *signs*. To do this he involves semiotics (Saussure 1966). The name "semiotics" is derived from the Greek word for "signs" and, as with "ritual" and "symbol," "sign" is another term that needs clarification. According to this approach, in addition to words, human beings use *objects* like the headpieces and other elements of the *Ẹpa* ceremonies to *communicate meanings* in a different way.

> I have suggested that carved masquerade headpieces (so called masks), with sculpted representations, associated artifacts (both natural and manufactured), drums and drum rhythms, dances, songs, mimetic acts, and people who take part in the rituals can be treated as a system of mixed semiotics in which each of the elements enumerated above gives us a clue to the significance of the headpieces.
>
> (Ojo 1979, 338)

While this form of analysis might seem to restore the headpieces to symbolic glory, what it actually does is acknowledge the role they do play in the meanings of these ceremonies. Their "artistic" (art for art's sake) status has been bracketed but, as the objects they are, they have been reinstated into proceedings whose overall purpose is to address deities and/or express indigenous priorities relating to a particular social concern. Along with the other components of the ceremonies, Ojo sees them as "icons, representations of and stimulus for religious and cosmological ideas, with immanent and transcendent meanings" (1982, 203–4).

As for fieldwork, his research (M.Phil.) and publications are replete with detailed participant observations of *Ẹpa* ceremonies all over Èkítí. On the sociological level he draws upon relevant background studies by various authorities related to the concerns and contexts underlying these three types of *Ẹpa* ceremonies. In the case of the mother-with-child ceremonies, in particular, this is indicated by his references to the status of barren women in the society; the shrines of deities relevant to the bearing of children; and studies of Yorùbá family values and structure.

Ojo concludes his discussions of *Ẹpa* by challenging yet another supposed characteristic of traditional cultures if applied to these Yorùbá festivals when they are classified as *rituals involving the mystical*. This is that when one of these ceremonies takes place, in some *magical* manner, what is represented as the desired outcome actually happens there and then simply because the ceremony has been performed: women will start to bear children; a town's defenses are reinforced; overall health is improved:

> It could be said of the Èkítí and the Yorùbá in general, that *religious* rituals are not ends in themselves but preludes to the pragmatic or technical solution of problems. For them then, such rituals are not therefore magic formulae for the solution of problems. It is recognized that performing rituals in order to seek help from *superhuman entities* is one thing, and *seeking a rational solution* is another.
>
> (1978, 466; my emphasis)

Communicating with the divine—religion—is one thing. Instigating practical, pragmatic, "this-worldly" measures to achieve those ends requires different kinds of actions. This is not to deny that there may be elements of the culture that involve magical beliefs (1978, 466–7). That can be true of people anywhere in the world. The point is that the belief in magic should not be taken as typical or definitive of Yorùbá culture.

Egúngún Ceremonies from *Ọ̀yó*

As a social anthropologist, one of Ojo's special interests is the objects that have been recast as African "art" by Eurocentric cultures. As part of the process of restoring the masks that feature in Yorùbá masquerades to their true role, Ojo undertakes detailed studies of the basic social concerns that give rise to these events in the culture. In the course of his fieldwork he makes additional discoveries about them that are relevant to the way in which the culture records its history.

According to the model of traditional culture, once a belief or practice is adopted it tends to remain in force, unchanged, for the indefinite future. Because change is discouraged, the historical consciousness of people in such cultures is said to be diminished. Their idea of time is cyclical rather than linear, in an atmosphere where events like the same masquerade ceremonies, which in part define the passage of time, are repeated over and over again. Ojo does not become involved in the cyclical versus linear time controversy on an explicitly metaphysical level. However, in the essay, "Doing Year," he explains how time is managed in the culture in one specific year. In communities where agriculture is a primary concern, climate is an important determinant of the festival timetable. If the rains are late (or early), that is likely to affect when the community will find it convenient to celebrate its festivals. There can be political or other economic developments that would have similar consequences. This demonstrates a temporal flexibility on the part of the Yorùbá, and also that there are always *reasons* for changes in the masquerade timetable (1996, 33).

He continues by pointing out that the terminology and orature associated with certain masquerade performances provides more explicit evidence of the conscious recognition of historical change on the part of the communities involved. "In practice, therefore, the festival often achieves more than mere religious expression and has material that can be an important source for the reconstruction of Yorùbá history *once the idiom is understood*" (Ogunba 1973, 88; my emphasis). This involves appreciation of a past that involved transformations and a future that may as well. Ojo will argue that such changes may involve innovation as well as modification, up to and including the introduction or even creation of new masquerades.

> The structure of a Yorùbá festival is usually such as to accommodate and integrate easily subsequent experience, apart from the fact that new festivals are established from time to time. The result, therefore, is that as one goes through the ceremonies of a typical Yorùbá community it is as if one is going through time itself with the dark past suddenly being illuminated and the present teeming with life.
>
> (Ogunba 1973, 108–9)

To ground his arguments for a historical consciousness on empirical evidence, Ojo turns to diffusion theory (Ojo 1974b; 1976). It has been established that Yorùbá culture overall is composed of a number of subgroups. Diffusionism suggests that cultural similarities between such subgroups may arise because they have copied or adopted things from one another rather than invented them independently and entirely on their own. Ojo favors a qualified form of the theory, as practiced by the anthropologists Franz Boas (1938; 1948) and S. F. Nadel (1951). Boas "advocated the plotting of distribution of traits in small contiguous areas …. He could only assume contact in geographically proximate areas" (Ojo 1974b, 317). This suits Ojo because the subcultures of Yorùbáland are contiguous and geographically proximate to one another.

In 1977 Ojo expanded his study of Yorùbá masquerades to include a type named as *"Egúngún,"* a term that is translated into English as "ancestors" (Yai 1996, 34). "The word *Egúngún*, masquerades, is often used to describe all masked figures found among the Yorùbá of Nigeria. It is, strictly speaking, applicable only to those found among the Ọ̀yọ́, hence *Egúngún Ọ̀yọ́*, Ọ̀yọ́ masquerades" (Olajubu and Ojo, 253).[15] To appreciate the significance of the attribution to Ọ̀yọ́, it is necessary to say something about the political empire that originated from that subculture. But first an aside about Ojo's continued use of the term "masquerade." He has reservations about using this word because it exaggerates the importance of the masks that are components of these ceremonies. However, he finds himself communicating with an international audience that continues to describe these events, pretty much exclusively, as "masquerades." It therefore appears it is to facilitate communication with those sources that he relents and continues to use this term in his published work.

The importance of the Ọ̀yọ́ kingdom to Yorùbá history generally is acknowledged. In the early 1600s this already successful regional kingdom set out to conquer the rest of Yorùbáland. It did so using a standing army that became famous for its horsed cavalry. Referring back to the subgroups of Yorùbá that were listed earlier on, by 1750 the Ọ̀yọ́ had conquered the neighboring kingdoms of Ẹ̀gbà and Ẹ̀gbádò (Akinjogbin 1980, 35). Not long after: "the empire of Ọ̀yọ́ covered a huge area, bounded to the north by the Niger [river], to the east by Benin [another kingdom in central southern Nigeria], to the west by the frontier of modern Togo and to the south by the mangrove swamps and lagoons that form a barrier between the sea [Atlantic ocean] and the interior" (Crowder 1980, 39–40).

"The bringing together of such a vast territory under a single administration was bound to have economic advantages" (Akinjogbin and Ayandele 1980, 135). There was a common language (Yorùbá), a common currency (cowries), important trade routes made possible by an efficient system of roads that incorporated towns as well as local and regional markets, and comprehensive law and order that for centuries provided security for those towns, roads and markets (Akinjogbin 1980, 36–44). Such an environment was certainly compatible with the large urban areas (let's call them "cities") that had also distinguished Yorùbáland.[16] When the empire finally fell victim to internal politics in 1830, commentators were still able to say: "[that] the security of these [trade] routes was still excellent during the early part of the 19th century, when central administration had broken down in Ọ̀yọ́, was admirable evidence of the efficiency of Ọ̀yọ́ rulers" (Akinjogbin and Ayandele 1980, 135).

Yorùbá masquerades involve specialized terminology and orature. As was pointed out, the various subgroups of the Yorùbá have their own distinctive dialects of the language. Ojo's overall fluency enables him to be sensitive to the presence of different dialects in masquerade performances. This also means he can recognize the presence of one dialect in a place where people normally speak another. As he has suggested, the word *"Egúngún"* was originally the name of a specific kind of masquerade that had its origin in Ọ̀yọ́. Yet, as detailed in the coauthored essay, "Some Aspects of Ọ̀yọ́ Yorùbá Masquerades," today this type of masquerade is found all over Yorùbáland. "Its ubiquity may be due to the movement southwards of Ọ̀yọ́ Yorùbá elements, the extent of Ọ̀yọ́ and later Ìbàdàn Empires, peaceful migration and cultural contacts with neighboring sub-groups" (Olajubu and Ojo 1977, 253). During the centuries the Ọ̀yọ́ Empire exercised hegemonic control, it is not surprising that elements of Ọ̀yọ́ culture diffused to the whole of Yorùbáland.[17]

Ojo and his coauthor detail two major types of Egúngún: "one connected with *ancestor worship* and the other with *entertainment*"[18] (253). Ancestral Egúngún is what he pays special attention to via his fieldwork. In that research he focuses on local Yorùbá accounts of Egúngún's origin; the occasions where there is clear evidence of the Ọ̀yọ́ dialect in orature associated with performances (Ojo 1983); as well as the various types of costumes, venues, and stages of the ceremonies. This involves detailed descriptions of Egúngún performances in Ọ̀yọ́, Ìbàdàn, Abẹ́òkutá, Gbọ̀ngán, Ìpétumodu, and Ìlá. In addition, information is provided about Egúngún performances in at least a score of other towns scattered across Yorùbáland.

Ojo then proceeds to identify other types of festivals of Ọ̀yọ́ origin that can be found in Èkítí. These involve a divinity named Òrìṣà Oko: "the songs, praise names and subsequent enquiries indicate that it was introduced from the Ọ̀yọ́ area" (1973, 26, 58). Again the presence of the Ọ̀yọ́ dialect in the festival's orature is clear. Ojo translates Òrìṣà Oko as the *deity of the farm and agriculture* and tells us that: "in his role as a warder off of catastrophes like soil infertility, drought, crop diseases, pests and lean harvests … some light is thrown on his appellation as the deity of the farm" (58).

Ojo wants us to understand that the processes underlying the spread of these masquerades can involve more than hegemonic considerations, more than a dominant subgroup imposing its beliefs and practices on other comparatively submissive subgroups. For example, the diffusion involving Egúngún that took place was as likely "due to the movement southwards of Ọ̀yọ́ Yorùbá elements, … peaceful migration and cultural contacts with neighboring sub-groups" (Olajubu and Ojo 1977, 253). In this case the Yorùbá subgroups were comfortable with incorporating a festival that paid tribute to their ancestors, as well as a variant for purely entertainment purposes. He therefore creates a framework that enables him to distinguish three different kinds of diffusion: (1) those that took place between different Yorùbá subgroups (Egúngún, Òrìṣà Oko); (2) those involving cross-overs from Yorùbá to other ethnic (non-Yorùbá) groups; (3) those involving cross-overs from other ethnic groups to the Yorùbá (Ojo 1976). Here considerations of time and interest limit the discussion to cross-overs internal to Yorùbá culture.

History and Innovation

Finally, there are at least two forms of Èkítí masquerades that Ojo introduces as evidence of both historical consciousness and creativity (1998; 2006). The first, Èlèfọ̀n, is a variety of Ẹpa that makes reference to specific wars or battles that took place in the past: "Masquerade festivals in small communities not only reflect the general history of the area, but that some of the elements of the festivals are linked directly with the bellicose events in the various communities during the turbulent years of the 19th century and even earlier" (1998, 449).

The second are a variety of children's masquerades known as *Ojíjá*. The way this festival is conducted in the town of Ìré is of special interest because there the organizers and performers are girls between the ages of five and fourteen. One performer is responsible for carrying the *Ojíjá* sculpture on her head,[19] an "exquisitely carved" figure "in the form of a mother with child" (Ojo 2006, 93). For every performance the girls compose the original songs that are part of the masquerade, which can represent current concerns such as:

> child kidnappers, political hoodlums who destroy the property of their victims even when heavy ransom money has been paid, … how six lorry loads of soldiers came to destroy a cannabis farm. On national issues, they sing about the change of the national currency from the British pound sterling to the Nigerian naira, as well as the change in traffic regulations from driving on the left to driving on the right. There was also the issue of unemployment among secondary school dropouts and eventually university graduates.
>
> (2006, 94)

Here is a translated selection of verses from a performance:

> Adediwure's father, are you listening?
> The amount of suffering we are undergoing
> Is most intolerable.
> Those sitting, those standing, are you listening?
> The children in our house in Lagos,
> The children in our house in Ọ̀yó,
> The children in our house in Ìbàdàn,
> Cannot find jobs.
> Is this what you call a good life?
> All the elders in Ìré,
> Help us to find a powerful force
> So that children who will make us famous,
> Children who will transform Ìré,
> Will be sent to us by Olódùmarè[20] in Ìré.
> Death will not snatch our children.
>
> (2006, 95–6; passages elided)

Conclusion

Ojo tells us that social anthropology in the African context will produce more accurate findings if the professionals involved are truly fluent in the appropriate languages and have significant firsthand experience of the relevant cultures. As professionally trained and himself a product of Yorùbá culture, he proceeds to do detailed studies of Yorùbá ceremonies that have been typed as "masquerades" because of the so-called "masks" that have been extracted from them and acclaimed as "artistic masterpieces" by Eurocentric interests in particular. His point is that this approach distorts the meanings of these ceremonies, thereby ignoring Yorùbá understanding of them as cultural events.

With respect to the masks, perhaps because they were objects that could be taken away, rather than having to be studied *in situ* like political systems or family structures, they could be isolated from African contexts and valued independently. Those involved often had no serious experience of the cultures and their languages. They therefore had no choice but to concentrate on the *forms* of the objects as a basis for understanding and value, both aesthetic and monetary. But, as Ojo reminds us, concentrating exclusively on *form* ignores the fact that it is usually paired with *content*:

> The separation of form from content is purely conceptual. In most cases it is impossible to separate the two. Especially when the objects under study are associated with indigenous "rituals" [masquerades, etc.]. In such cases, the form and content of the object constitute an organic whole which cannot be separated because a knowledge of the content is necessary in order to understand its form.
>
> (1982, 203)

On the basis of his own fieldwork he then proceeds to articulate the Yorùbá meanings of those objects and the ceremonies in which they play a part. As a result of his findings he is able to challenge those who characterize Yorùbá as a *traditional* African culture. The Yorùbá do articulate the meanings of the ceremonies, including their so-called "art" objects. Many of the ceremonies are deliberately reenacted to express specific social concerns. The ceremonies are not believed to have magical consequences. The ceremonies do evidence deliberate change and innovation. Cultural diffusion has played a significant role in that change and innovation.

Then there is the issue of vocabulary. The English-language terminology used to interpolate Yorùbá meanings and understanding is too often misleading. Why are religious or political ceremonies reduced to so-called "masquerades," events in Eurocentric cultures that are associated with pretense and entertainment? Why are the Yorùbá said to be "performing rituals," with the implications this has for change and innovation? Ojo therefore concludes that it would be best to dispense with use of the adjective "traditional" altogether:

> the point in dispute is the connotation attached to the word when used as a descriptive adjective …. it seems … that the word "traditional' has pejorative connotations perhaps because it replaced more value loaded words [e.g., primitive, "other"], used by foreigners in the study of African culture.
>
> But in suggesting other terms considered more "acceptable", are we solving the problem or complicating the issue? Do we in fact need such "descriptive" terms in the study of African culture at this point in the development of the Human Sciences? Our use of terms and concepts must take into consideration the people's culture (and tradition). We need *analytical tools and concepts which are acceptable to the people described*, scientifically precise for the analysis of the data available, and abreast of developments in cognate disciplines.
>
> (1992, ix; my emphasis)

We're accustomed to speaking of American culture, Indian culture, Japanese culture, etc. without qualifying adjectives. From now on it should be the same when we speak of Yorùbá culture.

In conclusion, the suggestion here is to treat Ojo as a pioneer and pathfinder where the study of Yorùbá art by Yorùbá scholars is concerned. Because he writes as an anthropologist his focus is on the social contexts that are responsible for the objects' creation and the roles they are meant to play. That provides the objects with meanings that relate directly to the existential concerns of the culture.

Notes

1 "the word 'anthropology' evokes more negative than positive feelings (Ojo 1992, viii)."

2 Yorùbá is a tonal language—a language that uses pitch to convey different meanings. It has three tone types: low, middle, and high. A syllable with a low tone is marked with a grave (`) accent. A syllable with a middle tone has no marking. A syllable with a high tone is marked by an acute (´) accent. In addition, the pronunciation of three letters can change if they have dot (.) subscripts. The pronunciation of the vowels "ẹ" and "ọ" change from long to short and "ṣ" is pronounced "sh." The phonetic pronunciation of the name "Ifẹ̀" is therefore "EE-fey" (with the small "e" pronounced as in the English language "fed").

3 "This is not to argue that the indigenous craftsman and his patron are not aesthetically motivated … but not in the sense of art for art's sake" (Ojo 1982, 204).

4 "travelers and explorers have been remarking on their [cities] existence from the end of the fifteenth century onwards" (Krapf-Askari 1969, 4; with a footnote reference to Pacheco Pereira's 2010 *Esmeraldo de Situ Orbis*).

5 "The 1952/3 Census listed 46 per cent of the Yorùbá population of Nigeria as 'urbanized' in the sense of living in settlements of over 5,000 people" (Krapf-Askari, 31–20). According to the 1952/3 Census: Ìbàdàn: 459,200; Lagos: 276,400; Ògbómọ̀ṣọ́: 139,500; Òṣogbo: 122,700; Ifẹ̀: 110,800; Ìwó: 100,000. There are another thirteen cities listed with populations ranging between 84,500 and 22,100 (Krapf-Askari, 59).

6 "Until quite recently, the masquerades of Northeastern Yorùbáland [Èkítí] have not received enough attention from scholars. Even now, published studies are confined to a group of related masquerades [*Ẹpa*] whose headpieces are in the form of large wooden sculptures which have aptly been described as being among the best examples of African wood carving" (Ojo 1981, 45).

7 Ojo references Turner (1969) in the essay being discussed (Ojo 1978, 463).

8 "In a study of the *Ẹpa* masquerade complex of N. E. Yorùbáland I have suggested that the carved *headpieces* (so-called masks)" (1974a, 6; my emphasis).

9 "Like other parts of Yorùbáland, the masked rituals of Èkítí form part of the *religious ceremonial* cycle of each town" (1978, 455; my emphasis).

10 "Owner of many children" (1978, 456).

11 "Owner of war" and "fight war fight war," equivalent to "warrior" (1978: 462).

12 "there is no evidence that the *Ẹpa* types of masquerade represent any deity" (1981, 47).

13 "the decent euphemism and urban sophistication for which the Yorùbá are remarkable" (Ogunba 1973, 93).

14 Here Ojo is describing a different kind of masquerade, but the generalization applies.

15 "the words *egúngún*, *eígún* or *egígún* (depending on ethnic group) are used for all masquerade types. *Egúngún* [note capitalization] is reserved for the type peculiar to the Ọ̀yọ́ Yorùbá group, the others are referred to by specific names such as *Gẹ̀lẹ̀dẹ́*, *Ẹpa* and *Agẹmọ*. Where local types exist side by side with the Ọ̀yó type, *Egúngún* is referred to as *Egúngún Ọ̀yọ́*" (Ojo 1983, 124).

16 See Krapf-Askari, 14–24 for a discussion of the reluctance to describe Yorùbá urban centers as "cities."

17 "although *Egúngún* is peculiar to Ọ̀yó Yorùbá and related groups, it has spread to peoples who do not belong to this group. These are: the Ẹ̀gbà, Ẹ̀gbádò, Ìjẹ̀bú Rẹ́mọ, Ijẹ̀sà, Ìgbómìnà and Moba (northern Èkítí). Also, it has taken root in places which were not originally part of the Ọ̀yó Yorùbá heartland, but now occupied by the Ọ̀yó Yorùbá. Some of these places are: Apòmù, Ìkìrẹ, Gbọ̀ngán, Ìpétumodu and Modákẹ́kẹ́, a town which to a stranger is inseparable from Ifẹ̀" (Ojo 1983, 124).

18 "Entertainment masquerades are variously referred to as *Alárìnjo* ('walk and dance') because they travel from place to place entertaining people; *Agbegijo* (take wood to dance) because the maskers use carved wooden headpieces; *Onídàn* (player of tricks) or *Labala* (a word of uncertain etymology). The maskers entertain people with dances and acrobatic displays at any time of the year. Some wear 'face masks' which are

caricatures intended to make people laugh. They also chant *iwì* (*Egúngún* poetry)" (Olajubu and Ojo 1977, 259).

"Among the Ọ̀yọ́ group and those groups to whom *Egúngún* spread, the oral poetry associated with *Egúngún* is either in Ọ̀yọ́ dialect or with overtones of local dialects among non-Ọ̀yọ́ Yorùbá groups" (Ojo 1983, 123).

19 "masquerading, or the use of the mask-like carving, whether by adults or children, is a serious matter" (Ojo 2006, 100).

20 The supreme deity.

References

Ajayi, J. F. A. and Akintoye, S. A. 1980. "Yorùbáland in the Nineteenth Century." In *Groundwork of Nigerian History*, edited by O. Ikime, 280–302. Ibadan, Nigeria: Heinemann.

Akinjogbin, I. A. 1980. "The Economic Foundations of the Ọ̀yọ́ Empire." In *Topics on Nigerian Economic and Social History*, edited by I. A. Akinjogbin and S. O. Osoba, 35–54. Ilé-Ifẹ̀, Nigeria: University of Ifẹ̀ Press Ltd.

Akinjogbin, I. A. and E. A. Ayandele. 1980. "Yorùbáland Up to 1800." In *Groundwork of Nigerian History*, edited by O. Ikime 1, 21–43. Ibadan, Nigeria: Heinemann.

Bascom, William. 1955. "Urbanization among the Yorùbá," *American Journal of Sociology*, 60, no. 5: 446–54.

Boas, Franz. 1938. *The Mind of Primitive Man*. New York: Macmillan.

Boas, Franz. 1948. Race, *Language and Culture*. New York: Macmillan.

Carroll, Father Kevin. 1956. "Yorùbá Masks: Notes on the Masks of the Northeastern Yorùbá Country." *Odù* 3: 3–15.

Crowder, Michael. 1980. *West Africa: 1000 AD to the Present Day*. Nigeria: Longman.

Derrida, Jacques. 1976. *Grammatology*. Translated by Gayatri Chakravorty Spivak. Baltimore, MD: Johns Hopkins University Press.

Hallen, Barry. 2006. "My Mercedes Has Four Legs: 'Traditional' as an Attribute of African Equestrian Culture." In *African Philosophy: The Analytic Approach*, edited by B. Hallen, 275–98. Trenton, NJ and Asmara, Eritrea: Africa World Press.

Krapf-Askari, Eva. 1969. *Yorùbá Towns and Cities*. Oxford: Oxford University Press.

Nadel, S. F. 1951. *The Foundations of Social Anthropology*. Glencoe: The Free Press.

Ogunba, Oyin. 1973. "Ceremonies." In *Sources of Yorùbá History*, edited by S. O. Biobaku, 87–110. Oxford: Clarendon Press.

Ojo, G. J. Afolabi. 1966. *Yorùbá Culture*. Ilé-Ifẹ̀, Nigeria and London: University of Ifẹ̀ Press and University of London Press.

Ojo, J. R. O. 1973. "*Òrìshà Oko*, Deity of the Farm and Agriculture among the Èkítí." *African Notes: Bulletin of the Institute of African Studies* VII, no. 2: Ibadan, Nigeria: University of Ibadan: 25–61.

Ojo, J. R. O. 1974a. *Ẹpa and Related Masquerades among the Èkítí Yorùbá of Western Nigeria*. Unpublished M.Phil. thesis, London University, UK.

Ojo, J. R. O. 1974b. "The Diffusion of Artefacts over a Limited Geographical Region." In *Symposium Leo Frobenius*. Cologne, Germany: UNESCO, pp. 317–36.

Ojo, J. R. O. 1976. The Diffusion of Some Yorùbá Artefacts and Social Institutions." In *The Proceedings of the Conference on Yorùbá Civilisation*, vol. 2, edited by I. A. Akinjogbin and G. O. Ekemode, 364–98. Ifẹ̀, Nigeria: Department of History, University of Ifẹ̀.

Ojo, J. R. O. 1978. "The Symbolism and Significance of *Ẹpa*-type Masquerade Headpieces." *Man* n.s. 13, no. 3: 455–70.

Ojo, J. R. O. 1979. "Semiotic Elements in Yorùbá Art and Ritual." *Semiotica* 28, nos. 3–4: 333–48.

Ojo, J. R. O. 1981. "Masked Dances of the Yorùbá Peoples." *The World of Music* 23, no. 3 (Masks II), *Journal of the International Institute for Comparative Music Studies and Documentation*: 37–51.

Ojo, J. R. O. 1982. "Art in Traditional African Culture." In *African History and Cultured*, edited by Richard Olaniyan, 200–23. Nigeria: Longman.

Ojo, J. R. O. 1983. "Masks, Masquerades and Masking Rituals as Sources of Historical Data." In *The Masquerade in Nigerian History and Culture*, edited by Nwanna Nzewunma, 118–33. Proceedings of a *Workshop Sponsored* by the School of Humanities and Department of History. University of Port Harcourt, Nigeria, September 7–14, 1980. Port Harcourt, Nigeria: University of Port Harcourt Press.

Ojo, J. R. O. 1992. "Foreword." In *Principles of Traditional in African Culture*, edited by M. Okediji, viii–x. Ibadan: Bard Books.

Ojo, J. R. O. 1996. "'Doing Year', Performance Patterns in Some Yorùbá Festivals." *Kurio: Africana, Journal of Art and Criticism* 2, no. 2: 28–40.

Ojo, J. R. O. 1998. "Reflections of War in Some Èkítí Festivals." In *War and Peace in Yorùbáland, 1793–1893*, edited by A. Akinjogbin, 443–50. Ibadan, Nigeria: Heinemann.

Ojo, J. R. O. 2006. "Gender Differences and Performance Styles in *Ojíjá* among Children in Two Èkítí Towns." In *Playful Performers: African Children's Masquerades*, edited by Simon Ottenberg and David A. Binkley, 89–101. New Brunswick, NJ: Transaction Publishers.

Olajubu, Oludare and J. R. O. Ojo. 1977. "Some Aspects of Ọ̀yọ́ Yorùbá Masquerades." *Africa: Journal of the International African Institute* 47, no. 3: 253–75.

Panofsky, E. 1970. *Meaning in the Visual Arts*. London: Penguin.

Pereira, Duarte Pacheco. 2010. *Esmeraldo de Situ Orbis*. Translated by George H. T. Kimble. London: Hakluyt Society.

Saussure, Ferdinand de. 1966. *A Course in General Linguistics*. Translated by W. Baskin. New York: McGraw Hill.

Turner, Victor. 1967. *The Forest of Symbols*. Ithaca, NY and London: Cornell University Press.

Wescott, Joan and Peter Morton-Williams. 1962. "The Symbolism and Ritual Context of the Yorùbá Laba Shàngó." *The Journal of the Royal Anthropological Institute of Great Britain and Ireland* 92, no. 1: 23–37.

Yai, Olabiyi Babalola. 1989. "Issues in Oral Poetry: Criticism, Teaching and Translation." In *Discourse and Its Disguises: the Translation of African Oral Texts*, edited by K. Barber and P. F. de Moraes, 59–69. Birmingham: University African Studies Series No. 1.

Yai, Olabiyi Babalola. 1996. *Yorùbá–English/English–Yoruba Dictionary*. New York: Hippocrene Books.

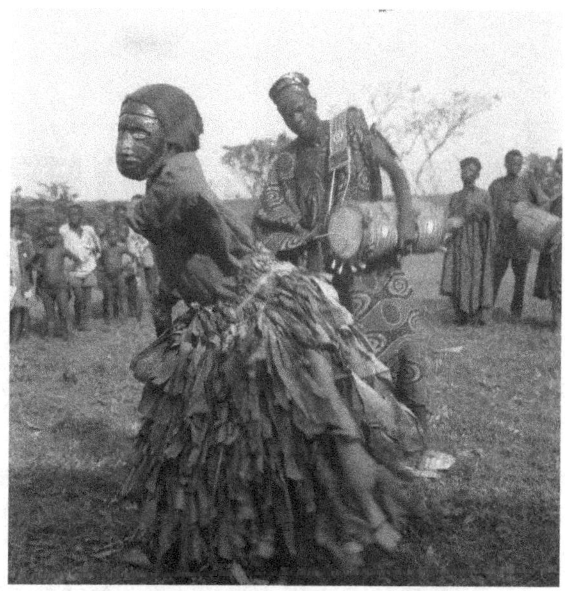

Figure 1 Egúngún Ceremony at Aiyétòrò, Nigeria (Photo: Frank Speed, 1968)

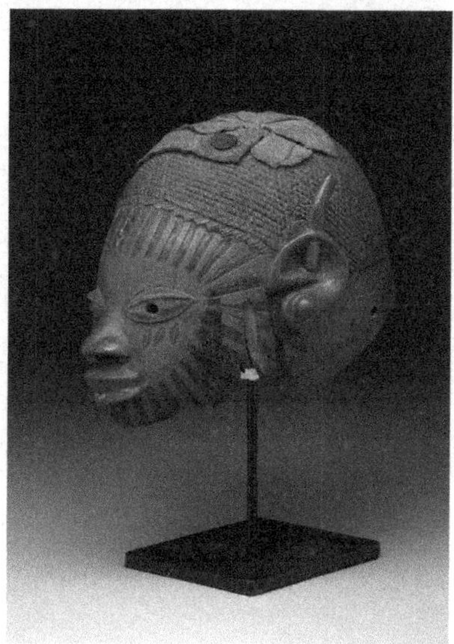

Figure 2 Gẹ̀lẹ̀dẹ́ Headpiece in Museum (Photo: Dallas Museum of Art, Dallas, Texas)

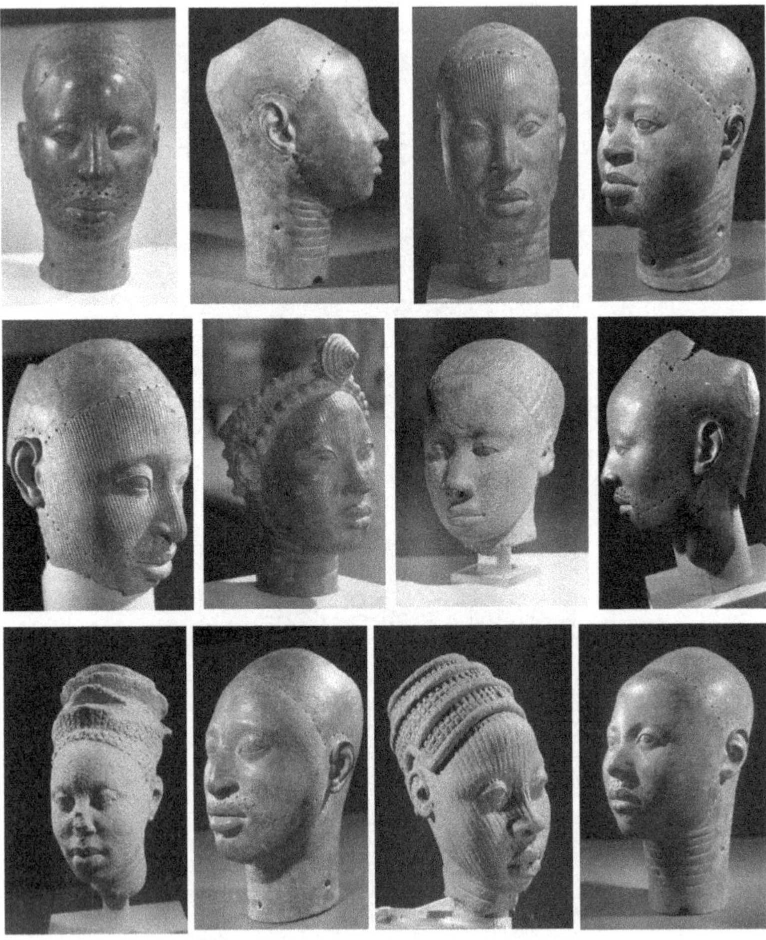

Figure 3 Various Ifẹ̀ Bronze and terra-cotta heads (Photo: Frank Speed, n.d.)

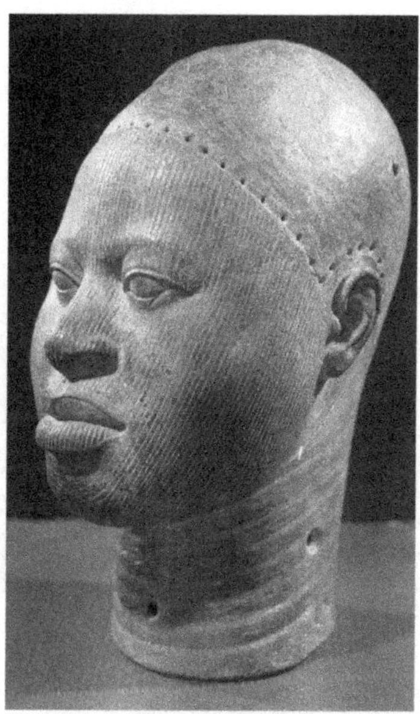

Figure 4 Ifẹ̀ Bronze Head (Photo: Frank Speed, n.d.)

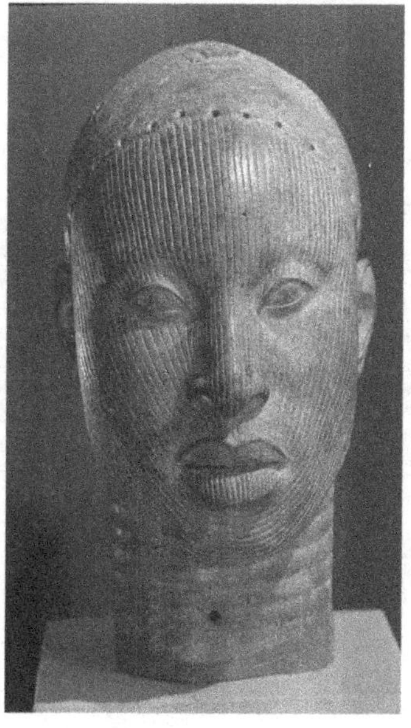

Figure 5 Ifẹ̀ Bronze Head (Photo: Frank Speed, n.d.)

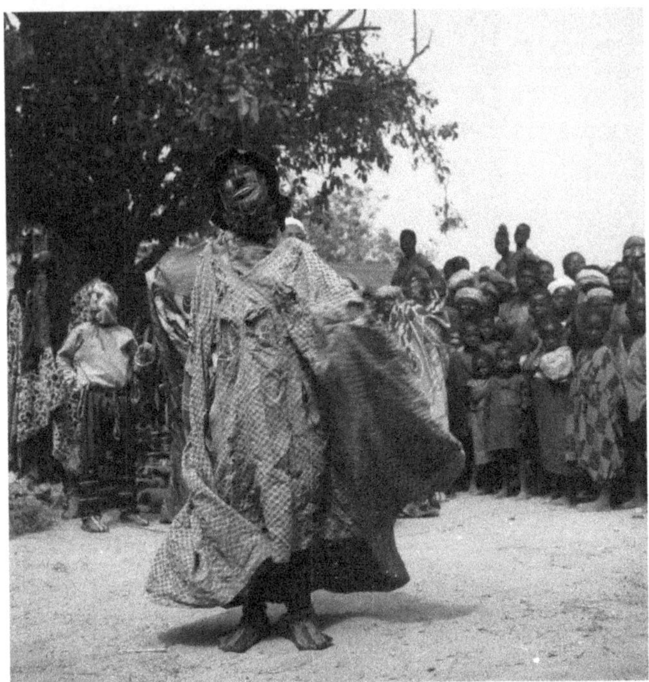

Figure 6 Egúngún Ceremony at Agbegijo, Nigeria (Photo: Frank Speed, 1968)

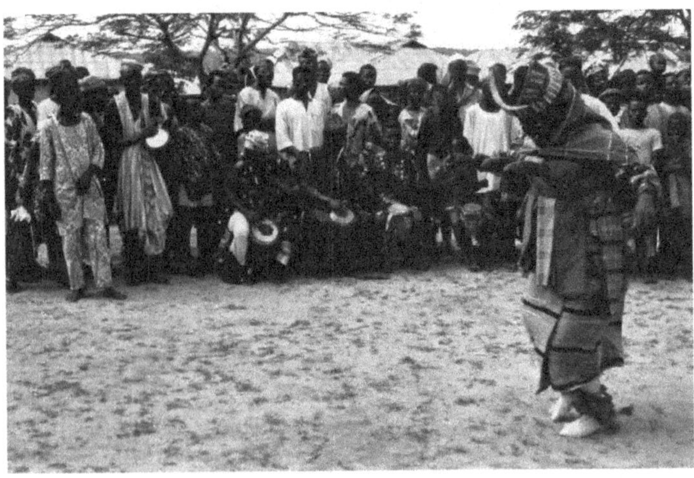

Figure 7 Gẹ̀lẹ̀dẹ́ Ceremony (Photo: n.p., Frank Speed, 1968)

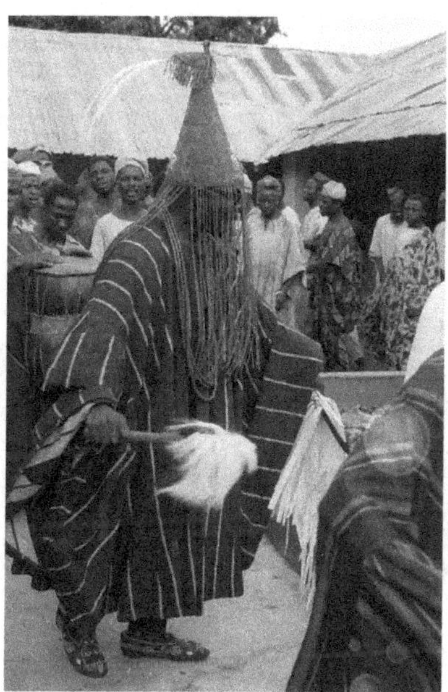

Figure 8 Ọba Sir Titus Martins Adéṣọjí Tadéniáwò Adérẹ̀mí (Atọ́batẹ̀lẹ̀ I), Ọ̀ọ̀ni of Ifẹ̀ (Photo: Frank Speed, 1973)

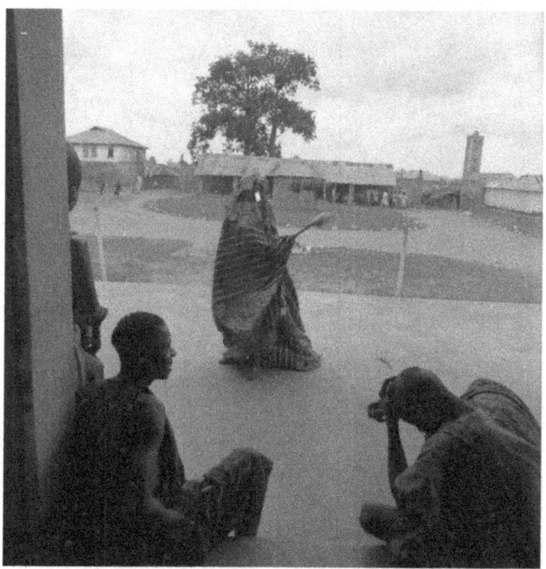

Figure 9 Egúngún Ceremony at Elewe, Nigeria (Photo: Frank Speed, 1969)

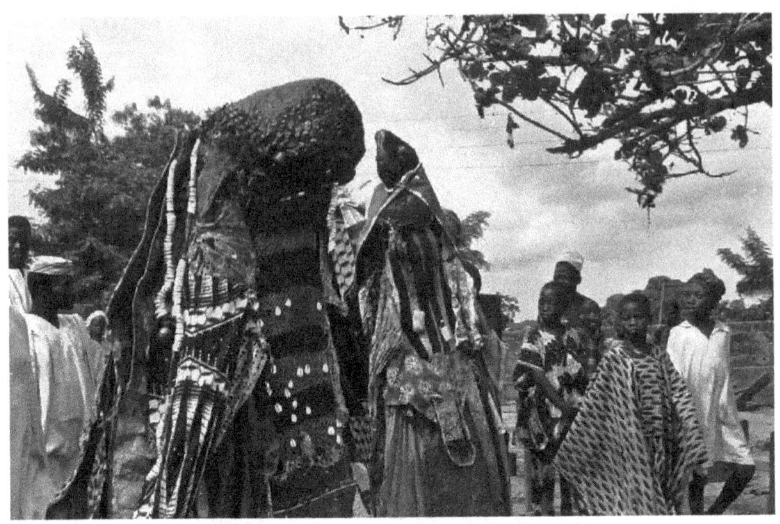

Figure 10 Egúngún Ceremony (Photo: n.p., Frank Speed, 1970)

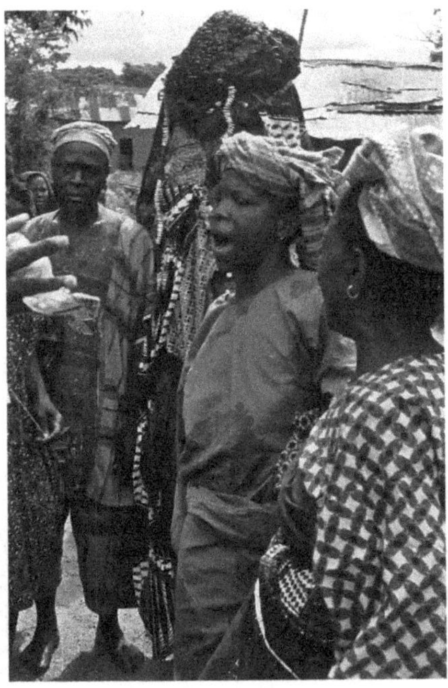

Figure 11 Egúngún Ceremony (Photo: n.p.,Frank Speed, 1970)

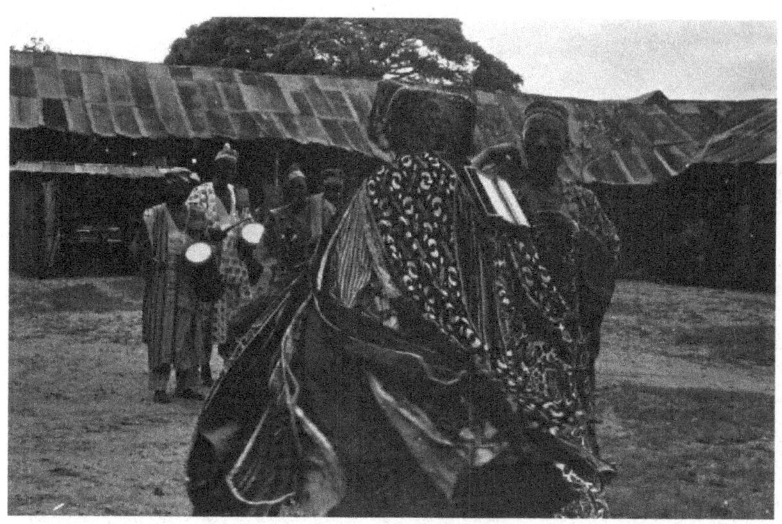

Figure 12 Egúngún Ceremony (Photo: n.p., Frank Speed, 1973)

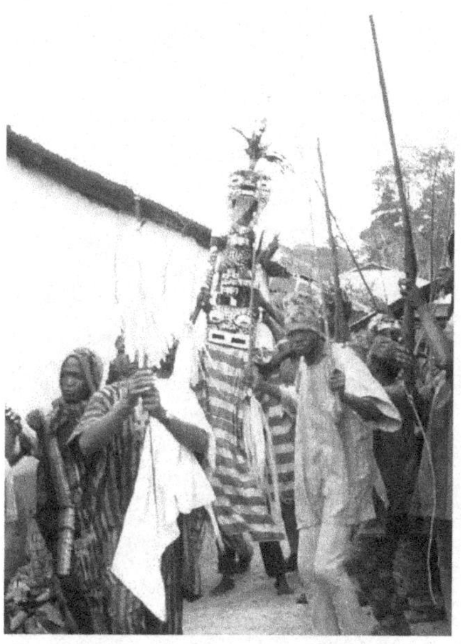

Figure 13 Ẹpa at Ògún Ceremony, Ifẹ̀, Nigeria (Photo: Frank Speed, 1973)

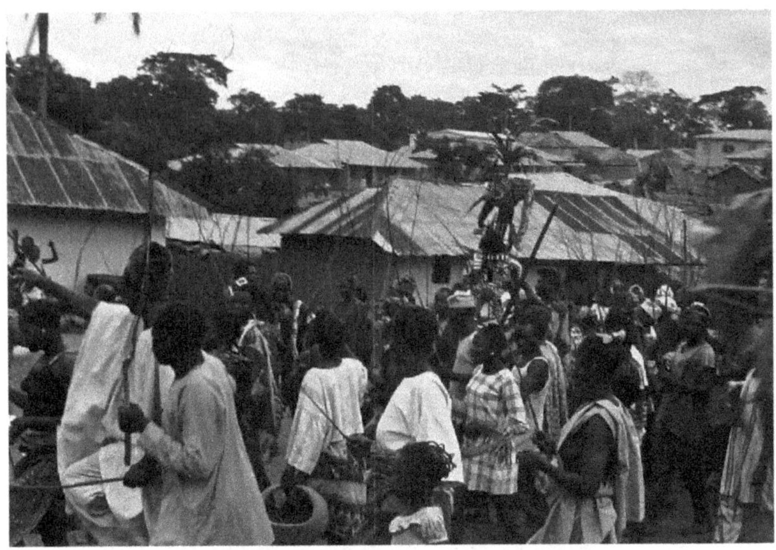

Figure 14 Ẹpa at Ògún Ceremony, Ifẹ̀, Nigeria (Photo: Frank Speed, 1973)

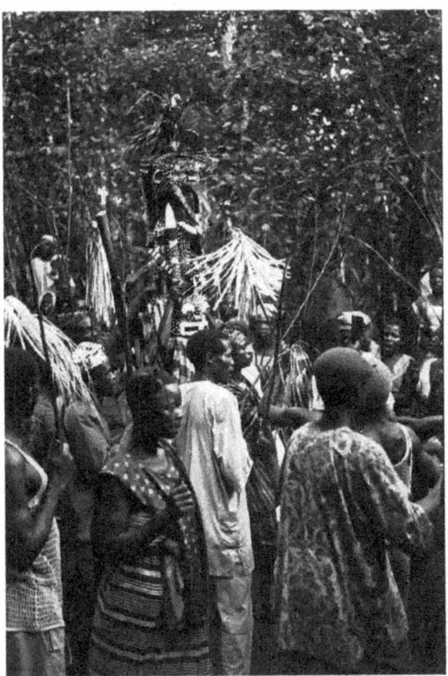

Figure 15 Ẹpa at Ògún Ceremony, Ifẹ̀, Nigeria (Photo: Frank Speed, 1973)

2

We Live in a Cosmos

Babatunde Lawal[*]

Introduction

When it comes to Yorùbá culture, Babatunde Lawal's cumulative work over the years evidences a number of critical methodological concerns. He appears to prefer a *philosophical* rather than *religious* framework for his analyses because it gives more accurate representation to the intellectual form and content—the character—of thought in the culture. Given the technical vocabulary associated with a *religious* framework, one is more likely to speak of a *world-view* and the relatively unreasoned *beliefs* and *practices* that define it.[1] Such beliefs and practices are more compatible, intellectually, with *faith* than with *reason*, and this serves to diminish their status as *theoretical thinking*. To avoid this, rather than a Yorùbá *world-view*, Lawal will speak of the Yorùbá *cosmos* and, rather than *beliefs*, he will reference the *theories*, the *philosophy*, and the *metaphysics/ontology* that define the systematic contents of that cosmos.[2]

> a number of scholars ... have called for a new critical approach that will allow *African traditions to be studied on their own terms*, instead of being viewed through Eurocentric lenses .... What is urgently needed ... is a *method* that *enables a given culture "to speak for itself* about its nature and various functions, rather than to read it, or analyse it, in terms

[*] Babatunde Lawal joined Great Ifẹ̀ as Research Fellow in 1966. He received the PhD in art history from Indiana University, USA in 1970. His thesis was entitled, *Yorùbá Ṣàngó Sculpture in Historical Retrospect.*

of ... theories borrowed whole from other traditions, appropriated from without" (Gates 1988, xix). Thus, this book will attempt to show that *Yorùbá culture has its own built-in theories,* by which much of its *artistic expressions* can be studied or comprehended.[3]

(1996, xvi; my emphasis)

This quote comes from what is perhaps Lawal's best-known publication, *The Gẹ̀lẹ̀dẹ́ Spectacle: Art, Gender, and Social Harmony in an African Culture,* a detailed study of a festival or event that some have misleadingly typed as essentially a masquerade.[4] In it he applies a methodology for understanding the artistic and aesthetic in Yorùbá culture that is meant to serve as a paradigm for African art history generally. Here is how he summarized that methodology years later:

Much of the data analyzed derives from field observations and interviews in Yorùbáland, where I have conducted art historical research since the 1960s. The fact that I conducted the field interviews in the Yorùbá language enabled me to play the role of a participant–observer and then follow up with questions pertaining to the semiotics of images and spectatorship. I have also made use of oral traditions, most especially the *Odù Ifá.* The latter is a collection of sacred divination verses on the *metaphysics* of the Yorùbá *cosmos,* the nature of the forces within it, and the rituals for harnessing those forces to solve human problems.

(2012b: 7; my emphasis)

Lawal finds the level of understanding that has been achieved by studies of Yorùbá culture based exclusively on fieldwork observations, interviews with informants, and formal analyses wanting. He is not suggesting that researchers who work in the African context should abandon use of these methodological tools that have become conventional to the study of African cultures. Indeed he uses them himself and, judiciously, at times incorporates the findings of others who do rely principally upon them.[5] "Much of my data derives from field observations and interviews in Yorùbáland" (2001, 498). His point is that, in the case of the Yorùbá, there are additional invaluable resources to be found in the culture's *oral traditions* and *literature*. These are places where one can literally hear the culture "speak for itself" and have access to "its own built-in *theories*," sources that will enhance understanding of its "artistic expressions."

These resources are inaccessible to many scholars because of their inadequate fluency in the Yorùbá language. This prevents them from having in-depth firsthand encounters with the traditions and literature when enunciated by members of the culture. Furthermore, since substantive portions of the literature have now been published in printed form in the Yorùbá language, even then it remains inaccessible to them (Lawal 1996, xxii). "An extensive use of oral tradition coupled with my own [firsthand] experience as a Yorùbá facilitated my study … from a perspective that would have been impossible had I depended solely on field observations and formal analysis" (1996, xxiii).

One genre of such literature that is particularly theory laden is that of the *Odù* that are instrumental to the knowledge system that has come to be known as Ifá divination.

> The Ifá literary corpus consists of two parts, namely, *Odù* and *ẹsẹ̀*. The corpus is divided into 256 distinct volumes which are called *Odù* and each *Odù* is sub-divided into numerous chapters which are called *ẹsẹ̀*. While the number of the *Odù* is known, the number of *ẹsẹ̀* in each *Odù* is unknown. This is due to the constant growth in the content of the *ẹsẹ̀ Ifá*, a growth which certainly does not affect the form of the text.
>
> (Abimbola 1976, 26)

A limited number of the *ẹsẹ̀ Ifá* have been transcribed and translated into languages other than Yorùbá. The English-language writings of Wande Abimbola, academic and *babaláwo*, have helped to introduce the Ifá corpus to international scholarship:[6]

> Ifá divination literature is perhaps the most accomplished product of Yorùbá traditional culture. Ifá is indeed the Yorùbá traditional body of knowledge embodying the deep wisdom of our fore-fathers. It is a complete system by itself in which all that the Yorùbá consider valuable

to them throughout the whole range of their experience from the very ancient times can always be found.

(Abimbola 1976, vi)

One of Lawal's important methodological innovations is that he will draw upon this knowledge system for his analyses so as to arrive at deeper understandings and explanations of why Yorùbá art is as it is and what that means for different contexts in the culture.

Traditional Art as Primitive

Lawal makes a point of deconstructing remnants of assessments of indigenous African art that characterized it as primitive, as the comparatively rough and unfinished product of craftsmen with limited intellectual and technical resources using rudimentary tools.

> an emphasis on Eurocentric theories led many Western anthropologists and art historians to regard the *stylized forms* of indigenous African art as "primitive" and a failed attempt to imitate nature (2020, 188). European art critics, influenced by evolutionist theory, mistook this [art] … for a failed attempt to imitate nature, and dismissed it as "primitive."
>
> (2010a, 184; my emphasis; passages elided)

Because of what were assumed to be their elementary skills, traditional Yorùbá artists were said to have been unable to create truly lifelike or naturalistic representations of the things portrayed. A further implication was that, had there been more time for a culture like that of the Yorùbá to evolve, those more advanced skills might have developed.

> As is well-known, the myth of primitivism is no longer taken seriously …. its assumption that naturalism was a late stage in the progressive evolution of art from the conceptual to the lifelike has been debunked (2010a, 184) …. The fact that the generality of African sculpture is "un-naturalistic" *does not mean that the traditional artist could not*

reproduce nature as it is, if he wanted to. That he possessed the skill to do so, when the *context warranted it*, can be observed in Ifẹ̀ and Igbo-Ukwu art whose naturalism ranks among the best in the world.

(Lawal 1987, 14; my emphasis; passages elided)

Art historians characterize a work of art as natural insofar as it is able to give detailed and lifelike representation to its objects. Indigenous African art was said not to be known for this, and so was assigned its own genre signified at first by the controversial word "primitive" and then by the less pejorative "traditional." Lawal finds this typology both offensive and mistaken. Ifẹ̀, a legendary Yorùbá city, is famous for the technically refined and lifelike terracotta and bronze heads produced there dating from the fourteenth and fifteenth centuries. Igbo-Ukwu, an Igbo town in southeast Nigeria, is also famous for the naturalism of the bronze pieces discovered there, dating from the twelfth and thirteenth centuries.[7]

It is the case that today art historians have become more open to relativities of style that avoid openly pejorative value judgments. But one can still ask a very important question: granted Yorùbá sculptural traditions and styles had and have their own integrity, why do artists in the culture choose to represent things as they do? *If there is indisputable evidence that Yorùbá artists could create so-called naturalistic or lifelike pieces, why did they choose not to in so many cases?* What sorts of artistic and aesthetic *criteria* were involved in the creation of these objects? In the case of the Yorùbá, these are questions that Lawal is convinced he can answer, and that his answers will put African art history on a different and fruitful trajectory. Here is a brief but tantalizing anticipation of his argument:

field research has revealed that the general disregard for naturalism in African art was a *deliberate choice* rather than the result of a technical deficiency. The practice seems to derive from the need to use *conceptual forms to encode cultural messages* (2020: 188) …. It is deliberate and has been influenced by different *cosmologies* that not only trace the *origin of art to supernatural beings*, but also identify the human body as a piece of sculpture animated by a vital force or soul. In other words, *art makes the invisible visible* in the physical world. The time-honored ritual still associated with the creation of sculptures and masks today clearly shows that *art in pre-colonial Africa was not so much concerned with imitating nature as with evoking its essence. Thus, stylization* hints at the *interrelatedness of the physical and metaphysical* (2010a, 184–5) .... The emphasis placed on the *spiritual aspects of reality* is partly responsible for the *"un-naturalistic" proportion* of traditional African sculpture. To arrive at this proportion, the traditional artist employed a special method of *Selective Realism*, which enabled him to emphasize the most important elements in a given situation.

(1987, 11; my emphasis; passages elided)

In what follows, consideration will be given to a select number of methodological innovations in Lawal's work. The first will involve examples of how the *Odù Ifá* can be used to enhance understanding of Yorùbá art and aesthetics. The second will be to detail the reasoning underlying an aesthetics of Selective Realism—of artists deliberately choosing not to create lifelike or naturalistic pieces. The third, which will be deferred to Chapter 5, is his account of the criteria the Yorùbá themselves employ for the conception, creation, and evaluation of art.

Yorùbá Cosmology

According to Lawal, becoming familiar with the Yorùbá model of the aforementioned *cosmos* is foundational to appreciating both the role played by the *Odù Ifá* and the reasoning underlying Selective Realism. For illustrative purposes, the cosmos is likened to a large calabash sliced horizontally in half to separate the top—the heavens—from the bottom—the earth. "The universe, according to the Yorùbá, is like a hollow calabash whose shape is more or less an elliptical spheroid with the greater axis across the rim of the 'hemispheres'.[8] The earth is on the lower hemisphere and the stars, sun and moon are in the upper" (Ojo 1966, 196).

The top half of the gourd/calabash—also called *Igbá Ìwà*, "the Calabash of Existence"—signifies the sky or heaven (*òrun, ìsálòrun*) the spirit world, and the domain of Olódùmarè [Supreme Being]. The bottom half of the calabash represents the primeval waters out of which the physical world (*ayé, isalayé*) was later created.

(Lawal 2012a, 219)

The heavens are home to a number of deities (*òrìṣà*) who can influence events on earth. Human beings came about when one of those deities, Ọbàtálá, was delegated by Olódùmarè, the Supreme Being, to descend to earth and create them: "the Supreme Being, Olódùmarè, is said to have commissioned Ọbàtálá, the arch-divinity, to mould man's physical body from clay" (Lawal 1976, 356). Lawal tells us that it was this event, and the carving techniques used by the deity to fashion the human body out of clay, as *the moment art (ọnà) was first introduced into the world* (2012b, 14).[9] The deity, in effect, acted as sculptor: "the human body is a divine work of art" (1987, 29).[10] The following *oríkì*, another literary form to be discussed in detail in Chapters 5 and 6, captures the moment:

> He molded the inner surface of the hand called the palm
> He molded the underside of the foot called the sole
> He molded the massive part of the body called the chest
> He created the refractive water balls called the eyes
> He molded the small pot called the skull
> The-Orisa-has-made-a-work-of-art, Owner-of-choice-clay ...

> *Oun ló dá pẹ́tẹ́ ọwọ*
> *Oun ló dá pẹ́tẹ́ ẹsẹ̀*
> *Oun ló dá àyà jànkàn, tí a npe ni ìgbá àyà*
> *Oun ló dá omi ójólójó, tí a npe l'ojú*
> *Oun ló dá orù rẹ́bẹ́té, tí a npe ní àtarí ...*
> *Osọnà, Alamòrere ...* (2005, 163)

A body of clay, however lifelike, is not alive. "The image (*ère*) turned into a living human being (*ènìyàn*) after receiving from the Supreme Being [Olódùmarè] the divine breath or soul (*ẹ̀mí*)—a form of *àṣẹ* (the enabling power)" (2001: 499). The *àṣẹ* is a *power* or *force* of Olódùmarè's that underlies and sustains the entire cosmos.[11] This creation and giving of life to humanity is an example of how the supernatural and natural can interrelate in the Yorùbá cosmos.

Deploying the *Odù Ifá*:
The Gẹ̀lẹ̀dẹ́ Festival and the Great Mother

Gẹ̀lẹ̀dẹ́ is one of the more important and popular festivals in Yorùbá culture that involves masquerades. In *The Gẹ̀lẹ̀dẹ́ Spectacle: Art, Gender, and Social Harmony in an African Culture* Lawal is as much social anthropologist as he is art historian:

> the ideals of the Gẹ̀lẹ̀dẹ́ society … are designed to promote the social and spiritual well-being of a given community …. The Gẹ̀lẹ̀dẹ́ society also endeavors to maintain good gender relations by advocating respect for motherhood …. There are two main reasons for this pro-female stance. One is that the preservation of humanity depends on the role of the female as mother; the other has to do with the linking of motherhood to a special power akin to witchcraft that can be used for good or evil.
>
> (1996, xiii–xiv; passages elided)[12]

As with Ojo this broader social anthropological perspective seems to be an essential methodological component of his approach: if you want to appreciate art in the context of Yorùbá society and culture, you must become fully informed about the social and metaphysical contexts for which it was created. This is what he has begun to do by introducing the foundational framework involving the Yorùbá cosmos.

Previous accounts of Gẹ̀lẹ̀dẹ́ also highlight the social and moral values endorsed during the course of the ceremony.[13] They generally agree it is designed to acknowledge, praise, and reinforce the important roles played by women/mothers in the culture. Additional moral values are also affirmed in the course of the ceremony that are applicable to both men and women because they promote the general welfare of the entire community. What will become of special interest here is the attention paid to the elusive and mysterious "more powerful" human mothers known as *àjẹ́* so that they, in particular, will not indulge in behavior that would qualify as anti-social.

However, Lawal is also doing art history and that discipline has been concerned principally with the headdresses, masques, or masquerades that are part of Gẹ̀lẹ̀dẹ́. Here is how he believes one should involve that discipline in a manner that complements the anthropological:

> Given their identification of the body as a work of art incarnating the soul on earth, *the Yorùbá use masquerade* for a similar purpose, that is, *to manifest the presence of invisible forces* on earth and *to visualize as well as dramatize concepts and values* deemed vital to the social and spiritual well-being of a given community.
>
> (2012a, 234; my emphasis)

Understanding why a festival like Gẹ̀lẹ̀dẹ́ occurs and incorporates the masques/headdresses that it does involves appreciating how the festival and its artistic components relate to the cosmos. Then the overall ceremony can be appreciated as more than a local moral exercise. It will be seen as a moment when the two different hemispheres of the cosmos—the heavenly and earthly—intersect and interact.

Ìyá Nlá or the Great Mother is a masque that appears early on in the festival. She comes out in the dark on the first night, with all lights extinguished, as a bearded white mask with a white cloth costume accompanied by drums, and dances slowly and wordlessly before the assembled community:

> The blackout heightens the awe. Soon the Ìyá mask arrives; she wears an all-white costume with a long train of cloth trailing on the ground behind her. Elders of the Gẹ̀lẹ̀dẹ́ society cluster round the mask, all singing the praises of Ìyá Nlá and the "powerful mothers," *inviting them to descend onto the arena and participate in the ceremony.* After dancing round the performance arena and encircling the marketplace—a ritual

aimed at warding off negative forces—the mask retires to the Gẹ̀lẹ̀dẹ́ shrine.

(Lawal 1996, 106; my emphasis)

Shrouded in mystery, Ìyá Nlá withdraws, never to reappear, leaving one to wonder about the identity of this mysterious Great Mother and why she is even part of the ceremony.

Lawal begins to use the *Odù Ifá* to understand Gẹ̀lẹ̀dẹ́ in an article entitled, "New Light on *Gẹ̀lẹ̀dẹ́*." There he draws upon the work of the ethnographer, Pierre Verger, and his account of a story from the *Odù Òsá Meji*:[14]

> After the creation of the Earth, Olódùmarè [Supreme Being] sent three *òrìṣà* [deities], including two males (Ọ̀bàìṣà and Ògún) and *one female (Òdù)* to administer it. To Ọ̀bàìṣà (another name for Ọbàtálá, the artist deity), Olódùmarè gave a special *àṣẹ*, with which to command and make things do his bidding, and to Ògún he gave the power of iron, hunting, and warfare. At first *the female òrìṣà was not given any special power*. Dissatisfied, *she returned to Olódùmarè to ask for her own power*. Olódùmarè replied, "You will be their *mother forever* …. You will *sustain the physical world* (Verger 1965, 202–5). With these remarks, Olódùmarè gave her a closed calabash (an image of the world) containing a special *àṣẹ* [power] symbolized by a bird (ibid.). When asked how she would use her power on Earth, *Òdù replied that she would use it to fight those who insult or disrespect her, but would not hesitate to use it to help those who adore her.*
>
> (Verger 204–5; as summarized in Lawal 1996, 31; my emphasis in part)

Note the ascription of "mother forever" which, Lawal argues, serves to identify *Òdù* as Ìyá Nlá, the Great Mother: "the first female goddess or Ìyá Nlá (the Great Mother)" (1996, fn. 5, 73). This is an important linkage because it now becomes clear that the masque known as the Great Mother or Ìyá Nlá is a powerful *òrìṣà*, a deity, who is made manifest on the occasion of Gẹ̀lẹ̀dẹ́. Moreover, She is a deity with a special power related to the control of things in the earthly portion of the cosmos. Here is a verse from the ceremony:

The one with the beautiful eyes, "My mother" of mothers
Who kills stealthily, and walks surreptitiously
"My Mother" of mothers,
The famous one of the night,
Who has water in the house but uses palm oil for her laundry,[15]
The entire community is in your hands.

Ẹlẹ́yinjú ẹgẹ́ o, Ìyà mi ìyá
Apákẹ́ṣẹ́, Arìnkẹ́ṣẹ́
Ìyà mi ìyá
Olókìkí òru
Olómi nlé f'epo fọ ṣọ
Ìyà mi ìyá.
Gbogbo ìlú d'ọwọ́ ẹ.

(1996, 128–9)

Lawal continues: "According to a story from the Ifá divination verse *Odù Ọsá Meji*, it was the Supreme Being himself, Olódùmarè, who gave the power of *àjẹ́* to the first woman [the *òrìṣà* Òdù, now identified as Ìyá Nlá or the Great Mother] (Verger 1965: 200–19)" Lawal 1996, 31). This is an important passage because the type of power (*àṣẹ*) given to the Great Mother is now more specifically identified as the *àjẹ́*. This *àjẹ́*, the power or spiritual agency of the Great Mother, "the Mother of All and the mother of mothers" (1996, 71), flows to and through a select number of the human mothers/women in her earthly domain. These women are known as *àjẹ́* in their own right, a term Lawal now translates using the English-language phrase "powerful mothers" (1996, 313) and more controversially by the English-language "witch" (1996, 30). At various points he makes reference to these women as the Great Mother's "earthly disciples, the 'powerful mothers'" (1996, 74), and to the Great Mother as "the grand matron of the *àjẹ́*" (1996, 73) or witches.

The cosmological information obtained from the *Odù Ifá* makes it clear that one very important reason for Gẹ̀lẹ̀dẹ́ is to praise and secure the metaphysical presence, power, and sustenance of the Great Mother for the entire community. This will then serve to persuade the human *àjẹ́*, the powerful mothers who are the Great Mother's earthly disciples, to also commit to the welfare of that community. In the end the aim is "to promote peace and social harmony by enjoining all members of a given community to interact with one another *as children of the same mother* and so refrain from anti-social activities" (Lawal 2002a, 10; my emphasis).

Lawal thinks there is "no exact equivalent in the English language" (Lawal 1996, 30) for the powerful mothers, the human *àjẹ́*. There is a popular stereotype that associates them with all sorts of terrible things, which is why the word "witch" comes to mind (Prince 1961). But there is a more measured view of *àjé* in the culture arising from Lawal's fieldwork that believes "there are two types of *àjé*, the good one (*àjẹ́ rere*) and the bad one (*àjẹ́ buruku*). A good *àjẹ́* uses her power to attract all the good things of life—to heal, to restore men's and women's fertility, to ensure safe childbirth, good harvest, and so on. A bad *àjẹ́* acts in the opposite direction" (Lawal 1996, 33). It appears that how the power is manifested or used depends upon the underlying character (*ìwà*) of the individual concerned.[16]

Because of the mystery surrounding her identity and involvement with Gẹ̀lẹ̀dẹ́, the Great Mother or Ìyá Nlá is particularly appropriate as a test case for Lawal's reliance upon the *Odù Ifá* as an additional explanatory source. The information provided by these narratives enables Lawal to conclude that the Great Mother deserves to be elevated to *the most important component* of the Gẹ̀lẹ̀dẹ́ festival: Gẹ̀lẹ̀dẹ́'s "*main function is to entertain Ìyá Nlá, the Great Mother*" (1978, 65–6; my emphasis). Lawal supports this by highlighting the enduring presence and influence of the Great Mother as the ceremony proceeds: "[another mask] speaks with the divine authority (*àṣe*) of Ìyá Nlá" (1996, 117); "[another mask] makes it absolutely clear that he is not speaking with his own voice but with that of Ìyá Nlá" (1996, 129); the numerous "songs of gratitude ... acknowledging Ìyá Nlá's blessings during the past year" (1996, 130).

Nevertheless, because of her multiple identifies and conflicted powers, in the end he concedes that "Ìyá Nlá remains something of an enigma. This is because she is Mother Nature" (1996, 71).

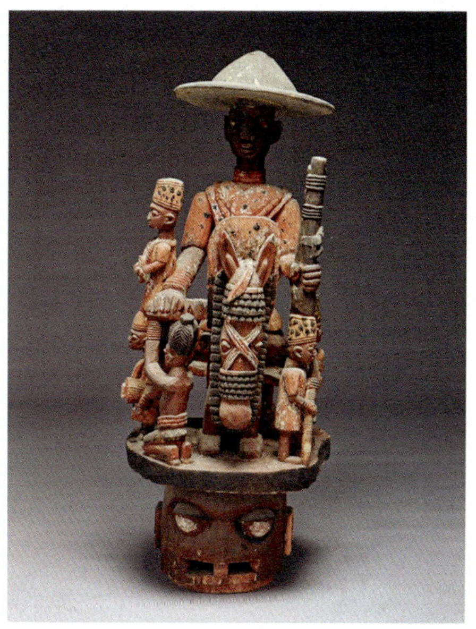

Plate 1 Ẹpa in Museum (Photo: Dallas Museum of Art, Dallas, Texas).

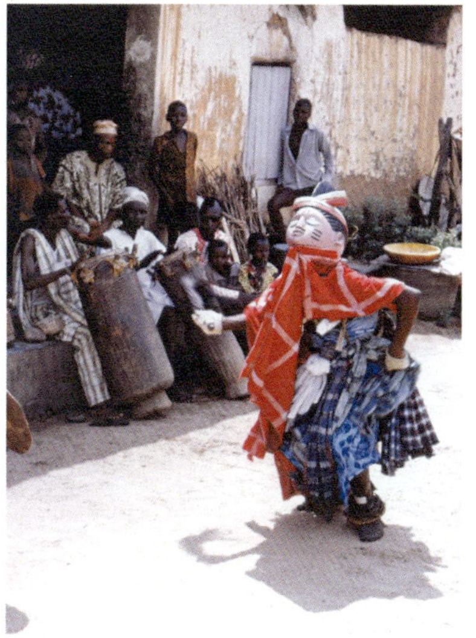

Plate 2 Gèlèdé Ceremony at Meko (Photo: Frank Speed, 1969).

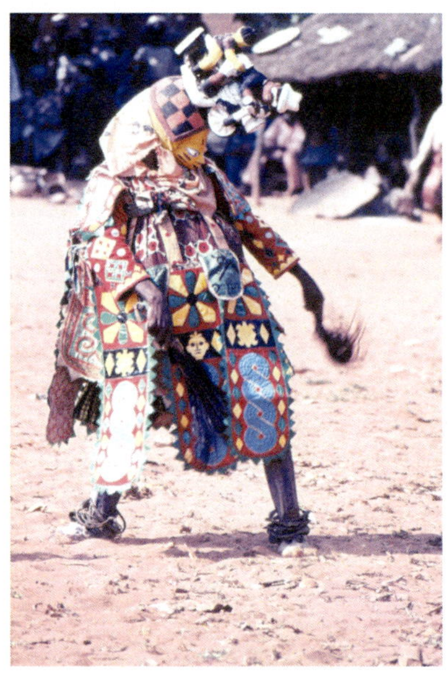

Plate 3 Gẹ̀lẹ̀dẹ́ Ceremony at Meko (Photo: Frank Speed, 1969).

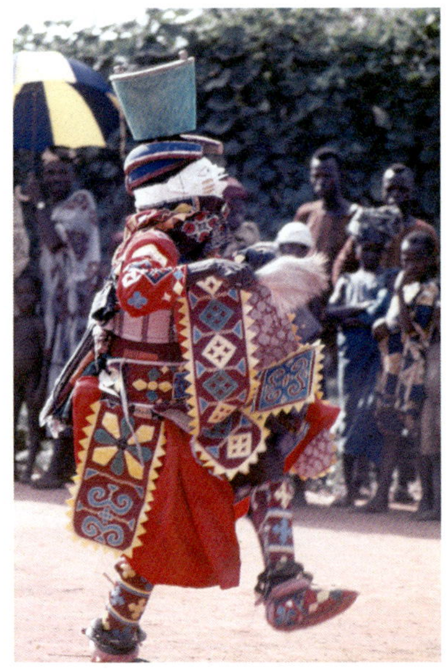

Plate 4 Gẹ̀lẹ̀dẹ́ Ceremony at Meko (Photo: Frank Speed, 1969).

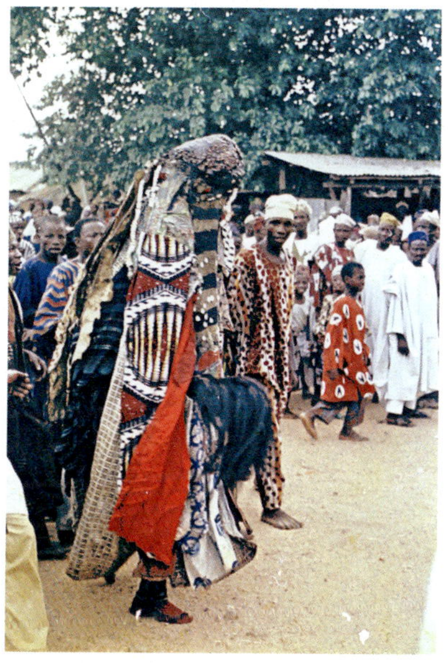

Plate 5 Egúngún Ceremony (Photo: n.p., Frank Speed, 1970).

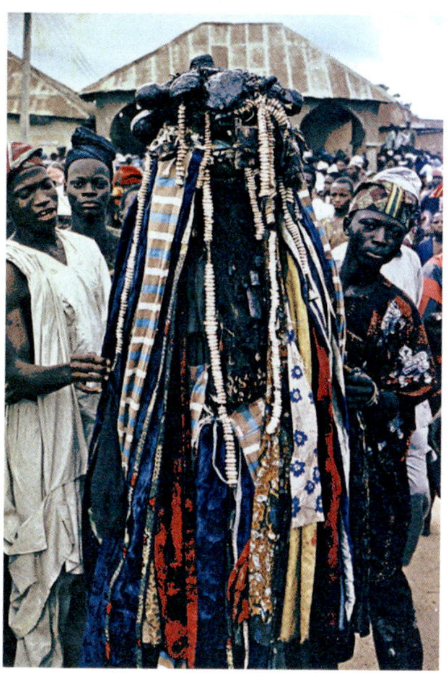

Plate 6 Egúngún Ceremony (Photo: n.p., Frank Speed, 1970).

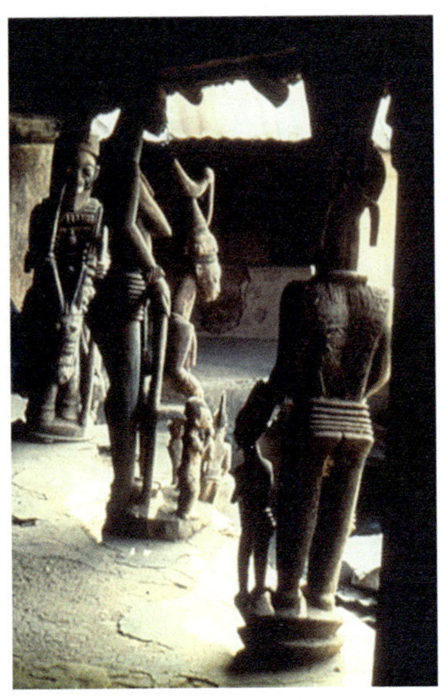

Plate 7 Ọba's Palace, Ìkẹ́rẹ́, Nigeria Veranda Post by Ọlọ́wẹ̀ of Ìsẹ̀ (Photo: John Picton, 1964).

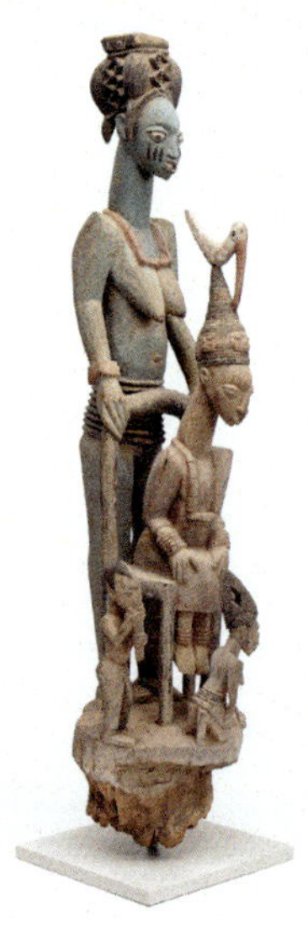

Plate 8 Ọba's Palace, Ìkẹ́rẹ́, Nigeria Veranda Post by Ọlọ́wẹ̀ of Ìsẹ̀ in Museum (Photo: The Art Institute of Chicago).

> She is *Yewajọbí, Ìyàmi, Ìyá* (the Mother of All and the mother of
> mothers), epitomizing the maternal principle in the Yorùbá cosmos,
> combining in her nature the attributes of all the principal female
> deities—Yemọja (mother of all waters), Olókun (sea goddess), Ọ̀ṣun
> (goddess of Ọ̀ṣun river), Òdù (founder of "witchcraft"), Oòduà
> (Earth goddess), Ilẹ̀ (Earth goddess), and Ọya (goddess of the Niger
> River).
>
> (Lawal 1996, 71)

Even if that is the case, now she is an enigma that has an origin, an
identity as an *òrìṣà*, a history, a place in the cosmos and a very
important role to play on the earth. Her presence in Gẹ̀lẹ̀dẹ́ is essential
and the secrecy attached to her person can be appreciated as a part of
her identity.

> Often identified as the first female in the Yorùbá universe .... She is
> *Yewajọbi, Ìyàmi, Ìyá* (the Mother of All and the mother of mothers),
> epitomizing the maternal principle in the Yorùbá cosmos .... the first
> female to whom the Supreme Being gave a special power (*àṣẹ*) in the
> form of a bird enclosed in a calabash, copies of which she presented to
> her disciples, the "powerful mothers" [*àjẹ́*].
>
> (1996, 71–3; passages elided)

There is of course much more to the Gẹ̀lẹ̀dẹ́ ceremony than the Great
Mother. The point here has been to provide an example of how Yorùbá
orature can be used to elevate an enigmatic "masque" to a cosmic
persona whose presence has profound consequences for the welfare of
the entire community.

Selective Realism

His arguments for Selective Realism also follow a cosmic path. In an
inaugural lecture presented at Great Ifẹ̀ in 1987 he argues that Yorùbá
art generally does not fall into the category of art for art's sake. His
title is "Art for Life's Sake: Life for Art's Sake," and in it he stresses the
functionality of art objects in the culture—their design is a consequence

of the jobs they are meant to do. Selective Realism is an appropriate phrase because the degree of naturalism or stylization of an art object is a function of the cosmic role it is meant to play.

Here is a simple example of how this works. Art objects in the culture are meant to be more natural or lifelike when their function is to give lasting and accurate representation to an actual person:

> The degree of realism in Yorùbá portraiture depends on which aspect is being emphasized. Naturalism is favored in most of the sculptures meant to recall the *physical likeness* of an individual, such as the terracotta and bronze heads from Ifẹ̀, as well as the àkó[17] second burial effigies that mark the last symbolic appearance of a deceased ancestor among the living.
>
> (Lawal 2002b, 82)

On the other hand when an art object is meant to represent the *spirit* of that ancestor subsequent to their funeral/burial or serve as the basis for communication with a deity or òrìṣà, the criteria governing representation change dramatically. "Sculptures placed on altars to communicate with the òrìṣà or the spirits of dead ancestors are often intentionally stylized to emphasize their non-material state of existence, even if they have a human essence" (2002b, 82). Since such things transcend the physical world—being lifelike or natural is no longer a priority. When an art object relates to the realm of the spiritual/metaphysical, stylization reigns supreme. This also applies to the masks involved in the ceremonies or festivals that have been typed as masquerades. When masks are meant to make metaphysical beings appear in the physical world, like the Great Mother or an ancestor (*Egúngún*), stylization predominates (Lawal 1981, 109).

This would appear to mean that the mechanism underlying Selective Realism involves a kind of sliding scale. At one extreme is the physical world requiring lifelike portrayals. At the other extreme is the metaphysical world requiring stylization. The further away the thing to be represented is from the physical world, the greater the degree of stylization, and the reverse. In between the extremes there is room for a diverse lot of objects that combine mixed degrees of both the lifelike and the stylized. This would apply to the many other masques that perform in Gèlèdé and portray things like the proverbial female and male as well as a variety of archetypal animals (Lawal 1996, 163). The same would apply to the carved superstructures of the headdresses, which portray a wide variety of people, activities, and things: twins, food hawkers, drummers, carvers, agricultural workers, tailors, and so forth (1996, 193–254). All are portrayed in an archetypal manner that combines elements of the lifelike and the stylized. In principle this scale can be used to rate innumerable art objects produced by the culture.

Conclusion: The Role of Art in the Yorùbá Cosmos—Art as the Metaphysical Facilitator

By situating art objects in the Yorùbá cosmos, Lawal remains committed to understanding and explaining them on the basis of their *metaphysical* or *ontological* character and status. That character and status can be elaborated by *theoretical content* derived from the *Odù Ifá*. This enables him to identify the Great Mother or Ìyá Nlá as a paramount *òrìṣà* whose involvement with the Gèlèdé spectacle proves to be essential to the promotion of communal welfare. In numerous essays he uses theoretical content derived from the *Odù* to understand a variety of art forms in the culture (1985, 1995, 2002a, 2008).

When it comes to the events or festivals that have been typed as "masquerades," in fact the function of many of the masques that distinguish them is to enable elements of the heavenly sphere of the cosmos to transition from the invisible to the visible and thereby be made manifest on earth. He goes so far as to apply the trope of the masque to the Yorùbá account of human creation. Since the *èmí* soul is said to be eternal and to undergo an indefinite cycle of reincarnations, its present and future bodies can be viewed as a succession of crafted masks for it to wear.

To return to his caustic remarks about "primitive" African art: inadequately informed observers of Yorùbá culture saw pieces deliberately created to be unnatural as unsuccessful attempts to produce lifelike or natural representations by artists with limited technical and intellectual skills. In fact the functions of those pieces required that they *not* be lifelike or natural. This is because one of the most important *functions* of "art" is to facilitate interaction between the heavenly and earthly, between the invisible and visible, between what can easily be given representation and what cannot. All of these examples serve to underline the fact that art in the culture serves any number of important functions and that approaching it as an end in itself, as art for art's sake, promotes misunderstanding.

Notes

1   "The religious function of the art is often emphasized at the expense
      of the social and aesthetic ones" (1996, xiii). Robin Horton compares
      applying a theoretical model with a religious model in his "African
      Traditional Thought and Western Science (1967)" and "African
      Conversion" (1971) essays.
2   "The philosopher Pythagoras first used the term *kosmos* for the order of
      the universe (https://en.wikipedia.org/wiki/Cosmos)"; "Metaphysics is
      the branch of philosophy that studies the fundamental nature of reality
      (https://en.wikipedia.org/wiki/Metaphysics)."
3   He references the work of two African philosophers: Paulin Hountondji's
      African Philosophy: Myth and Reality (1983) and V. Y. Mudimbe's *The
      Invention of Africa* (1988), texts that are well known for their critiques of
      misleading representations of the cultures of Africa.
4   Note the absence of the word "masquerade" from the title of his book.
5   "My theoretical approach combines linguistic, visual, iconographic,
      contextual, and anthropological analyses reinforced by the findings of
      other scholars" (Lawal 2020, 189).
6   "*Babaláwo*" is the Yorùbá title for a diviner. The standard literal English-
      language translation is "father of secrets."

7 A more detailed critique of Africa when portrayed as the "dark" continent is to be found in Lawal 2010b.

8 Hollowed out pumpkins or melons qualify as calabashes.

9 Lawal extends his philosophical model here when he categorizes this Yorùbá account of human being as Yorùbá *ontology* (1977, 51). Ontology is the subdiscipline of philosophy concerned with what exists and the nature of existence.

10 "He thus became the sculptor-divinity" (Idowu 1962, 21).

11 "the Yorùbá trace the origin of the universe to a supreme creator called Olódùmarè, 'the Eternal One and Ultimate Cause', the generator of the *àṣẹ. Àṣẹ* is a vital force or power that enables the sun to shine, the moon and stars to glitter, the wind to blow, the rain to fall, and the rivers to flow; it gives form to the formless, motion to the motionless, and life to living things. This power sustains the cosmos" (Lawal 2012a, 218–19).

12 "Among the various informants, there are three common explanations of the word Gẹ̀lẹ̀dẹ́. One, that it is an onomatopoeia for the leisurely and relaxed gait of an obese woman, alluding to the mythical image of Ìyá Nlá [see below] as the potential pot-breasted mother; the nursing mother with the rolling buttocks (*Ìyá ọlọ́yọ̀n orùbà; Abiyamua bìdí jẹ̀lẹ́nkẹ́*) .... Two, that it connotes a phenomenon treated with indulgence (i.e. Gẹ̀—lẹ̀—dẹ́). Three, that it refers to something that cools and relaxes (i.e. Gẹ̀-ẹ̀—lẹ̀-ẹ̀—dẹ́-ẹ́). In addition, some informants etymologize the word as follows: *Gẹ̀* = 'to pet or indulge'; *Èlẹ̀* = 'carefulness'; *Dẹ́* = 'to relax'" (Lawal 1996, 75).

13 J. R. O. Ojo had some things to say about Gẹ̀lẹ̀dé in the previous chapter. Prior to Lawal the most important study of Gẹ̀lẹ̀dé was that of Henry and Margaret Thompson Drewal (1983).

14 Pierre Fátúmbí Verger (1902–96), was an ethnographer and *babaláwo* in his own right. He was a Visiting Professor in the Great Ifẹ community during the 1980s. His text (1965) contains the Yorùbá-language originals and his French-language translations. In line thirty-seven of the Yorùbá-language *Odù*, Olódùmarè addresses the deity Òdù [the different tone marks indicate reference is being made to an *òrìṣà* rather than the Odù used to name the volumes of Ifá divination] as "Ìyá," which Verger translates into French as "*mère*" (mother).

15 Lawal footnote: "This is an indirect reference to blood; the palm oil is reddish in color" (1996, fn. 35, p. 129).

16 See "The Secrecy of the Àjẹ́," chapter 3 of Hallen and Sodipo, 1996: *Knowledge, Belief and Witchcraft: Analytic Experiments in African Philosophy* for an account of similar views.

17 For *àkó* sculpture see R. Abiodun 1976, "A Reconsideration of the Function of *Àkó* Second Burial Effigy in Ọ̀wọ̀," *Africa* 46, no. 1: 4–29; and B. Lawal 1977, "The Living Dead: Art and Immortality among the Yorùbá of Nigeria," *Africa* 47, no. 1: 50–61.

References

Abimbola, Wande. 1976. *Ifá: An Exposition of the Ifá Divination Corpus.* Ibadan, Nigeria: Oxford University Press.

Abiodun, Rowland. 1976. "A Reconsideration of the Function of *Àkó* Second Burial Effigy in Ọ̀wọ̀." *Africa* 46, no. 1: 4–29.

Drewal, Henry J. and Margaret Thompson Drewal. 1983. *Gẹ̀lẹ̀dẹ́: Art and Female Power among the Yorùbá.* Bloomington: Indiana University Press.

Gates, Henry Louis Jr. 1988. *The Signifying Monkey.* New York: Oxford University Press.

Hallen, Barry and J. Olubi Sodipo. 1996. *Knowledge, Belief and Witchcraft: Analytic Experiments in African Philosophy.* Stanford, CA: Stanford University Press.

Horton, Robin. 1967. "African Traditional Thought and Western Science." *Africa* 37, nos. 1–2: 50–71 and 155–87 (Reprinted 1993 *Patterns of Thought in Africa and the West: Essays on Magic, Religion and Science,* 197–258. Cambridge: Cambridge University Press).

Horton, Robin. 1971. "African Conversion." *Africa* 41, no. 2: 85–108.

Hountondji, Paulin. 1983. *African Philosophy: Myth and Reality.* Bloomington: Indiana University Press.

https//en.wikipedia.org/wiki/Cosmos.

https//en.wikipedia.org/wiki/Metaphysics.

Idowu, E. Bolaji. 1962. *Olódùmarè: God in Yorùbá Belief.* London: Longman.

Lawal, Babatunde. 1970. *Yorùbá Sango Sculpture in Historical Retrospective.* Unpublished PhD thesis, Indiana University.

Lawal, Babatunde. 1976. "The Significance of Yorùbá Sculpture." In *The Proceedings of the Conference on Yorùbá Civilization,* edited by Isaac A. Akinjogbin and O. Ekemode, 356–63. Ilé-Ifẹ̀, Nigeria: Department of History, University of Ifẹ̀.

Lawal, Babatunde. 1977. "The Living Dead: Art and Immortality among the Yorùbá of Nigeria." *Africa* 47, no.1: 51–61.

Lawal, Babatunde. 1978. "New Light on Gẹ̀lẹ̀dẹ́," *African Arts* 11, no. 2: 65–70; 94.

Lawal, Babatunde. 1981. "The Role of Art in Òrìṣà Worship." In *The Proceedings of the First International Congress of Orisa Tradition and Culture*, 100–118. Ilé-Ifẹ̀, Nigeria: Department of African Languages and Literatures, University of Ifẹ̀.

Lawal, Babatunde. 1985. "*Orí*, the Significance of the Head in Yorùbá Sculpture," *Journal of Anthropological Research* 41, no. 1: 91–103.

Lawal, Babatunde. 1987. *Art for Life's Sake; Life for Art's Sake* (Inaugural Lecture Series), Ilé-Ifẹ̀, Nigeria: Obafemi Awolowo University Press.

Lawal, Babatunde. 1995. "*À Yà Gbó, À yà Tọ́*: New Perspectives on *Ẹdan Ògbóni*." *African Arts* 28, no. 1: 36–49; 98–100.

Lawal, Babatunde. 1996. *The Gẹ̀lẹ̀dẹ́ Spectacle: Art, Gender, and Social Harmony in an African Culture*, Seattle and London: University of Washington Press.

Lawal, Babatunde. 2001. "*Àwòrán*: Representing the Self and Its Metaphysical Other in Yorùbá Art." *The Art Bulletin* 83, no. 3 (September): 498–526.

Lawal, Babatunde. 2002a. "Behold the Mask: A Yorùbá Scholar's Experience." In *Facing the Mask*, edited by Frank Herreman, 8–13. New York: Museum for African Art.

Lawal, Babatunde. 2002b. "*Oríloníse*: The Hermeneutics of the Head and Hairstyles among the Yorùbá." *The World of Tribal Arts/ Le Monde de L'Art Tribal* VII, no. 2: 80–99 (Reprint from *Hair in African Art and Culture*, edited by Roy Sieber and Frank Herreman, 93–109. Munich, London and New York: Prestel and Museum for African Art, 2000).

Lawal, Babatunde. 2005. "Divinity, Creativity and Humanity in Yorùbá Aesthetics." In *Before Pangea: New Essays in Transcultural Aesthetics*, edited by E. Benitez, 161–71. Sydney, Australia: Sydney Society of Literature and Aesthetics (Also 2005 in *Literature and Aesthetics* 15, no. 1: 164–74).

Lawal, Babatunde. 2008. "*Èjìwàpò*: The Dialectics of *Twoness* in Yorùbá Art and Culture." *African Arts* 41, no.1 (Spring): 24–39.

Lawal, Babatunde. 2010a. "The Yorùbá Double-Axe Staff (*osé-Ṣàngó*): Tradition, Transformation and Recontextualization." in *GEO-GRAPHICS: A Map of Art Practices in Africa, Past and Present*, edited by Anne-Marie Bouttiaux and Koyo Kuoh, 184–91. Brussels, Belgium: Center for Fine Arts.

Lawal, Babatunde. 2010b. "After an Imaginary Slumber: Visual and Verbal Imagery of 'Awakening' Africa." *Word & Image, A Journal of Verbal/Visual Enquiry* 26, no. 4 (October-December): 413–28.

Lawal, Babatunde. 2012a. "*Ayélojà, Òrunn'ilé*: Imaging and Performing Yorùbá Cosmology." In *African Cosmos: Stellar Arts*, edited by Christine Kreamer, 217–43. New York: The Monacelli Press in collaboration with Washington, DC: Smithsonian National Museum of African Art.

Lawal, Babatunde. 2012b. *Visions of Africa: Yorùbá*. Milan, Italy: 5 Continents Editions.

Lawal, Babatunde. 2020. "One's Head Is One's Creator: The Interconnectedness of Word and Image in Yorùbá Art." In *Speaking of Objects: African Art at the Chicago Art Institute*, edited by Constantine Petridis, 96–115; 188–95. Chicago, IL: Art Institute of Chicago and New Haven and London: Yale University Press.

Mudimbe, V. Y. 1988. *The Invention of Africa: Gnosis, Philosophy, and the Order of Knowledge*. Bloomington: Indiana University Press.

Ojo, G. J. Afolabi. 1966. *Yorùbá Culture: A Geographical Analysis*. London: University of London Press.

Prince, R. 1961. "The Yorùbá Image of the Witch." *The Journal of Mental Science* 107, no. 449: 795–805.

Verger, Pierre Fátúmbí. 1965. "Grandeur et Décadence du Culte de *Ìyámi Òṣòrùngà* (Ma Mère la Sorcière) chez la Yorùbá." *Journal de la Société des Africanistes* 35, no. 1: 141–243.

3

Yorùbá Artistic Criticism

Robert Farris Thompson[*]

Introduction

This text also tells a story that illustrates how wrong things can go when one culture (Eurocentrist) approaches another (Yorùbá) with the assumption that the two are categorically different from one another. In the case of the Yorùbá that is a misconception the American art historian, Robert Farris Thompson, sets out to challenge and correct. Thompson wants to free the Yorùbá, in particular, from negative stereotypes portraying the African intellect as primitive, traditional, or as an "Other." The methodology he crafts to accomplish this and the results of its application will, however, prove to be controversial.

The methodologies involving African art have their own history. In the case of the Yorùbá, since many art objects were already on display in Eurocentric museums and private collections, they could be accessed independently from their culture of origin. This was compatible with a methodological approach known as *formalism* and produced accounts such as the following:

> Yorùbá figure carving shows certain very distinctive characteristics. The figures are lively and show great variety, every posture is attempted, and the trunk and body no longer remain on one axis. Forms are rounded, but are kept clear-cut and decisive; there is the usual African

---

[*] Robert Farris Thompson was for many years Professor of the History of Art at Yale University, USA. He received his PhD from Yale in 1965 for a thesis entitled *Yorùbá Dance Sculpture: Its Contexts and Critics*.

tendency towards enlarged heads and great reduction in the size of the legs. The form of the head is usually unmistakable; the general shape of the face is naturalistic, with pointed chin and large brow; the features are strongly marked. The eyes are long and pointed at each end, with the lower lid nearly as large as the upper, and the pupil of the eye is gouged out. The nose is broad at both root and base, with well-marked nostrils. The mouth protrudes, is thick-lipped, and does not narrow at the ends, which are slightly upturned. The ears are set high and well back on the head. Faces are cicatrized on the cheeks, and sometimes on the forehead, with tribal markings.

(Trowell 1970, 72)

This methodology treats art objects quite literally as visual *forms* that are then described in scrupulous empirical detail. But pure description does not say anything about how the objects relate to their cultures of origin. Who created them? What role did they play? Art historians recognized that to have this deeper understanding they would have to do fieldwork in the cultures concerned that would enable them to answer these kinds of questions. The problem with fieldwork arising from participant observation and information provided by informants is that it is inevitably secondhand. As time passed there came to be a supplementary demand for a different kind of information that would be comparatively firsthand: what one American scholar described as the "like-they-see-it" or "insider's view" of the art objects.[1] By this was meant how do Africans themselves, in this case the Yorùbá, view the creative process and evaluate the objects that are its outcome.

It is one thing to describe art. It is another to evaluate it. Viewing is not necessarily a passive process. It can involve evaluation, and that must involve criteria, subjective or shared, that are applied in order to create and appreciate an art object. Judging the origin and relevance of the criteria that are being applied also becomes important. When some African art objects were eventually assigned masterpiece status by Eurocentric connoisseurs, the criteria invoked were not of distinctly African origin.[2] A demand for more specific information about the criteria, if any, that Africans themselves apply for the creation and appreciation of art objects continued to be made.

In 1973 this demand appeared to be satisfied, in rather dramatic fashion, with the publication of an essay by the American art historian, Robert Farris Thompson, entitled "Yorùbá Artistic Criticism." The text of that essay is republished in this chapter as an example of how "listening" to the people of another language culture with the best of intentions can be subject to error. Here is how Thompson describes the contents of the essay:

> Eighteen indigenous criteria of sculptural excellence are presented in this section. Each criterion, a named abstraction, defines the categories of elegance by which Yorùbá recognize the presence of art. No single Yorùbá provided all these ideas. Canonical notions developed by the investigator were discussed with individual Yorùbá sculptors who sometimes added important insights or refinements of their own.
>
> (1973, 29)

Why did art historians wait so long to enquire after such criteria? Possibly because the objects involved had been thought to be fashioned by individuals who were as much primitive craftsmen as "artists" and therefore incapable of being guided by, much less articulating, anything like the aesthetic criteria and values that are associated with art in Eurocentric cultures. That is perhaps one reason why the contents of Thompson's article were received as somewhat sensational in international art historical circles.

Thompson wants to liberate the Yorùbá from the models of traditional Africa that make people there incapable of being critical and valuing the arts of their culture. Thompson begins his essay by outlining how he carried out the fieldwork that led to his findings. He first acquires a number of pieces of Yorùbá sculpture. He then begins to visit a variety of Yorùbá towns and villages where he puts the sculpture on display, in search of individuals (critics) who will comment on their artistic properties. "Potential critics moved in the curious crowds of bystanders which always formed around the writer, his wife, and assistant" (1973, 26).

> The crowd was then asked, while pieces of sculpture brought out for study were still in the sunlight, was someone willing to rank

the carvings for a nominal fee and explain why he liked one piece over another.

(1973, 26)

The individuals who do respond to Thompson's initiatives come from a wide variety of occupations: chiefs, priests, artists, traders, farmers, and civil servants, apparently almost everyone and anyone in Yorùbá culture.

Thompson tells us he was inspired to be so open-minded about who qualifies as a critic by a passage from an earlier essay published by the American anthropologist, Paul Bohannan, arising from his fieldwork on the Tiv of Nigeria. Thompson quotes the passage selectively in his text, for some reason omitting the single sentence that best expresses the viewpoint he was to adopt: "And in Tiv-land, *almost every man is a critic*" (Bohannan 1961, 94; my emphasis). This methodological tenet, of treating every member of Yorùbá culture as, in principle, a competent artistic critic will be challenged by Yorùbá art historians in succeeding chapters.

These critics have to be compensated monetarily because, according to Thompson, "Yorùbá critics will not criticize with style and precision unless it is made financially worth their while …. the *quality* of the data of the fieldworker may reflect the amount of money allocated to aesthetic research" (1973, 20–1; my emphasis; passages elided). In Yorùbá culture, that the *quality* (rather than *quantity*!) of information obtained in such circumstances is a function of remuneration also is more than questionable. This will be evidenced by methodological and empirical challenges that will be made in Chapters 4 and 5 to the artistic criteria Thompson claims to "reveal."

African, in particular Yorùbá, art historians were placed in a difficult position by Thompson's publication. That Yorùbá "critics" are credited with indigenous artistic guidelines and values is one thing. Whether the *specific criteria and values* enunciated by Thompson should be endorsed is another. Scholars like Babatunde Lawal and Rowland Abiodun had for long been doing research on Yorùbá aesthetics and the question was whether they would confirm, amend or challenge outright the criteria and values enunciated by Robert Farris Thompson.

Let's begin here with Thompson's heralded "insider's view" of how the Yorùbá themselves value their art.

The Thompson Text: Yorùbá Artistic Criticism

There exists in Subsaharan Africa, locked in the minds of kings, priests, and commoners, a reservoir of artistic criticism. Wherever tapped, this source lends clarity to our understanding of the arts of tropical Africa. The Eurocentric scholar may assign value to a work which would elicit equal praise in the compound of a traditional king, assuming the work and critics were from the same African society, but he cannot assume that the reasons for his choice are present in the mind of the native critic.[3]

Africans may admire works of art, or categories of artistic expression, which a Westerner, in the ethnocentric conviction that he had mastered all the relevant issues, might pass over in ignorance. African criticism enriches, in these cases, our sense of definition. By definition I mean the identification and characterization of expressive media which, like African dancing, might pass largely unanalyzed through the filter of scholarship. Conversely, consideration of African judgment of African art protects the student from the dangers of reading into a work of art aesthetic principles which might not be present in the native imagination.

More important is the fact that African aesthetics opens onto African sensibility. Aesthetic criticism suggests the relation of art to emotional ideals. These ideals, in turn, reveal the hidden unities which impose meaningful design upon the face of a culture. The mosaic may, of course, be apprehended only in fragments by members of the society.

Contexts of Yorùbá Artistic Criticism

Yorùbá art critics are experts of strong mind and articulate voice who measure in words the quality of works of art.

Yorùbá artistic criticism may occur at a dance feast where the excellence of sculpture and motion becomes a matter of intense concern. In Iperu-Rẹmọn, Nigeria, "loads" (headdresses) for the *Orò* cult are judged competitively on the basis of sculptural and choreographic appeal. Similarly, in Ajilete, Nigeria, "battles of dance" decide which quarter at a given festival has triumphed and brought glory to the town. The elders of Igogo-Ekiti critically observe the dance movement of young men who aspire to the honor of carrying the senior headdresses of the local *Ẹpa* cult. Young men of legitimate birth, physical, moral, and artistic powers are chosen. In this way festivals provide a setting of criticism.

In addition to the cult context, where critical activity seems to increase under the stimulus of expressive sounds and sights, artistic criticism seems to flourish among the Yorùbá in those situations where money provides auxiliary excitement or agitation. In the market, workshop, and other places, the quality of a work of art can become the essence of commercial transaction. Here aesthetic products again meet articulated conventional tests of quality. An apprentice, for example, who has attempted to sell an indifferent example of his work to a bona fide patron may find himself called into the workshop of the village master where the master criticizes him (Cordwell 1952, 292). The master indicates, either by carving a new piece or by improving the finish of the unsatisfactory work, proper control and care. He tells the carver what went wrong with the work and warns him to do better. The criteria of the master are frequently regarded as trade secrets, which explains why so few have been shared in the past with Westerners.[4]

Mutual criticisms among sculptors are an especially sensitive source of information about Yorùbá aesthetics. When a master carver impugns the abilities of a lesser carver, his gestures and facial expression can be as eloquently derisive as his words. Alaga of

Odo-Owa, for example, dilated his nostrils with disgust when he met a carelessly rendered *Ẹpa* headdress at Egbe: "A! A! the juju gourds are unpleasingly lumpy. The face of the man is crooked. *O burú tó bẹ́ẹ̀ gẹ́*—it's as bad as bad can be."

Apart from important chiefs and mutual friends, Yorùbá critics will not criticize with style and precision unless it is made financially worth their while. This does not mean that they are professional. It simply means that Yorùbá live traditionally in a world of money, personal honor, and entourage. By acts of generosity a Yorùbá leader proves to his entourage that he is worthy of their acclaim. By the same token, the Western student proves by remuneration that he merits the honor of shared qualitative data. The size of a Yorùbá ruler's entourage is a mark of his generosity and importance (Bascom 1951, 496); the quality of the data of the field worker may reflect the amount of money allocated to aesthetic research. This is in character with the importance that the Yorùbá give to spending money on oral skills. Drummers, for example, find livelihood in the praise of rich men, and one woman of Ikare has earned 75 pounds a year in recompense for prayer of surpassing beauty and force.[5]

The oral art of criticism also moves within the sphere of money. It is certain, moreover, that few traditional Yorùbá make gratuitous statements of opinion on any subject in the presence of foreigners. No informant ever discussed with me the notion of multiple souls, but this did not mean that such a belief was not indigenous, as the researches of P. Amaury Talbot (1926, 261–2) and William Bascom (1960) attest. We must therefore weigh the following report with special care:

> I have never heard a spontaneous discussion on the form, proportion
> or expression of a piece of sculpture—although I have lived twelve
> years in Yorùbá country and have moved a great deal among priests
> and worshippers in shrines full of religious carvings.
>
> (Beier 1963, 6)

This does not imply an absolute lack of spontaneous discussion of aesthetic merits in Yorùbáland. It may mean that outside the festival, the commercial transaction involving sculpture, the admonitions of master to apprentice, the mutual criticisms among sculptors, and so forth, it is rare. Entrance into a shrine full of carving clearly does not guarantee an audience with a traditional critic. After all, do Roman Catholics analyze the aesthetic merits of cathedral images when at worship?

A Westerner may be lucky enough to overhear some fragment of spontaneous criticism. By chance I observed a mother of twins abuse an apprentice because he had brought her an image which she said did not resemble a human being. Again by chance I observed the head of the Mękǫ *Gèlèdé* cult motivate his hired carver, by worriedly knitting his brows, to rectify certain proportional improprieties.

Is it possible to distinguish criticism to paying outsiders from in-group criticism? In both instances critics name abstractions and cite common terminology in order to define the qualities which distinguish aliveness from, say, woodenness. However, it seems likely that critics who are also master carvers may rise to a higher level of nuance and precision in their conversations about quality. In point of fact, some sculptor-critics use a set of analytical verbs which are as sure in effect as the defining strokes of their adzes. These verbs grant them the power to measure the relative weight and shading of linear properties with an accuracy which might well provide astonishment in the West.

As in the professional jargon of the social scientist, the proliferation of conceptual vocabulary among the better Yorùbá critics "corresponds to an intensely sustained attention toward the properties of reality." This is an instance of Levi-Strauss' important observation that in their appetite for objective knowledge we have one of the most neglected aspects of the thinking of those whom some still dare to call primitive (Levi-Strauss 1962, 5).[6]

Cross-Cultural Identification of the Critic

Yorùbá qualitative criteria are consensual. This means they are matters of opinion, widely shared, but perhaps only fully comprehended by the guardians of philosophic thought. The best example of the latter are the priests of the divination cult. Yorùbá aesthetic criteria are perhaps best nuanced by sculptor-critics who lend to their words their special insights of process and form. But the roots of the criteria lie with the common people without whose supporting testimony the fabric of aesthetic thought loses conviction and certainty.

Aesthetics among the populous Yorùbá people is thus the sum of simple statements about artistic quality and the sum of the verbal characterizations which qualify these statements. When the qualifications are weighed it is found that the simplicity of the vocabulary is only apparent. On the other hand, a Westerner might validly draw from random audiences the following conclusion:

> I have seen people dancing and singing for a new work of art—but its merits as art are not normally discussed. It is possible to hear comments on the craftsmanship. Slovenly surface treatment in a piece of sculpture, and any kind of quick careless work will be condemned.
>
> (Beier 1963, 6)

Identification of the African Critic: The art critic in a traditional African society may be identified first on the basis of whether he has voiced elements which imply a theory of elegance or excellence in art. Secondly, one notes whether the critic successfully applies this theory to particular cases. In the process, it is possible to distinguish the critic from the appreciator (Ballard 1957, 194).

Appreciators identify with a work of art; in their vision the physical facets are in sharp focus, while aesthetic facets are blurred. An example: one evening while the harmattan blew chill into the air, a young man attempted to evaluate a twin statuette by the light of a native lamp. He dealt with the practical virtues of the cap depicted on the image's head; its flaps, he said, protect one from the cold. He had identified with the subject matter. A critic emerged from the shadows around the lamp and criticized the appreciator's lack of insight. He made comments about posture and vigor and qualified one of his standards. Appreciators only identify. Critics both identify (richly reflecting cultural preoccupations) and criticize (on the basis of normal elegance).

The most important criterion of identification of African critics is that their standards of judgment be qualified. Estimation of quality on grounds of coiffure may, if no further reasons are given, reflect associative values. Coiffure characterized in terms of delicacy of line and spacing does indeed constitute aesthetic criticism.

Judgments of better or worse imply an aesthetic when they are qualified and if the qualifications prove to be fairly systematic. Whatever else true criticism is, it is an applied aesthetic. Traditional African critics may qualify their remarks with subordinate clauses, as it were, in which the reasons behind each choice are spelled out and where, ideally, the reasons for the reasons are also given. At one end of the continuum of judgments one monitors the simple statement that such-and-such a work is "good"; in the middle one finds characterizations of aesthetic flavor, for example, "the features are handsome"; at the opposite end of the continuum one encounters aesthetic substance, as when a critic remarks on the delicacy of the modeling of lips.

One meets surprises. One may discover a rationale which is wholly "cultural" in flavor. Thus an Oke-Iho critic found fault with the carved image of a devotee in a shrine because the face was not beautiful. Why? Because the mouth was carved open. Why this objection? Because a fly (one of the traditional messengers of evil) might enter the mouth or dirt collect within the oral cavity (Yorùbá fear imprecations uttered when the mouth is dirty, especially early in the morning).

Associative values, even of the most magico-religious nature, and true aesthetic sensibilities are not mutually exclusive any more than possession of the skill of reading and writing prevents one from worshipping the traditional Yorùbá gods.

Yorùbá Art Critics: Their Character and Contribution

The presence of sculpture in Yorùbá country, together with a tradition of artistic criticism, provides a basis for the understanding of the relation of African sculptors to art itself.

As Bohannan has commented, definition of artistic criticism depends upon study of critics, not artists (see Smith 1961, 94):

I was wrong in my field work because, Western fashion, I paid too much attention to artists, and when artists disappointed me I came away with nothing. When I return I shall search out the critics. There are as many reasoned art critics in Tiv society as there are reasoned theologians or political theorists, from whom we study Tiv ideas about their religion and politics.

Bohannan's conclusions gave direction to my program of study. He taught me to expect little from artists as informants on quality. Early in my field work I asked a Yorùbá sculptor which were his finest works and was not surprised to hear that all of his works were fine. At the end of my field work I returned to his compound. This time he spoke of form and quality in sculpture although he still evaded analysis of his own works. What had opened his lips about quality? Rapport, *per se*, had little to do with it. What had happened was this: thanks to conversations with critics I now possessed some of the vocabulary of the Yorùbá aesthetic. The sculptor confronted with the critical language of his peers is the sculptor partially disarmed.

The Collapse of "Primitive Art"

Criteria of primitivism in the main do not apply to the traditional Yorùbá, which means that one must rethink the status of the arts and criticism of this important African people. For example, here are some of the characteristics of "primitive culture" (Hsu 1964), 1) non-literacy, 2) small-scale settlements, 3) isolation, 4) lack of historical records, 5) low level of technical achievement, 6) social relations based primarily on kinship, 7) nonindustrialization, 8) lack of literature, 9) relative homogeneity, 10) nonurban setting, 11) general lack of time reckoning, 12) moneyless economy, 13) lack of economic specialization, and 14) endowment with an overpowering sense of reality where everyday facts have religious and ritual meaning.

Only four of these criteria really apply to the Yorùbá. It is true that Yorùbá were nonliterate before the coming of the Europeans to their shores. They based their social relations primarily on kinship (and they still do). They were not industrialized; they were endowed with an overpowering sense of reality (many still are). But their cities were not small in scale, nor were they isolated. Yorùbá urbanism, Bascom (1959, 29–44) indicates, predates the European penetration and probably was ancient. Court singing kept historical records alive (Biobaku 1955). The technical achievement of the Yorùbá craftsmen is an historic fact.[7] Equally complex were and are the many genres of the rich oral resources of traditional Yorùbá literature—hunters' ballads, ancestral songs, praise poems, divination verses, proverbs, and so forth.[8] Yorùbá traditionally had a sense of time reckoning and a cowrie-shell currency.[9] Economic specialization, both in degree and incidence, was striking. If some traditional Yorùbá are endowed with an overpowering sense of reality, it is difficult to see where their attitude differs from that of clergymen or philosophers in the West.

The issue of nonliteracy and industrialization seems important only to those for whom it is important to preserve the concept of "primitive art." Lack of factories and a high incidence of illiteracy have never prevented scholars from classifying the world of Gothic France as a civilization.

It is possible to stress, as definitively "primitive," the "absence of any political organization which is necessary before man-power can be trained and utilized for the construction of roads, aqueducts, or monumental architecture" (Wingert 1962, 6). However, we know from the history of Yorùbá architecture that a mighty rampart, the *eredo*, surrounded the inner kingdom of the Ijebu (Lloyd 1962, 15–22). The ancient holy city of Ilé-Ifẹ̀ was superbly walled. Monumental royal architecture, necessitating politically organized units of communal labor, adorned the ancient cities of Ekiti.[10]

It is interesting that a recent artistic geography of "primitive art" excludes the arts of the Andes. Is Great Benin or Ancient Ifẹ̀ more primitive than Chan-Chan? The separation of the civilizations of the world into great, in contrast to primitive, categories of culture appears meaningless when applied to simpler societies. The collapse of "primitive art" as a workable concept is nigh.

Once the mask of primitivism falls, what will we see? We may discover that the vision of African aesthetics as rudimentary or functional only projected our own weakly developed means of verbalizing the visual constituents of fine African sculpture. It is just possible, for example, that Yorùbá critics surpass all but the most professional of Western students of Yorùbá art in fluency of verbalization. To match the level of competence with which a Yorùbá cultivator estimates artistic quality, one would have to deal with a specialist of Western art. Wherever and whenever Yorùbá critics of Yorùbá sculpture analyze sculpture, they do so with conviction and swiftness of verbalization.

Yorùbá Critics: Selection and Profession

Artistic criticism was not requested in any village or town until data about carvers, dating of works, names of woods, and so forth had been collected. This art historical research served as a kind of lure. Potential critics moved in the curious crowds of bystanders which always formed around the writer, his wife, and assistant. The crowd was then asked, while pieces of sculpture brought out for study were still in the sunlight, was someone willing to rank the carvings for a nominal fee and explain why he liked one piece over another? Owners sometimes immediately made clear that they did not want to participate—"to put it to another person," a twin image owner protested once. Almost without fail someone would step forward and immediately begin to criticize the sculpture. The rare delays did not stem from lack of verbal skill. Rather some informants were simply afraid that their efforts would not really be compensated. Others wished to study the works with care in the light, turning them around and testing their profile and mass. The volunteer-critics were, with two exceptions, male.

Eighty-eight critics offered their services.[11] None was a full-time professional, as far as could be determined, but as two entries in Bowen's *Grammar and Dictionary of the Yorùbá Language* of 1858—*amẹwà* "to be a judge of beauty" and *mẹwà* "to be a judge of beauty"—broadly suggest traditional Yorùbá have long had a concept which substantially overlaps our own notion of the connoisseur.[12]

But if Yorùbá critics are not professionals, many of them prove to be leaders of opinion in other areas. Sixteen informants were village chiefs, nine were heads of traditional cults, four presided over quarters of towns, fifteen were artists, eleven were in trade, and seven were in the employ of the Nigerian government. All drew upon their importance of self-esteem as the basis for their authority. In the male-oriented Yorùbá world it was not surprising that only two women appeared as critics. But also many of the images under discussion were twin images and women are the owners of these images. As such, they were understandably reluctant to rank their own possessions.

Yorùbá criticism is not the prerogative of kings or of politically important persons. Almost anyone is free to criticize art if he (or she) so desires. Thus 20 cultivators, some of them of very humble economic means, balanced the simplicity of their material possessions against the riches of their mind. Their powers of qualitative characterization compared favorably with the commentaries of kings. Neither king nor commoner, however, could improve upon the insights of the sculptor-critics of Northern Ekiti. If the excellence of criticism is intellectually ranked among the Yorùbá, the ranking depends upon the critic's individual talent and degree of familiarity with the forms of art.

Name, approximate age, village, profession, and religion were tabulated insofar as possible. In this way it was discovered, for example, that practicing Christians and Muslims used the same criteria by which worshippers of traditional Yorùbá gods judged art. But only 19 exclusively Christian and five exclusively Muslim responded. The remainder (64 critics) were practicing devotees of one or more of the traditional Yorùbá gods.

The variable of ownership seems pertinent. Of a total of 88 informants, only 32 actually owned the pieces of sculpture under discussion. They may have possessed sculpture in their own compounds but none of them offered to fetch and analyze their own possessions. This suggests that Yorùbá more readily evaluate sculpture when it belongs to somebody else.

Nevertheless, 32 critics saw no harm in ranking their own possessions provided they were paid for doing so. But no mother of twins was ever persuaded to judge her own twin statuettes. Years of ritual had made these images seem alive. In point of fact, twin mothers handle their statuettes lovingly. Some explain that they are alive. One cannot expect a mother in such circumstances to play favorites. To do so is positively dangerous: the spirit of a slighted twin may strike the mother with sterility or cause her to "swell up" and die. In the Aworri bush village of Ayobo, a middle-aged critic had begun an interesting recital of the "proper" physiognomy of the *ibejì* face when suddenly he cut himself short and became silent. When asked to resume the thread of his argument, he refused and stated firmly: "We cannot so abuse these *ibejì*. We are afraid of what they might do to us."

The Artist as Self-Critic

An American photographer was once asked to rank and edit his works for an exhibition catalogue. He replied bitterly that he would rather edit his own children. There is little reason to believe that less emotion attaches to the works which Yorùbá sculptors create or that they might rank in public their own works with pleasure. Compare Bohannan's experience among the Tiv: he asked a calabash carver which was his favorite design, and the artist reasonably replied that he normally liked the one he was working on, so he liked them all.

Yorùbá carvers had a stock reply for Justine Mayer Cordwell when she asked them to evaluate their preference of one form over another: "I do whatever the customer orders." In the light of this and similar admission heard in Yorùbá country from carvers, it seems likely that when sculptors rank their works equally, they do so with an eye to commercial advantage and that, in any event, inability to criticize their own works is shammed. I did not embarrass the Alaga of Odo-Owa (formerly known as Bamgboye) with direct questions about the qualities of his recent work, but I could not fail to note the enthusiasm with which he led me around the *Ẹpa* headdresses which he carved before 1955 and which were of good quality and the sadness which came into his face when he stood before his last *Ẹpa* headdress, at Obo Ayegunle, carved in 1959 when his physical strength had declined.

It is significant that the carvers and blacksmiths who served as critics judged the work of rivals and not their own handiwork. Their gusto and precision might well have evaporated had they been asked to analyze their own creations. Nevertheless, one Yorùbá sculptor, Bandele Areogun, has proved willing to criticize (at least retrospectively) his own works.[13]

Identification of Basic Criteria: Conversation with critics was straightforward. When an Ẹ̀gbádò critic observed that the lineage marks on the face of an image pleased him, a simple pointing question, *nítorí kíni* (Why?), sufficed to elicit an aesthetic response.

All responses were translated into English in the following manner: 1) the field interpreter wrote out a verbatim text of the critic's comments on the spot and checked it with him, 2) the field interpreter and the author wrote out together a rough translation of the comments on the spot and checked it with the critic, 3) the translations were evened out and polished at the author's base at Lagos or Ilé-Ifẹ̀, 4) finished typescripts of vernacular text and English translation were rechecked for accuracy and searched for nuances of idiom and vocabulary by Mr. Samuel Adetunji of Ilesha in New Haven, Connecticut.

When I analyzed the comments of the 88 critics, common denominators of taste emerged, representing the rationale behind the individual choices. This rationale is the "Yorùbá aesthetic."

Yorùbá Aesthetic Criteria

Eighteen indigenous criteria of sculptural excellence are presented in this section. Each criterion, a named abstraction, defines the categories of elegance by which Yorùbá recognize the presence of art. No single Yorùbá provided all these ideas. Canonical notions developed by the investigator were discussed with individual Yorùbá sculptors who sometimes added important insights or refinements of their own.

Before examining the criteria in detail the general Yorùbá notion of the aesthetic will be discussed.

The Yorùbá Notion of the Aesthetic

To speak of a native aesthetic presupposes basic questions. First, have the Yorùbá a notion of the aesthetic? The answer, as might be plain by now, is "yes." Artistic sensibility, mixed with a hint of the hierarchy of the beautiful, is a clear power of the following verse from the oral literature of divination:

Anybody who meets beauty and does not look at it will soon be poor.
The red feathers are the pride of the parrot.
The young leaves are the pride of the palm tree.
The white flowers are the pride of the leaves.
The well-swept veranda is the pride of the landlord.
The straight tree is the pride of the forest.
The fast deer is the pride of the bush.
The rainbow is the pride of heaven.
The beautiful woman is the pride of her husband.
The children are the pride of the mother.
The moon and the stars are the pride of the sun.
Ifa says: beauty and all sorts of good fortune arrive.

(Beier and Gbadamosi 1959, 30)

Discrete visual phenomena intersect: beautiful possessions (verandah, wife, children) whose quality the owner maintains or protects; ephemeral beauty (leaves, flowers, rainbows) at its prime; the beauty of more permanent things, earthly and celestial, which a sensitive man does not take for granted. Prize these things, the god of divination warns, for mental richness creates material wealth.

Aesthetic impulse alone brought together these felicities; their unifying aspect was beauty. The poem has the effect of an *aide-mémoire*: it safeguards, as it were, the natural resources of Yorùbá aesthetic experience.

It is clear that a classification of visual powers, systematically developed, does not constitute mere function or utility. On the contrary, the moral is clear: aesthetic sensibility brilliantly embarks a man upon his career.

This poem, as well as other passages which might be cited from the oral literature of the Yorùbá, refutes the assumption that Africans lack experienced appreciation of natural beauty for its own sake. Yorùbá, for instance, greatly admire the quality of verdancy which is implicit in one line of the poem and explicit in the common phrase, *ilẹ̀ yìí tútù yọ̀yọ̀*, "this land is verdant" (Abraham 1958, 658).[14]

If it is accepted that Yorùbá truly appreciate physical beauty, the next question is: have the Yorùbá a notion of aesthetic quality in sculpture; have they precise criteria by which to analyze the constituents of the beautiful in plastic expression? The answer again is yes. The plastic order of Yorùbá sculpture is so striking as to stimulate an immediate awareness of its concrete manifestations in the minds of native critics. They speak fluently of the delicacy of a line, of the roundness of a mass. This eliminates the general question of whether or not Yorùbá identify the aesthetic components of form.

Art as Use—the Pidgin English of African Aesthetics: Few old-fashioned ethnologists dreamed that the peoples they investigated experienced aesthetic responses. And they never dreamed that "primitive man," himself conversant with art and noting few men of like experience among the emissaries from Europe he met in the nineteenth century, might be addressing to Westerners the same reproach.

Some traditional Yorùbá seem to assume a white man's ability to perceive aesthetic import in art is weak or underdeveloped. One illustration must suffice: asked why he was most proud of a certain carved divination dish, a diviner at Ilobi replied: "It is a container of good divination things." Outwardly, he was "incapable of aesthetic analysis." But inwardly, he had assumed that utility was the only trait a foreigner might comprehend. When assured of the true direction of the inquiry, he spoke at once of quality.

The alleged lack of aesthetic among ethnographic peoples may well have derived from a kind of conceptual pidgin which arose when "civilized" and "primitive" man met and spoke of art, neither believing the other capable of aesthetic analysis. Thus, as Bohannan observed, the Tiv weaver keeps his best piece for his mother-in-law and sells his worst piece to foreigners who, presumably, would not know the difference (See Smith 1961, 92). The Fon brass caster sells the coarsest of his creations to foreigners and excellent pieces in traditional styles to indigenous patrons (Herskovits 1938, 358).[15] An Anago Yorùbá wood sculptor, although locally noted for an especially sensitive handling of earth colors, permits enamel paint to be splashed in garish patterns over commissions for Westerners, obliterating the fine cuts of his knife, because "that is what those Europeans like." In the process, Western and African prejudices are mutually reinforced.

Yorùbá Qualitative Criteria

[1.] **Midpoint Mimesis:** A value of Eastern art is exemplified by the story of the dragon which was painted with such aliveness that the creature flew out of the ink and into the air. The Western parallel tells of the birds who pecked at painted fruit. "What is the similar African story?" Mr. Kenneth Murray (1961, 100) has asked.

The following African version, a precious fragment of the oral literature of the Yorùbá, documents equal attention to shape, detail, and vitality, but these Western-sounding preoccupations dissolve in a solvent of native irony.

Motinu and the Monkeys is a fable about a beautiful girl, Motinu, who meets a magnificently handsome man near the Yorùbá city of Owo. The man is actually a monkey in disguise who tricks Motinu into marrying him and moving to his forest eyrie where he transforms himself back into his true state and the hapless girl is forced to drum dance music and fetch wild corn for her captor and his chattering friends. By chance Motinu meets a hunter, when alone in the woods one day, and he promises to rescue her. The hunter's stratagem is a capsule rendering of the traditional Yorùbá notion of mimesis:

> On his return to Owo, the hunter called on a woodcarver in the town. He described to the carver Motinu's hairstyle, and tribal markings and asked him to make eight little images of her. When these had been carved and painted, the hunter carried them to the bush when he knew he would find Motinu alone, and then together, they set out quickly for Owo. Every few miles, the hunter dropped one of the carvings in a conspicuous place along the track. (The hunter) knew that these images would delay the monkeys when they tried to follow them ....

When the monkeys reached the first image they were very curious indeed and sat down to chatter and argue.

> "What is this," they said, "that bears such a strong resemblance to Motinu? ... growing tired of it, they threw it away into the bush and went on in pursuit of their lost Motinu ... Each image they came to exasperated the monkeys more and more, and when they came upon one they would pounce on the image in anger and smash it up, chewing the pieces afterwards till nothing remained. By this means Motinu and (the hunter) were able to escape.

(Fuja 1962, 47–9)

This fable, to begin with, qualifies the degree of realism Yorùbá critics desire: the village connoisseurs are pleased by conventionalized human faces sharpened with touches of individuality (lineage marks and coiffure). The monkeys, unlike the birds of the West, were not deceived. There was no reason that they would be, for one of the aims of the Yorùbá sculptor is to strike through the individual personality of men and women to arrive at general principles of humanity.[16]

The monkeys puzzled over the images and, in a sense, appreciated their mimetic qualities—"What is this, that bears such a strong resemblance to Motinu"—but never did they confuse art with reality. Thus the fable summarizes Yorùbá mimesis: the formulation of general principles of humanity, not exact likeness. Light touches of portraiture (hair, scars, dress) redress the balance in favor of individuality, yet not to the degree where even the vilest monkey cannot distinguish likeness from equivalence. Mimesis to modern traditional Yorùbá means the cultivated expression of resemblances (*jíjọra*), not likenesses. It is "midpoint mimesis" between absolute abstraction and absolute likeness.

This is brought out by the vocabulary of the 20 critics who applied this criterion to their arguments. A single sentence, *Ó jọ ènìọ̀n* (It resembles a person), was the modal expression although an alternate phrasing, *Ó dàbí ènìọ̀n* (It looks like a person), was also heard. A healthy recognition of the limitations of illusion is implied in the verb *jọ*. Witness the common phrase, *ó jọ bẹ́ẹ̀* (It seems to be the case). It is therefore significant that Yorùbá critics qualify mimesis with a phrase which makes clear a desire for generalization. They did not say that carvings resembled specific personalities.

[2.] Hypermimesis: Some of the reasons why Yorùbá art comprehends mimesis as a process sited somewhere between abstraction and exact likeness can be found in the critic's rationale for disapproving of a work. Amos Tutuola plants one clue in his Yorùbá folk novel, the *Palm-Wine Drinkard*, which is based upon traditional mythic themes. At one point the hero of the novel encounters his own portrait in wood and is frankly terrified (Tutuola 1952, 68):[17] "Our own images that we saw there resembled us too much." There can be something sinister about absolute mimesis. Why? One reason seems magical. A master carver of Ẹfọn-Alaiye, Owoeye Oluwuro, told me that a traditional *Èfọn* sculptor, before he initiated any important commission involving the carving of human eyes, mouth, and nose, had to make a sacrifice of sugarcane, dried maize with red palm oil, and pigeon to prevent the entrance of ugliness into his carving. What kinds of ugliness? A wrinkled man's wrinkles, a warty man's warts. If his adze slipped, as it were, and he began to carve the unpalatable truth in some of the faces which he saw around him, the danger existed that these very features might be transmitted to the face of his next-born child.

To one Yorùbá critic a slight hint of individual expression sufficed to incur censure: "[One carving's mouth] comes out to form a laugh. That is bad." The lips of an ideal statue ought to be pursed. Such lips reflect impersonal calm.

Perhaps the most decisive factors behind the limitations placed upon mimesis in Yorùbá art are aesthetic ones: the assumptions of the native critic (that sculpture be smooth, youthful, erect, and so forth) would be violated by direct rendering of the rough skin, gaunt appearance, and ruined posture of an elderly man.

[3.] Excessive Abstraction: Related to the notion of mimesis, on a negative grid of disapproval, is the notion of excessive abstraction. Fine sculpture, to the Yorùbá, is not too real, but neither does it absolutely depart from natural form. For example, a North Oyo critic stated that "if a person's ears were all round like that they would talk about him" and condemned a work of art while he went on to laud another piece with relatively realistic ears.

Carvers are amused by apprentices who fail to imprint human quality upon the principal masses of their work. Bandele Areogun once studied a carved house column by Ayantola of Odo-Ehin and commented derisively:[18] "It looks like an *àpótí*," and then laughed. In making this comparison with *àpótí*, a common Yorùbá term for box, Bandele had impugned the ability of his rival to enliven brute timber with human presence.

[4.] Visibility: Twenty-nine critics stressed this quality. A master sculptor, the Alaga of Odo-Owa, heartily concurred with their emphasis: "One knows from the visibility of the face and other parts of the image whether the work is beautiful." The artist used, as did some of the critics, the precise Yorùbá word for visibility, *ifarahòn*.

Some critics phrase the idea without refinement and simply assign importance to sculpture of full, well-finished, organic details. Thus a critic of Tede: "the tribal marks are well cut … I like the eyelashes, they help make the face attractive … the hairdress is exact … all five fingers are complete … all five toes are complete. The other carvers did not show the toes so visibly."

But sculptors lend to their criticism a vocabulary of astonishing accuracy and range. Their words describe to begin with, the stages of the process of carving. Bandele Areogun of Osi-Ilorin distinguishes four divisions in the making of sculpture:[19] 1) the first blocking out, 2) the breaking of the initial masses into smaller forms and masses, 3) the smoothing and shining of the forms, 4) the cutting of details and fine point of embellishment into the polished surfaces of the prepared masses.

Alaga of Odo-Owa views the process slightly differently: 1) the measuring of the wood, 2) the blocking out of the head, occiput, chest, torso, buttocks, thighs, legs, and feet in that order, 3) the smoothing and polishing of all masses, 4) the incising of details into the polished masses. Alaga insists that "above the shoulders the head must be readily visible." Visibility as criterion therefore is an assignment of the initial stages of adzework (are the major masses visible?) and the terminal stages of knifework (are the smaller embellishments and linear designs visible?).

The privilege of visibility must not be abused: as the Alaga told me, a sculptor must not only block out a schematic eye (*yọ ojú*) which provides as gross visibility and relief, he must also "open" the eye (*là ojú*) with sensitive lining. Visibility refers, therefore, to clarity of form and to clarity of line.

Let us consider the last quality first. Linear precision is largely a matter of knifework, whereas plastic clarity is summoned from the brute mass of the chunk of the log by means of adzework. Although knifework falls under Bandele's fourth category of *fínfín* in Osi-Ilorin, this final stage cannot be described solely by means of the root verb *fín*, which means to carve or incise. Bandele uses an extended set of special verbs, each with its own nuance:[20] 1) *là*, which refers to the "lining" of eyes, mouth, fingers, ears, and toes, 2) *lọ*, which refers to the "grooving" of brass bracelets, 3) *gé*, which refers to the cutting of waistbeads and other forms of beads, 4) *fín*, which refers to the "incising" of coiffure, sash, fringes, and special patterns and designs.

Bandele criticizes, for example, the lack of visibility of a certain cult container by means of these special verbs: "The mouth remains; they have not lined it. They have not incised the sash. They have grooved the sash."

The fact that a lexicon of linear qualities exists suggests the depth of the Yorùbá aesthetic. Bandele uses verbs of line to estimate swiftly those carvers who have (or have not) liberated fine points of human appearance from the larger masses of the wood.

Alaga of Odo-Owa and Mashudi Latunji, who works in the faraway town of Meko in the province of the Ketu, use much the same sort of verbs Bandele employs in their criticisms. Like their colleague, the latter artists criticize the finishing of small detail, the rendering of its visibility, in terms of lining and incising and grooving but they criticize the cutting of coiffure and interlace patterns with the verb *dì*, which means, literally, to tie. Alaga insists one may judge the excellence of the rendering of cloth in sculpture by means of the verb *sán*. Thus: *Ó san bàntẹ́ dádá*—"He rendered the loincloth well." This refers, literally to the tying on of the garment.

The apparent lack of specialized vocabulary in the criticisms by non-carvers might suggest that Yorùbá criticism is intellectually stratified. Bandele, the sculptor, said: "They have not lined the eyes." But a carpenter (with no artistic pretensions) said: "The beautiful face has eyes which have lids and the ugly faces have lidless eyes." Yet all critics of Yorùbáland hold the artist responsible for as complete a grid as possible of human anatomic coordinates. Carvers seek to express generalized principles of humanity. They must carve them, nonetheless, with ultimate sharpness of clarity and focus.

Thus the notion of linear connoisseurship is highly developed among traditional Yorùbá. Symptomatically, the art of cicatrization in traditional times was of paramount importance, both as mark of lineage membership and aesthetic concern. Verbs of linear analysis in sculpture find a parallel in the language of the cicatrix specialist. This professional, like sculptors, has a verb for different visual effects. He cuts (*bu*) *àbàjà* marks, slashes (*ṣá*) *kẹ́kẹ́* marks, digs or claws (*wa*) *gombo* marks, and splits open (*la*) *Ẹ̀fọ̀n* marks (Abraham 1958, 301).

Relation of verb to sculptural effect seems meaningful. *Kẹ́kẹ́* marks are bold; when they are faint, they are allegedly called *gòmbọ́*, a fact which might be conveyed by the concept of slashing the former and clawing the latter. *Efọn* marks indeed seem to split open the flesh of the cheek.

Since antiquity, Yorùbá have adorned their cheeks with lines. They associate line with civilization. "This country has become civilized" literally means in Yorùbá "This earth has lines upon its face" (Abraham 1958, 399). "Civilization" in Yorùbá is *ilàjú*—face with lined marks. The same verb which civilizes the face with the marks of membership in urban and town lineages civilizes the earth: *Ó ṣá kẹ́kẹ́*; *Ó saiko* (He slashes the *keke* marks; he clears the bush). The same verb which opens Yorùbá marks upon a face, opens roads and boundaries in the forest: *Ó lanon, Ó la aala; ó lapa* (he cut a new road; he marked out a new boundary; he cut a new path). In fact, the basic verb to cicatrize (*là*) has multiple associations of the imposing of human pattern upon the disorder of nature: chunks of wood, the human face, and the forest are all "opened," like the human eye, allowing the inner quality of the substance to shine forth (Abraham 1958, 399, 400, see also 602 as to *sa*).

This history of associations with the tradition of cicatrization sharpens the eye of the Yorùbá critic and gives the sensitive noncarver the knack of talking about clarity of line with conviction. For example, an Aworri critic insisted that the coiffure on what he considered inferior sculpture was "too faint" and that the lines of good sculptural versions of hair must be seen. An Ijesha critic with a single comment—"the eyes really show on *Èfọ̀n* pieces"—went to the heart of his taste for linear visibility.

Another sample criticism: Ojelabi of Oluponon admired an image because the face was "visibile" and there was "a boundary line for the hair." These comments and many others which could be cited prove that noncarvers, with the simple vereb *họ̀n* (becomes visible), are able to defend their tastes when judging sculpture which does or does not satisfy local feelings about linear visibility.

Visibility, as has already been pointed out, also refers to clarity of form. An Ijebu cultivator judged one twin image excellent on the ground that its forehead was "more visible than the other [piece]"— (*Otowá ó họn jù eléyi lọ*). At Ṣepeteri a critic admired the nose on an image because it was readily visible. The taste for crispness of form affects the criticism of abstract shapes and ornament as well: a young citizen of Ajasse-Ipo viewed four carved door panels in the palace of the local chief and found the criterion of visibility the decisive means of distinguishing the best patterns. As in the discussion of line, plastic clarity is expressed by the verb *họn* or grammatical units constructed from this verb.

Artistic integrity is also a factor which must be taken into account. This point might not have been documented but for the comment of a critic from the west of Igbomina country who singled out the sharp visibility of an image and added that "If you want to marry a person you have to see the body completely." Plastic and linear clarity become a matter of candor: all parts of the body are presented to the court of the eye. Visibility in this sense means that the honest carver has nothing to hide; he nakedly exposes his imagination. He does not conceal an inability to portray a complicated hairdress under a cap or headtie.

To Bandele of Osi-Ilorin the head and the hands of images are the essential aspects of plastic clarity. "Don't we," he asked Kevin Carroll didactically, "look at the face at the top of the *Ẹpa* headdress first and then we look at the hand? Those two places we first take notice of. The body is not so difficult." If the face and the hand of the *igi* (superstructure) are carved with proper conscientiousness the carving will become readily visible and therefore good and therefore beautiful.

[5.] Shining Smoothness: Yorùbá who invoke the quality of visibility simultaneously invoke the quality of luminosity. Alaga of Odo-Owa told me that when he finishes a work of art he stands back to examine the "shine" of the work, the polished surfaces and the shadows in between the lines of incisions.

This taste for luminosity appears to have considerable historical depth. We may infer that the Yorùbá-influenced city of Great Benin reflected, as early as 1668, the Yorùbá quest for luminosity in art (in this case architecture) as visual stimulus, for early explorers duly documented the extraordinary polish of the earthen red walls of Benin (Roth 1903, 160–1).

Eleven modern Yorùbá critics shed light on the nature of this canon. Onamosun of Iperu recalled: "When my father (Taiwo Olejiyagbe) objected to low quality in my early work he sometimes lashed me with a flywhisk. I did not make any serious slips of quality after I got the hang of carving from observing my father's work day after day. But if he told me to carve an image very smoothly and I failed to comply, I would be punished. The smoothing (*işé dídón*) was done with a knife, with the side of the knife."

An Aworan lineage head asserted that smoothness was a matter of skill: he praised the straightness of the hand of a sculptor and then commented upon his luminous touches of polish.

Headmen at Ilogbo-Aworri and Ipole-Ijesha made clear that they demanded smoothness and shining qualities in sculpture. Speaking of cheeks, a priest of Erinle at Oke-Iho said: "The cheek (of this image) is beautiful; it is not swollen but rather shining" (*Eèkée ó dára, kò wú, sùgbón ó dón*).

Creative enjoyment of art by Yorùbá critics relates to the notion of luminosity in remarkable ways. Thus a cultivator at Odo-Nopa in the kingdom of the Ijebu:

> One image is ugly and can quickly spoil. Its maker did not smooth the wood. Another image was carved so smoothly that one hundred years from now it will still be shining, if they take proper care of it, while the ugly image will rot regardless.

One might compare this fragment of criticism (which seems to raise luminosity to talismanic powers of preservation) with a more idealized Yorùbá notion of beauty as "guard" or "amulet," which is present in the pages of Amos Tutuola. Here is a passage from his *Palm-Wine Drinkard*:

If bombers saw him in a town which was to be bombed, they would
not throw bombs on his presence, and if they did throw it it would
not explode until this gentleman would leave that town because of his
beauty.

(Tutuola 1952, 25)

When Yorùbá critics discuss luminosity, they almost unfailingly use the
verb *dọn*. The qualities conjured by the verb intermesh with aesthetic
implications associated with the initial stages of carving. Thus Bandele:[21]
"We know a carver's work is good if he has blocked it out well and by
the shining smoothness of the wood" (*t'o ba ti bu ona, ti o ba ti lena ona
lile da... nipa igi didọn*). Onamosun of Iperu and Bandele explain that
iṣé dídọn technically mean the smoothing of the forms of sculpture,
respectively with a knife of Remon and with a knife and chisel in
Northern Ekiti. Kevin Carroll has informed me that the old smoothing-
tool in Ekiti dialect was called *unkan* and consisted of a handle and
cutting edge formed from one iron bar. Bandele's phrasing refers to the
Yorùbá sculptor's intent to smooth down the surface of his wood so
that it reflects light and seems to shine, as if from an inner source. The
smoothness-shining duality emerges as both cause and effect. Surfaces
are so smoothed that they give back the lights of intelligence which
went into their making.

We are now prepared to suggest the background of one of the most
striking of the habits of the Yorùbá artist—his penchant for carving
facial traits in (to academic Western tastes) excessive relief. The issue
cannot be treated, of course, apart from other notions of quality. Linear
and plastic clarity combine with shining smoothness to illumine the
artistic intent behind this habit of carving.

The rounded shapes of the face of a Yorùbá image have been
smoothed so as to reflect light whether in sunlight or in shade. Eyes
in protrusion cast meaningful shadows against the glowing surfaces of
the face. The ink of shadow is calculatingly split below or above the
eyes (according to the source of light), the better to mark off their form
against the shine of the face, the better to make them "readily visible."
The short durational values of Yorùbá music propel sculpture in the

dance with staccato movements that blur the vision. Shadow against shining surfaces acts as a countereffect to this blurring.

Moreover, Yorùbá appreciate distinct intensities of shadow. I have observed Alaga turning a carved comb around in sunlight, testing the beat, as it were, of its rhythmic shadowed incisions. I have also observed a critic at Tede turning a twin statuette around in the sunlight, turning the image around several times, observing the flow of shadows.

Yorùbá recognize that deliberate excrescences and edges in sculpture cast darkened silhouettes which may be "read," as an abstract image, at considerable distance by an observer. Moreover, in the blur of the dance or under the shadows of a verandah, refinements of form must be made readily visible. Alaga tells us that the shadows between or within incisions and the shadows beneath or above relief are beautiful against the polished surfaces of the whole of a sculpture.

The eye primed to appreciate the canon of shining smoothness, as the foil of shadow, distinguishes master from apprentice in works of art. The adzemarks of the master, where the edges show, shine, while the adzemarks of the apprentice lack formal separation and do not shine.

We must be careful to point out that Yorùbá seem to prefer the relative or moderate enunciation of any given criterion. An absolute polish, mirror-like and glittering, is as foreign to their art as is sculpture in which no attempt whatsoever has been made to polish surfaces. Moreover, as Kevin Carroll has usefully reminded me, the woods which Yorùbá sculptors use are generally smooth in texture. And even the moderate or generalized shining of Yorùbá sculpture is broken in some areas with crosshatching, and other designs, sometimes extensively.

One of the most interesting extensions of the Yorùbá taste for luminosity is the depiction of clothing. Because Yorùbá artists devoutly desire to create well polished surfaces that reflect large amounts of light, they do not treat substances, which in reality are soft, with realistically softened textures. When a Yorùbá carves a headtie, turban, cap, or gown, he exaggerates its bulk and polishes it to a high sheen. Drapery conventionally has a consistency which resembles sheet metal far more than it does cloth. The soft twists of the turban of the Muslim cleric—a favored theme in recent *Gẹlẹ̀dẹ́* carving of the Yorùbá southwest—harden in the hands of a sculptor. Loose or folded twists of female headties (*gèlè*) stiffen into architectonic forms. Èṣù, the trickster, in one instance wears a cloth cap which in sculpture becomes as unyielding as an iron helmet.

Thus the Yorùbá aesthetic hardens and polishes the representation of the soft substances of life so that they will shine in harmony with the luminous whole of the image, so that the edges of a turban or a gown will cast the same strong shadows cast by the eyes in expressive relief or by multifaceted foreheads and torso areas. Just as the sound of hard, metallic percussion dominates much Yorùbá music—Yorùbá iron bells and gongs are distinctive because of their high pitch (King 1961, 11)[22]— so the creation of hard, almost metallic polished surfaces dominates Yorùbá sculpture. With respect to representation of clothing, and even hair, Yorùbá sculptors discover luminosity by thickening widths and polishing surfaces and sides.

A verandah post by Alaga which he carved for the house of a chief at Ekan-Meje *ca.*1931 demonstrates most tangibly to what extent he successfully acquired the aesthetic of luminosity.[23] The distinction between the smooth radiance of the head and coiffure of the central figure and the duller luster of the unfinished structural support above the head of the figure is decisive: Hair, cloth, and flesh glow with equal intensity.

The Yorùbá sense of luminosity is especially refined. Hunters in Yorùbáland are sensitive to this quality and have, for example, a word (*rekina-rekina*) to describe the glittering effect of sunlight shining on wind ruffled water.[24] And in their ballads and salutes hunters generally admire the gleaming surfaces of the pelt of a wild beast as they might have admired, when in town, the luminous refinements of a carved image.

[6.] **Emotional Proportion:** Yorùbá notions of proportion form a dialogue between the permissive and the prescribed. Critics countenance certain dimensional liberties when they are charged with tradiţional sanction of aesthetic expression. Critics approve sculptural composition set in "social perspective" where the sculpture indicates seniority by gradations of scale. At all times, however, critics rank sculpture upon a theory of relative proportion. The members of a king's entourage must be carved in proportion to one another, regardless of their scale in relation to the monarch.

A Ketu paradigm: the late Duga of Meko finished, probably before 1955, a striking headdress for the local cult of *Gèlèdé*. The headdress is surmounted by an *Àlùfáà* (the Muslim cleric), carved standing in a canoe with a helper. Two teakettles flank the canoe. The cleric counts his beads. The size of his rosary is overpowering; the beads fill his hands as a chunky width of Manila hemp rope might fill them. This is a splendid example of fusion of proportion and empathy. The usage of "emotional proportion" contrives to communicate the psychological importance of a thing, as opposed to strict measurement. Duga enlarged the beads of the cleric for at least two purposes: 1) so that they would "read" easily in the motion of the dance, 2) in conformance with their role in the important Islamic ritual of *dhikr*—"telling beads"—in solitary communion with Allah and the Prophet (Trimingham 1961, 93). The size of the rosary translates its fascination in the eyes of non-Muslim Yorùbá who recognize the power *dhikr* acquires from use in initiation and cult practice.

Duga framed the canoe bearing the cleric and helper between two teakettles. These are strikingly out of proportion to the cleric and the canoe, but they are convincingly related to the dimensions of the head of the mask which serves as infrastructure. All Yorùbáland has observed Muslim cattle-drivers from the north of Nigeria halt by the sides of roads and streets to pour ablutions from teapots. Recognition of the teakettle as a mark of modern Islam in West Africa would be immediate. Their symbolic dimensions are no more startling than the diminutive or heightened renderings of the Christian cross which are not taken as literal measurements of the True Cross but are tokens of faith.

Yorùbá share a notion with Heraklitus: a man's character is his fate. Yorùbá sculptors enlarge the human head to mark its importance as the seat of character, the part conversant with destiny. Heads, as wisdom symbols, mark the visual climax. But exaggeration of the head must not be ludicrous.

In the clear-cut instances of standing figures, the components of judicious proportion are swiftly identified by critics. Alaperu of Iperu minced no words: "The thighs are too thick for the body." Of a certain carver's work he said: "Bako carves figures with eyes too open. The lower part of the lid is too stretched out." A minor lapse of conception by the hand of the local master, Onamosun, did not pass unremarked: "Actually the height of the figure shows some grace. So far as I look at the cheeks and the nose I like what I see. Only the eye is a bit out of proportion." Significantly, the proportion of the head (which was slightly exaggerated) was not mentioned.

The criticism of Abinileko of Otta provided another source of Yorùbá thinking about proportion in carving. Abinileko, who in 1964 presided over the Oruba quarter of the capital of the Aworri subtribe, had been a tailor in his youth, and kept a cloth measuring tape in a wooden chest as a memento. He applied this measuring instrument to a judgment of the relative merits of the works of Labintan and Salawu, two sculptors of Otta. The bases of his judgment were two *Gẹ̀lẹ̀dẹ́* headdresses which he took down from nails on the walls of his parlor. "Labintan is the better carver," Abinileko began, tapping the best headdress with a stick. Breadth (*ìbú*) was to his mind an important variable. Labintan had conceived a human nose, for example, with pleasingly moderate measurements while Salawu had not. The critic reached for his measuring tape and marked off two and a half inches for the breadth of the ugly nose, one and a half for the finer nose.

He then compared mouths. Labintan's was two inches long, Salawu's three. He commented: "Labintan's mouth looks like the mouth of a person but Salawu's does not" (*Ẹnun tí Lábíntán rí bi tí ẹnu ènìọ̀n, ṣùgbọ́n ti Salawu kò jọ ènìọ̀n*).

He dissected further deficiencies: "Salawu's forehead is too close to the edge of the headgear. The distance from cap to the top of the nose is too short." He buttressed this point with a measurement: two and a half inches described the distance between nose and hat in the image by Labintan, one and a half for Salawu.

Precise measurements are by themselves merely descriptive. But the critic analytically used measurement as a means of arriving at a concrete notion of proportion.

Moderation in small things, not too broad the lips, not too short the forehead, might be suggested as the sum of these notions. The use of a Western instrument here does not vitiate the traditional grounding of this exercise, for the measuring tape was simply a replacement of African prototypes. Thus Ketu sculptors use the length of the blade of their knives as a rough module to secure the proportion and symmetry. Finally, Kevin Carroll has observed Bandele of Osi-Ilorin "often use a measure of hand length, finger length, and knuckle length."

As he wove his way through a complex argument about the aesthetic merits of Eyinle cult figures, an Oke-Iho critic made several observations which help us to understand how Yorùbá view the proportion of facial traits. The critic liked one chin because it was not short (*kò kúrú*). He condemned the dimensions of another sculptor's version of the human chin with metaphor: "It is not beautiful. The chin rushes into its house" (*Kò dá; àgbòn kó sílé*). The lower lip of the mouth on this piece was neglected; the lower margin of facial outline and the lower lip had been made to coincide, as in a mode prevalent among the Western Ijọ. The fine piece, on the other hand, displayed a suitably fleshy chin. The metaphor was apt, the chin of the inferior face did indeed seem to rush into the mouth and disappear.

The same critic found the lips of one figure "decently proportioned" (*Ó wa mogi-mogi*) and "terrible" on another figure. The "terrible" mouth was too big.

In conclusion, man is the module. As Alaga told me: "if the image represents a big man, the eyes must be big, if the image is small the eyes must be small." But inspiration and imagination are part of the process: "These measurements we use," Mashudi told me, "God gives them to us. No one is using the white man's instruments when they carve at Mẹkọ. We take our measurements from our heart."

[7.] Positioning: This concept overlaps the notion of proportion. Alaperu, for instance, analyzed the proper placement of parts of the body. "The ears are good, well-fixed, not too far down, not too far up." Eleven critics made similar commentaries. Jogomi of Ajilete laid equal stress upon the correct placing of the navel. Otuşoga of Odo-Nopa was disgruntled by a nose which he felt had been placed too high upon a face.

Yorùbá hunters attach importance to elision in recitals of their traditional ballads. Thus a Yorùbá was once documenting the ballad of the monkey when another Yorùbá interrupted: "No. Do not write it so, it does not sound sweet like that" (Collier 1953). The latter informant then proceeded to elide eight words to satisfy his tastes. On the other hand, there were many words which he did not run together, for as the distinguished late authority on Yorùbá linguistics, Professor R. C. Abraham, was forced to admit, there is no underlying principle about elisions (Abraham 1958, xxxi).

By the same token, Ogidi of Igogo-Ekiti imitates the natural position of the shoulders and navel in his sculpture, but he connects the upper lip to the edge of the nose. One elides for the sake of visual concord but there does not seem to be a fixed principle. Other North Ekiti carvers take pains to separate the nose from the lips.

[8.] Composition: The aesthetic spacing of things in relation to one another is a complication of the art of siting. Positioning of traits by means both mimetic and emotional becomes a more elaborate task of relating individuals (sometimes individuals, things, and animals) within a single composition.

On a minor level Yorùbá composition means the pleasing articulation of limbs in spatial terms. Alado of Ado-Awaiye characterized his pleasure in the graceful placement of the hands of a figure which embellished his own divination container. The curve of the wrist and the arm, the naturalness of the gesture, were stated as pleasing qualities.

Onamosun of Iperu reported that "one of the things that people are talking about when they see my work is my carving of the hands without detaching them from the body, with the outer side of the hand flat." The design element to which the carver refers is one of the striking qualities of his mode of figural composition.

Olodoye of Ijero-Ekiti briefly adumbrated a few compositional qualities. He liked the suppleness of the placement of a child within a mother's hand and he also expressed pleasure in the placement of a twin on the mother's back. Unfortunately, he did not qualify these remarks. It is possible that a cultural factor, namely the Yorùbá intense appreciation of motherhood and children, guided his remarks more than aesthetic discernments.

As to free siting, critics, did not discuss the matter but it seems probable that blendings of permissive and prescribed actions again apply. For instance, the members of a senior person's entourage are carefully positioned, normally, so that when seen full-front they do not obscure the view of their master.

[9.] Delicacy: Sixteen critics spoke of this quality, one of the few aesthetic notions for which we have scraps of nineteenth-century literary evidence. Thus the explorer Richard Lander in 1830: "The natives of that part of Africa appear to have a genius for the art of sculpture. Some of their productions rival in point of delicacy any of similar kind I have seen in Europe" (Quoted in Allison 1956, 18). Lander was an ethnocentric outsider but his disadvantages did not preclude a striking observation at an early date of one of the informing qualities of Yorùbá sculpture.

Samuel Johnson, himself a Yorùbá, understood the relevance of delicacy to the appreciation of other Yorùbá arts. Here is a comment on coiffure written in the 1890s:

> Hair is the glory of the woman. Unmarried ones are distinguished
> by their hair being plaited into smaller strips, the smaller and more
> numerous the plaited strips the more admired.
>
> (Johnson 1921, 101)

Traditional connoisseurs of the arts of hairdressing today still nod in agreement with the notion of delicacy and closeness of spacing.

The more closely spaced the braids, the more braids can be made to embellish the head. This taste informs the commentaries of modern traditional critics of Yorùbá sculpture. Thus an Ẹgbádò diviner at Ilobi characterized the aesthetic appeal of a certain divination dish in terms of its numerous faces and their diminutive eyes. "Small eyes" (*ojú kékeré*), he added, make an image resemble a person.

Delicacy of eye cut and lining was a concern of an Ẹgbádò and an Ijesha critic. The former liked the eyes of a twin image at Ajilete because the lids were thin (*ipénpéjú tínrín*); the latter remarked the pleasing smallness of eyes and used the identical phrase employed by the Ilobi diviner, *ojú kékeré*. An Ijebu critic isolated the element of delicacy in the aesthetic character of a carved version of hairstyle. He stressed the sensitive rendering of the plaits, saying literally that the "cuts" or "lines" were thin.

Smallness suited the tastes of the Ijebu critic when applied to the field of linear ornament. Smallness of anatomic mass provoked a different reaction. The critic denounced the slimness of an *ibeji*'s arm with the same adjective with which he had praised the fineness of line: *Èyìí tínrín jù lọ* (This one is thinner than the other). A thin line is beautiful, a very thin mass is not. Thus one must take pains to plot the usage of verbs which predict quality in Yorùbá criticism according to context and subject matter. Linear delicacy is a matter of admiration. But excessive delicacy or thinness in the portrayal of human mass is condemned. It may be that the latter quality is associated with the sinister, as suggested by a phrase in the pages of the Yorùbá novel *Simbi and the Satyr of the Dark Jungle* (Tutuola 1955, 73). "Their bodies were withered for fear." Ideally, the human frame in Yorùbá sculpture is carved with attributes full, vigorous, and fleshy. It is the shape of confidence.

To return to linear finesse: a carpenter of Ṣepeteri used an interesting verb in relation to this quality when he admired an especially sensitively carved *ibeji* and remarked that the coiffure was "just like a crown," an appropriate simile for its well-finished elegance of form. He refined his remark with a verb which seems to conjoin the notions of delicacy in coiffure which Samuel Johnson had documented some 74 years before. "I like the lines of the hairstyle," he said, "[Each] is small and tightly spaced" (*Ó wẹ́ dáda*). The verb *wẹ́*, according to Mr. Samuel Adetunji, describes both delicacy of line and spacing.

Yorùbá critics require delicacy in portrayals of human morphology. An Ajilete critic liked the ears on an image because they were small; an Oke-Iho critic voiced the same thought with the same phrase (*Ó kéré*). This speaker condemned versions of ears which were "conspicuously" (*Ó họ̀n gbagdagbagda*) visible. This is interesting because it not only qualifies the notion of grossness as the opposite of delicacy, but it also refines the notion of visibility. Elements which are conspicuous—too visible—are indecorous. The aesthetic import of *kéré*, like *tínrín*, depends upon context. There is a difference between a delicate nose and a nose which is simply too small. The vanishing nose is censured with the phrase *Ó kéré*.

Thus four words, at least, form the Yorùbá vocabulary of delicacy: 1) *kékeré*, "small," referring to the delicacy of mass; 2) *kéré*, "is small," referring to delicacy of mass in the context of approval; 3) *tínrín*, "narrow," referring to delicacy of line, both as to fineness of outline and as to sensitivity of grooving or incision patterns (*Tínrín* when applied to mass may acquire a negative denotation); and 4) *wẹ́*, literally "is slender," referring to linear delicacy in a special sense—tiny lines spaced closely together in neat parallel incisions.

Clear-cut definitions of the verbs' meanings emerge in contexts in which subtle sculpture stands beside brutal works. Taiwo of Ajilete said of sensitivity incised lineage marks: "That cicatrization pattern pleases me. It is tiny and spaced tightly together and not conspicuously big" (*Ilà nã wùn mi. O wẹ́ dáda. Kò tóbi gbagdagbagda*).

Yorùbá oppose in their diction the synonyms and antonyms of the delicate as skillfully as, in their traditional songs, the manifestations of romantic and practical love are opposed, as in the stanza "love is of many kinds, one love says 'if you die let me die with you,' another love says 'if you buy the soup I will buy the yam!'" The antonyms of the delicate in the parlance of Yorùbá critics are "big" and "blunt," as illustrated by the peculiarly expressive phrase *tóbi gbagdagbagda* (conspicuously big). The dull or blunted edge is not aesthetic. The fine edge is aesthetic. This notion overlaps to a great extent Western notions. Thus a common dictionary definition:

> *Fine.* 1. Exquisitely fashioned; delicate ME. 2. Not coarse; delicate in structure, a texture … very thin or slender.

[10]. Roundness: Fourteen critics defined roundness as an aesthetic handling of carved outlines and full spherical mass. As regards curved outlines the comment of an Igbomina critic is a useful introduction: "I prefer the chin of one image—the other is flat and sharp—for the best chin is moderate." Examination of the images he held in his hands as he judged them revealed that what he meant by "moderate" was pleasingly rounded, not angular.

The idea of full spherical mass was explored by Alaga of Odo-Owa. Alaga explains that the ideal form of the "pot mask," which serves as the helmet of the *Ẹpa* feast dancer, is rounded. He made signs of disgust when he stood before an *Ẹpa* headdress in Yagba territory which he felt failed to measure up to this standard. Alaga elaborated: "The pot-mask is not beautiful; it is not finished, it is not rounded" (*Kòkò kò dá; Kò ṣe pé; kò ṣe róbótó*). He referred to his own work as model. Failure to round major and minor masses not only destroys art, in Alaga's opinion, it can impair the prime mimetic function of art. Thus he found that small calabashes on the same headdress were lumpily rendered and therefore not realistic and not beautiful. Calabashes must be specially rounded.

Mashudi Latunji spoke of the rounding of the forms of good Gẹ̀lẹ̀dẹ́ masks. He alleged that carvers "invent" roundness after close observation of reality: "We use our eyes to observe how things are round." There is art historical truth to what he says. The basic roundness of Yorùbá art is especially evident in the art of Ketu, the ancient Yorùbá town under whose cultural influence Mashudi's own town of Mẹkọ lies. Mashudi has indeed used his eyes to absorb the penchant for rounded mass which characterizes the style range of Ketu.

The unified rounding of small masses in relation to larger masses is a hallmark of fine style. In Egba sculpture the eye often flattens to follow the curve of the temple. Ogundeji of Iseyin, in contrast to the Egba solution, rounds the sphere of the exaggerated eyes he carves so that when viewed in profile they are congruent with the rounded mass of the forehead. Ogidi of Igogo-Ekiti vividly rounds off all elements of his images; his works stand on rounded limbs; concave lines articulate arms from rounded torso; convex lines articulate fusions of loin and leg. Each marked division of mass is achieved with fluent curvilinearity.

Criticism of human buttocks where represented in sculpture brings the Yorùbá love of rounded shapes into focus. Jogomi of Ajilete likes his buttocks rounded and "human." By inhuman he means sharp protrusion. The head of the Shango cult in Ila-Orangun made the same distinctions. Departure from the idea of the rounded rump met with amusing ribaldry in an Ijebu village: "If a man wants to copulate, or if a man wants to have an affair, he would quickly and easily be able to do what he wants to do [with this image] as its buttocks resemble those of a real person. But the second [image], its rump is raised up, its rump [stands up] high at the back" (*Ó se dó fún ọkùnrin, ti ó bá jẹ́ wípé ọkùnrin ba fẹ́ bá lò pọ̀, ó lè tètè rí ṣe neg kan ti ó fẹ nítoríwipé ìdí rẹ dàbí ti ènìòn. Ṣùgbọ́n èkejì ìdí rẹ̀ wà lókè, kole rete di giga ẹyìn ni ìdí rẹ̀ wà*).

[11.] Protrusions: A pleasing bulge, as opposed to displeasing or incompetent bulges, may be denoted by the verb of action, *yọ*, "sprouted," qualified by an appropriate adverb. Thus a critic of Ṣepeteri extolled the tactile structure of a nose quite simply: "It bulges" (*Ó yọ gbunñgbu*). "You can hold the beautiful nose with your fingers," he added, "you cannot do this with the unattractive nose." This criterion seems to distinguish the sculptural from the schematic. Moderate bulges are thus an accepted part of roundness.

[12.] Nonpleasing Protrusions: A definite vocabulary defines this negative taste. The modal response of the critics was *ó yọ síita*, "it protrudes," and it was used, for example, by critics at Oke-Iho and Ilobi to portray, respectively, a jutting forehead and a jutting chin. The verb is rooted in the currency of abuse, as in the Yorùbá phrase "he is troublesome" (*Ó yọnun*), meaning literally, "he is mouth protruding."

The verb *yọ* by itself, of course, is neutral; adverbs shade the quality of the protrusion. Thus *ètèerèé yọ dòdò* describes a pendulous lip, *ó lẹ́nun dòdò* a drooping mouth (Abraham 1958, 141).[25] Here the adverb *dòdò* denotes a sagging curve of flesh. An Aworri critic used this word to characterize what he felt was wrong with the pectorals of a male *ibejì* image. A deliberate usage of this effect in Yorùbá art occurs in satiric sculpture for the *Egúngún* cult. One mask, now in the collection of the Nigerian Museum, lampoons a nineteenth-century enemy of the Yorùbá, the Dahomean, with a striking depiction of sagging jowls.

[13.] Sinister Bulges: In general, rounded masses define Yorùbá sculpture. Excessively curved swellings are not, however, looked upon with favor. One critic declared that swollen cheeks were bad art and puffed out his own cheeks in demonstration.

The verb this critic employed to denote swelling (*wú*) has sinister connotations. *Oríimí wú*, literally "my head is swollen," means "I remember something which makes me apprehensive" (Abraham 1958, 673).[26] *Oríi wíwú*, "the remembrance of a terrifying event," is another example.[27] Then there is the singularly cheerless phrase, *Á wú kó tó bẹ*, "Things will be worse before they are better."[28]

Amos Tutuola draws upon this folk fear of unusual swelling in his *Palm-Wine Drinkard*:

> I noticed that the left hand thumb of my wife was swelling out as if it was a buoy, but it did not pain her. [A] child came out from the thumb. He began to talk to us as if he was ten years of age. I was greatly terrified. I was thinking in my mind how we could leave the child in the farm and run to the town, because everybody had seen that the left hand of my wife had only swelled out, but she did not conceive in the right part of her body as other women do.
>
> (Tutuola 1952, 31; see also p. 32)

An excrescence which is sited "in the right part of the body," forming the "obstetric line" which defines the belly of a pregnant woman, does not of course generate fear, although it is infrequently seen in Yorùbá sculpture. At least one obviously pregnant woman appears as a theme, carved with humorous intent, for the *Ẹpa* feasts of the town of Ipoti-Ekiti. Outside of the context of rational expectation a swelling shape recalls pathology and is to be feared. An Ẹgbádò mother warned Kenneth Murray once that if he kicked an *ibejì* image about, as he was kicking about an abandoned celluloid European doll, he would swell up and die. A strange bulge of earth in the court of the priest of Orò at Iseyin is held dangerous: "if someone steps on Ota Orò they will swell up and die immediately." Fear of swelling, in fact, may well be diffused throughout West Africa.

Under the pressure of similar beliefs, an Ijebu cultivator immediately related the swollen upper arms of an *ibejì* figure to pathology: *Ó tún wú bí ẹní pé ó dùn* "It is swollen doubly like a person in pain." An oral literary reflection of this visual prejudice is the ballad of the Scarlet River Hog or *Túùkú*: "River-Hog, a swelling has ruined your beauty" (*Túùkú, kókó ba ojú jẹ́*, literally, "river-hog protruberance spoils face") (Abraham 1958, 656).[29]

[14.] Pleasing Angularity: Roundness is not an immutable law. One of the strengths of the Yorùbá aesthetic is its flexibility. Yorùbá critics may waive their tastes provided that novel departures are phrased with richness of human expression. Mr. William Fagg (1963) of the British Museum once told me: "The Yorùbá roundness is not to be found in the works of Agunna of Oke Igbira. Agunna is more ascetic, concentrating the chin and the mouth into one point."

Within the style range of Ẹfọn-Alaiye, for example, there is a mode (much favored by chiefly patrons in Ilesha) whereby the chin is crisply pointed. Samuel Adetunji, a native of Ilesha, has described the effect: "You really notice the chin on *Èfọ̀n* carvings. They carve chins which look like a blade." To Eṣo of Ipole-Ijesha *Èfọ̀n* chins were "pointed" (*ṣónṣó*).

Ṣónṣó thus describes the sculptural concentration of human attributes into points. It is a usage slightly elevated from common speech where the verb acquires an occasionally whimsical tinge, as in the phrase "he has a pointed nose." But *ṣónṣó* implies something more than a physical state, according to Samuel Adetunji. In its most refined nuance, the verb connotes boldness; it reflects character. Eṣo of Ipole invoked this special power of the word. This was entirely in keeping with the heroic stance and pose of fine Ẹfọn-Alaiye sculpture. The bold sharpness of the Èfọn chin seems to be a prerogative, interestingly enough, of the generalized representation of mounted warchiefs and kings in the Ilesha area.

The elements and counter-elements of the Yorùbá notion of roundness briefly reviewed include canonic roundness described as *róbótó*; pleasing bulges are greeted with the phrase *ó yọ gbunñgbu*; negative bulges described by a language apparently borrowed from abuse; sinister bulges fall under the verb *wú*; and, finally, one aspect of a pleasing angularity, at least, is characterized by the word *ṣónṣó*. Yorùbá in general admire roundness but will accept sharp, angular, or bulbous shapes if these present aesthetic credentials which are clearly legible. Eṣo of Ipole, for example, not only detected the expression which went into the making of an abstract mode of *Èfọn* chin, but he measured its visual impact with a verb nuanced with boldness.

[15.] Straightness: This quality ranks with roundness as a geometric trait of essential character in fine sculpture. Yorùbá define straightness as upright posture and, by extension, balanced alignments and symmetry. When Bandele of Osi-Ilorin was asked by Kevin Carroll why he used to stand back from his work at Oye-Ekiti and look at it from a distance the sculptor replied: "We were looking at the straightness of the work" (*Gígún iṣé l'a nwò*), "So that it would not be crooked" (*Kí ò máà wọ*) (Father Kevin Carroll, personal communication).

Sculpture must stand erect. This is one of the first demands made upon an apprentice striving to master the art of sculpture. At a later point in his career he can assume that the problem of straightness has been mastered, and he can concentrate his energies upon more challenging aspects of form. But in the beginning (and perhaps forever for third-rate carvers) the matter of alignment is a matter of paramount concern. Bandele confessed his own fledgling uncertainties: "I did not look to the quality of shining smoothness but to the straightness. If you will remember I wasn't as good then as I am now. At that time I did not know the art of blocking the main shapes out of the wood as I do now" (Father Kevin Carroll, personal communication).

If Bandele's enunciation of the problem is enlivened with memories of the mastery of process and form, the noncarving critics' detections of this quality are equally to the point. The head man of Ilogbo told me that he found the stooped posture of an *ibejì* not beautiful (*kò dá*). In Central Ekiti a critic liked the back of an *ibejì* because it was straight, while the back of a rival piece was not straight (*ò gún*) and, therefore, inappropriate.

I observed Ajanaku, a fine blacksmith of Ẹfọn-Alaiye, at work in his workshop on an iron staff. The staff was surmounted by an iron bird with an iron plume sprouting from the back of its head. The blacksmith in the last stages of the work attended to the straightening of the neck of the bird and to the straightening of the staff supporting the bird. He took the staff in his tongs and placed it in the sand upright and studied it critically before he was satisfied with the *gígún* (straightness) of the total effect.

That the testing of the staff for straightness was a mental process which did not operate at a subconscious or subliminal level, in a manner suggested by Ralph Linton (1958, 11–12), was clearly demonstrated the next time Ajanaku was visited. On this occasion one of the sons of the blacksmith took over the anvil.

The straightening of the bird's neck was not to the taste of the father. Ajanaku softly told his son to reheat the neck of the bird in the furnace and to straighten it out, so that it would not be crooked (*Kí ò mà wọ́*). The son complied. In the glowing "charcoal" of palm kernels he turned the neck of the bird around several times, holding the object with his tongs. With pincers freshly moistened in water he bent the neck of the bird, now cherry-red, just behind the crest behind the bird's neck. At last the neck was suitably erect. Ajanaku smiled. He then told his son to bend the wings of the bird slightly down; this formed a pleasing visual contrast to the rigid axis of the neck and spike.

Here a blacksmith is communicating with verbal commands a canon of straightness tempered with contrast. Pointing commands are the means of the qualification of canons. Mere physical example does not suffice. At some point the master must put into words what has gone wrong.

[16.] Symmetry: The calming virtues of symmetry are a constant in Yorùbá art. The serene lips of a twin image find reflection in the balanced disposition of the image's hands. When a woman kneels and presents her offering in a container, her hands fold symmetrically around the bottom of the object; when a warrior sallies forth on his mount his hands, if free, touch the reins at precisely mirrored points. Even the theme of a bird pecking a snake, potentially a scene of random coils and agitated posture, becomes, in the hands of Duga of Mẹko, a concrete manifestation of pure form in even-sided resolution.

Alaga spoke of the nature of symmetry from a sculptor's point of view. Quite characteristically, he inextricably merged the concept with notions of straightness and siting. "One always positions the ears equal to each other," he asserted, "and one always keeps the ears and the eyes on the same line." He continued: "But there are some carvers [laughter] who are like small children and these put the ear on the jaw and do not think of the place of the eyes at the time they block out the ears and the mouth."

A sculptor in Ketu declared that a good carver never works without careful measurements either by adze-nicks or knifed incisions on the log, so that he can balance one effect against another as forms emerge from the raw chunk of the wood. One works quickly, he explained, but one does not work so hastily that one blocks out shapes which are not "straight." As a model of his ideal, he pointed to his own work, a headdress representing a market woman with wares on a tray atop her head. The wares were symmetrically disposed in a criss-cross of minor and major masses.

The critics made comments about straightness in the sense of symmetry, though not with the sophistication of carvers' commentaries. They spoke, for example, of the symmetry of lips, and one critic traced with his finger imaginary lines as he discussed the symmetrical disposition of facial traits and headtie on a Thundergod dance wand.

Straightness is extremely important in what might be phrased the *Ẹpa* cult aesthetic. Here it is canonic among the dancers who carry headdresses during feasts. The canon not only reflects the practical necessity of avoiding the dangerous tilting of the heavy superstructures during the ceremony but also links the prolonged straightness of the architectonic forms of the sculpture to the postures of the dance.

Allusions to the importance of straightness may be found in classical Yorùbá poetry. One example is the sixth line of the divination verse quoted near the beginning of this paper. Another exists in the class of Yorùbá poems known as *àròfọ̀* (literally jokes, as in the term *aláàròfọ̀*, witty person) which are verses aimed at abstract subjects. As their title implies, they probe the assumptions of daily life with irreverence:

> Why do we grumble because a tree is bent
> When, in our streets, there are even men who are bent?
> Why must we complain that the new moon is slanting
> Can any one reach the skies to straighten it?

> (Hodgkin 1960, 326)[30]

Sculptors, however, are more committed than the makers of the oral arts. But they may approach the canonical with equal levity in the prescribed areas of moral inquisition, satire, and psychological warfare.

[17.] **Skill:** Yorùbá esteem skill. There are suitable means of phrasing the rare knowledge of the artist. A frequent source is the *oríkì* or praise names. *Oríkì* are attributive names. They express a man's most noble qualities, real or imagined. For males they often bear heroic connotations. Thus the *oríkì* of a sculptor may allude not only to his skill but magnify the quality on an heroic scale.

Consider the *oríkì* of Taiwo of Ilaro, an excellent sculptor who died around 1920 and whose early twentieth-century work is found in the study collections of the Royal Ontario Museum at Toronto. In the province of Ègbádò, Taiwo was widely known under his attributive name of *Onípàsónòbe* which means possessed of a knife like a whip.[31] It is a miniature poem in praise of artistic cunning. Such was the skill of the late Taiwo that he summoned shapes, as with a whip, out of brute wood with his knife and made the shapes do as he bid them.

[18.] Ephebism: This is perhaps the most important criterion. It is, in a sense, the resolution of all the canons in combination. Ephebism means, broadly, the depiction of people in their prime. In accordance with this canon, critics pose this question: Does the image make its subject look young?

Yorùbá sculpture is a mirror in which human appearances never age. In Ipokia, for example, an old priest pointed to a robust image and said with pride: "That stands for me." Yorùbá art idealizes seniority. Divination poetry tells us wisdom is the finest beauty of a person.[32] Ergo, what could be more appropriate than to flatter the moral beauty of the elders with the physical beauty of the young?

Moreover, the actual physiognomy of the senior devotee often resists the flawless seal of Yorùbá sculptural form. To imitate the masters of Yorùbá life and religion as they really are would deny the Yorùbá idea of sculpture from self-realization.

Critics led me to these conclusions. Thus the wife of the village blacksmith at Ilishan: "I like that carving—it makes the Oba look so young." Study of the carving she criticized validates her judgment. Cheeks are firm, stance is sure, chinline is strong. The waist is slim and youthful, and the chest is muscular, if slightly androgynous.

At Shaki an *Egúngún* worshipper pursed his lips and parried a request for artistic criticism of twin images with a question: "Between a beautiful young woman and an old woman which would you prefer for a wife?" The expected reply was given. The informant was amused for he had led his interrogator into corroborating his argument. "I like one image best," he then stated, "because it is carved as a young girl while the other three are like old women."

This ranking was one of the very few which did not coincide with the opinion of the present writer. Three twins which seemed slender and youthful to the writer and his wife were the very pieces which seemed old to the informant. What caused the divergence of views? The informant pointed to the breasts. The breasts of the "old" women were high, as if shrunken and withered, while the breasts of the "young" girl hung down and gave the impression of fullness.

A more important reason, however, was probably the erosion of features through ritual washing. The facial traits of the "old" pieces had been somewhat worn away by time and use. It is of interest that the informant was not swayed by the sumptuous money garments, made of cowries, which adorned two of the nonfavored *ibeji*.

A critic of Ilogbo-Aworri immediately censured the hunched shoulders and fleshy pectorals of an *ibeji* image. Good images, he said, were carved as youths, not old men. A critic at Ifaki-Ekiti made substantially the same point and added "The chest of a young man should look like this," pointing to a hard, polished surface. "It is beautiful because it makes the image look young."

Critics characterized the alleged age of an *ibeji* (female) at Ṣepeteri on the basis of breasts. A favored image had breasts of equal length. "It resembles a young girl" (*Ó dàbí ọmọnge*). A rejected image had breasts which sagged, with the right breast longer than the left, a not infrequent phenomenon among Yorùbá mothers whose children have favored one nipple over the other while nursing. Asiru of Ṣepeteri made this point concrete: the most elegant *ibeji* possessed breasts of the same length and consequently resembled a young woman.

Abinileko of Otta established that ephebism can control the judgment of Gẹ̀lẹ̀dẹ́ masks: "Labintan's cheek looks like the chin of a young man, but that of Salawu resembles someone who is middle-aged" (*Àgbọ̀n ti Lábíntán dàbí ti ọ̀dọ́mokùnrin ṣùgbọ́n ti Salawu dàbí ti àgbàlágbà*). The main source of satisfaction with Labintan's image was that it had the look of a young boy.

The vocabulary of ephebism is simplified. It consists essentially of the key verb *jọ* (resembles) in combination with substantives denoting the quality of being young. Ephebism, as a criterion, is a logical interpretation of certain of the visual constituents of Yorùbá sculpture. For example, roundness connotes the vigorous period of existence, for human faces tend to become angular in old age.

Coiffure also points in the direction of youth. *Irun àgògo*, a bridal mode of the nineteenth century Oyo, is frequently used in sculpture.[33] The high-keeled structure of the hair to a Yorùbá immediately recalls the fresh beauty of the bride.

Mashudi of Mẹko reveals that one motive for the use of ephebism is commercial advantage:

> If I am carving the face of a senior devotee I must carve him at the time he was in his prime. Why? If I make the image resemble an old man the people will not like it. I will not be able to sell the image. One carves images as if they were young men or women to attract people.

The Yorùbá aesthetic qualifies the notion that Africans never seem to carve their subjects as of any particular age. The intent of the Yorùbá sculptor is to carve a man at the optimum of his physical beauty between the extremes of infancy and old age. Even where a beard indicates maturity the brow of a Yorùbá sculpture may glow with the freshness of early manhood.

Seen as a whole, the Yorùbá aesthetic is not only a constellation of refinements. It is also an exciting mean, vividness cast into equilibrium. "The parts of this image are beautiful," an Oyo elder once said, "because they are equal to one another." Each indigenous criterion is a paradigm of this fundamental predilection. Thus mimesis, as traditional Yorùbá understand it, is a mean between absolute abstraction and absolute likeness; the ideal representational age is the strong middle point between infancy and old age; the notion of visibility is a mean between faint and conspicuous sculpture; light is balanced by shade. That beauty is a kind of mean is explicitly stated by Tutuola in *Feather Woman of the Jungle*: "She was indeed a beautiful woman. She was not too tall and not too short; she was not too black and not too yellow."

Yorùbá color preferences extend these beliefs. One schoolboy once stated on a questionnaire given by Justine Cordwell that his favorite color was blue because "it usually gives some attraction to the eyes. It is midway between red and black. It is not too conspicuous as red and is not so dark as black. It is cool and bright to see." He spoke with the full authority of his ancestors. Most significant was the notion of blue, a highly favored traditional Yorùbá color, as a mean between red and black.

Yorùbá sculptors impose a truce upon the elements of their works, the elements themselves expressed in moderation. Even in the field of Egúngún sculpture, where in order to suggest visitations from the world of the dead much license is allowed, one finds bestial and human attributes coexisting in a dignified manner because they have been balanced. Then, in turn, the sculpture will be balanced on the top of a dancer's head, and he himself will probably make symmetrical gestures with a pair of flywhisks as a countereffect to his occasional impassioned twirlings.

Increase and fertility are important preoccupations. But of themselves they constitute no more than the instincts of a beast. Yorùbá artistic criticism seems to be saying that force or animal vitality must be balanced by ethics, the moral wisdom of the elders. Ethics in this special sense would be the peculiarly human gift of finding the tolerable mean between the good and the bad, the hot and the cold, the living and the dead, to safeguard man's existence.

Notes

1   Henry J. Drewal 1990, 35.

2   The orthography in the Thompson text is his own.

3   My intellectual debts incurred in the making of this paper are legion. First of all, I should like to thank the generosity of the Ford Foundation

and The Concilium for International Studies at Yale for two generous grants which allowed me to study Yorùbá responses to artistic quality during three field trips over the period 1962–1965. Secondly, I should like to thank Kenneth Murray and Father Kevin Carroll for a thoughtful criticism of the text and William Fagg, Leonard Doob, George Kubler, and Vincent Scully for many insights. Finally, I am grateful to Alan Merriam, Roy Sieber, and Warren d'Azevedo for many courtesies and for the example of their works. I also warmly thank Lila Hopkins Calhoun for clerical assistance and my wife, Nancy, for excellent criticism and sustained enthusiasm.

4 Thus Cordwell (1952, 292): "none of the master carver informants would become more explicit about what it was that they would say to another carver in pointing out why and how the carving was not good."

5 Ikare informants told me very simply that beauty of voice is also considered by those who judge the quality of oral skills.

6 Thus: "Comme dans les langues de métier, la proliferation conceptuelle correspond à une attention plus soutenue envers les propriétés du réel."

7 See Murray (1938?). As to one of the monuments of Yorùbá metallurgy see Williams (1964, 152). "[The 'anvil' of Ladin], a drop-shaped block of iron 30 inches high with a girth of 41 ½ inches, still stands in the compound of the Ooni of Ifẹ. It was believed by Frobenius to be of cast iron, a claim which would suggest furnaces capable of generating temperatures in the region of 1,550 C. The block on close inspection, however, appears to have been built up from lumps of wrought iron which in any case represents a high degree of metallurgical skill."

8 An excellent survey of Yorùbá literary types is *Yorùbá Poetry* by Beier and Gbadamosi (1959).

9 As documented by D'Avezac (1845, 78): "markets … operate on a money basis—based on the cowrie shell, called *owwo*." On pp. 81–3 D'Avezac discusses the Ijebu Yorùbá concept of the week, month, and year.

10 See, for example, Roth (1903, 157–91). See also Weir (1933, par. 101). "The official residence of the Ologotun is maintained by the townsfolk and the share of the work is allocated as follows: (1) By all the town (a) the entrance gate to the forecourt known as *enu geru* (b) the forecourt known as *ode gbaragada* (c) the second court known as *ode useroye* (2) By

the Uba quarter (a) the court for council meetings known as *ode ayigi*." Weir documents similar information in his *Intelligence Report on the Ikerre District of the Ekiti Division of the Ondo Province* (Lagos: December 31, 1933).

11 I have since this time interviewed many more critics. Eventually I hope to ploy differences of taste by ethnic sub-group, though the task may prove difficult.

12 Bowen (1858). Amewa seems formed of *a mọ̀n ẹwà* "Knower (of) beauty," just as "lawyer" (*amọ̀fin*) is literally a "knower (of the) law" (*A mọ̀n òfin*).

13 Quoted in a personal communication to the author from Father Kevin Carroll of the Roman Catholic Mission, Ijebu-Igbo.

14 The details of spelling are taken from Abraham (1958). Thus, for example, I spell "*enia*" as he does, phonetically *enion*. Abraham's *Dictionary* is likely to stand for years as a standard reference and to facilitate thus the easy use of his intricately organized materials, I have used frequently his own system of orthography.

15 Thus: "Most of these commercial pieces exhibit a lack of feeling so marked that they can easily be distinguished from the figures made for Dahomeans, on which time and effort are lavished in the best traditional manner." Compare Kenneth Murray's experience with Suli Onigelede, a woodcarver of Lagos, circa 1946: "Suli … had some *ibeji* (twin statuettes) … unfortunately he smothered them in bright green enamel as he thought Europeans would like them so, in spite of my instructions to use native colours" (Murray n.d., unpublished manuscript).

16 Cf. a brief summary of the problem of portraiture in African sculpture may be found in Bohannan (1964, 152–3).

17 These are described as real portraits "for remembrance."

18 For these and other remarks by Bandele I am indebted to the kindness of Father Kev who shared the insights of this famous son of Areogun of Osi-Ilorin in a letter dated February 29, 1964.

19 Father Carroll has published the Ekiti Yorùbá terms for these stages in his "Three Generations of Yorùbá Carvers," *Ibadan* No. 12 (June 1961), p. 23.

20 These are points from tape-recorded conversations with Bandele which Father Carroll has shared with me.

21 Quoted in a personal communication from Father Kevin Carroll.

22 King (1961, 11). Bells and gongs are made "visible" to the ear, as it were, because of their high pitch.

23 Nigerian Museum, Lagos (KCM 381). The housepost once stood in a courtyard in the house of the Elegbe.

24 Collier ("Yorùbá Hunter's Salutes," p. 54): "Some hunters say *rekina rekina* which I understand to mean 'glistening' or 'glittering'—like the sun shining on wind-ruffled water, I was told …"

25 See *dòdò* (Abraham, p. 141).

26 *Wú* (Abraham, p. 673).

27 Ibid.

28 Ibid, p. 672.

29 Abraham's translation has greater focus than an earlier version of the *ijala* of the Red River Hog by F. S. Collier who rendered the Yorùbá "animal … with swelling on his face."

30 From E. L. Lasebikan, "The Tonal Structure of Yorùbá Poetry," *Presence Africaine* No. 8–10 (1956), p. 49.

31 Mr. Kenneth Murray collected this information at or near Ilaro.

32 Cf. Beier and Gbadamosi (1959, 30): "Wisdom is the finest beauty of a person. /Money does not prevent you from becoming blind/ Money does not prevent you from becoming mad."

33 *Agogo* coiffure also, of course, denotes subservience to a deity.

References

Abraham, R. C. 1958. *Dictionary of Modern Yorùbá*. London: University of London.

Allison, Philip. 1956. "The Last Days of Old Òyó." *Odù* 4: 18.

Ballard, Edward G. 1957. *Art and Analysis*. The Hague: Martinus Nijhoff.

Bascom, William. 1951. "Social Status, Wealth and Individual Differences among the Yorùbá." *American Anthropologist* 53, no. 4: 490–505.

Bascom, William. 1959. "Urbanism as a Traditional African Pattern." *Sociological Review* 7, no. 1: 29–43.

Bascom, William. 1960. "Yorùbá Concepts of the Soul." In *Men and Cultures*, edited by A. F. C. Wallace, 401–10. Philadelphia: University of Pennsylvania Press.

Beier, Ulli. 1963. *African Mud Sculpture*. Cambridge: Cambridge University Press.

Beier, Ulli and Bakare Gbadamosi. 1959. *Yorùbá Poetry*. Lagos: Black Orpheus.

Biobaku, Saburi O. 1955. "The Use and Interpretation of Myths." *Odù* 1: 12–17

Bohannan, Paul. 1961. "Artist and Critic in an African Society." In *The Artist in Tribal Society*, edited by Marian W. Smith, 85–94. New York: Free Press of Glencoe.

Bohannan, Paul. 1964. *Africa and Africans*. Garden City, N.Y.: Natural History Press.

Bowen, T. J. 1858. *Grammar and Dictionary of the Yorùbá Language*. Washington, DC: Smithsonian Contributions to Knowledge.

Carroll, Father Kevin. 1961. "Three Generations of Yorùbá Carvers." *Ibadan* 12.

Collier, F. S. 1953. "Yorùbá Hunters' Salutes." *Nigerian Field* 18, no. 2: 1.

Cordwell, Justine Mayer. 1952. *Some Aesthetic Aspects of Yorùbá and Benin Cultures*. Unpublished doctoral dissertation, Northwestern University, Evanston, Illinois, USA.

D'Avezac, M. 1845. *Notice sur le pays et le people des Yebous en Afrique*. Memoires de la Societe Ethnologique, II. Paris.

Drewal, Henry J. 1990. "African Art Studies Today." In R. Abiodun, National Museum of Art, et al. *African Art Studies: The State of the Discipline: Papers Presented at a Symposium Organized by the National Museum of African Art, Smithsonian Institution, September 16, 1987*, 29–62. Washington, DC: National Museum of African Art.

Fagg, William. 1962/3. *Nigerian Images*. London: Lund Humphries.

Fuja, Abayomi. 1962. *Fourteen Hundred Cowries: Traditional Stories of the Yorùbá*. London: Oxford University Press.

Herskovits, Melville J. 1938. *Dahomey*, Vols. I and II. New York: J. J. Augustin.

Hodgkin, Thomas. 1960. *Nigerian Perspectives*. Oxford: OUP.

Hsu, Francis L. K. 1964. "Rethinking the Concept 'Primitive.'" *Current Anthropology* 5, no. 3: 169–78.

Johnson, Samuel. 1921. *The History of the Yorùbás*. Lagos: Church Missionary Society Bookshop.

King, A. V. 1961. *Yorùbá Sacred Music from Ekiti*. Ibadan: Ibadan University Press.

Lasebikan, E. L. 1956. "The Tonal Structure of Yorùbá Poetry." *Presence Africaine*, n.s. No. 8–10: 43–50.

Levi-Strauss, Claude. 1962. *La Pensee sauvage*. Paris: Librairie Plon.

Linton, Ralph. 1958. "Primitive Art." In *The Sculpture of Africa*, edited by
     W. Fagg and E. Elisofson, 9–17. New York: Praeger.
Lloyd, Peter C. 1962. "Sungbo's Ersko." *Odù* 7: 15–22.
Murray, Kenneth. n.d. *Notes on the Arts and Crafts of Lagos and Colony*.
     Unpublished manuscript.
Murray, Kenneth. 1938? *Native Minor Industries in Abẹ̀òkúta and Ọ̀yọ́
     Provinces*. Unpublished manuscript. Lagos.
Murray, Kenneth. 1961. "The Artist in Nigerian Tribal Society: A Comment."
     In *The Artist in Tribal Society*, edited by Marian W. Smith, 95–114.
     London: Routledge and Kegan Paul.
Roth, H. Ling. 1903. *Great Benin*. Halifax: F. King and Sons.
Smith, Marian W. 1961. *The Artist in Tribal Society*. London: Routledge and
     Kegan Paul.
Talbot, P. Amaury. 1926. *The Peoples of Southern Nigeria*. Vol. II. London:
     Oxford University Press.
Thompson, Robert Farris. 1965. *Yorùbá Dance Sculpture: Its Contexts and
     Critics*. Unpublished PhD thesis, Yale University, New Haven, CT.
Thompson, Robert Farris. 1973. "Yorùbá Artistic Criticism." In *The
     Traditional Artist in African Societies*, edited by Warren d'Azevedo,
     19–61. Bloomington: Indiana University Press (republished 2006 in
     The Anthropology of Art: A Reader, edited by Howard Morphy and Morgan
     Perkins, 242–69. Malden, MA: Blackwell Publishing).
Trimingham, J. Spencer. 1961. *Islam in West Africa*. London: Oxford
     University Press.
Trowell, Margaret. 1970. *Classical African Sculpture*. London: Faber and Faber.
Tutuola, Amos. 1952. *The Palm-Wine Drinkard*. London: Faber and Faber.
Tutuola, Amos. 1955. *Simbi and the Satyr of the Dark Jungle*. London: Faber
     and Faber.
Weir, N. A. C. 1933. *An Intelligence Report on Ogòtún District, Èkítí Division,
     Òndón Province*, Lagos.
Williams, Denis. 1964. "The Iconology of the Yorùbá." *Africa* 34, no. 2:
     139–66.
Wingert, Paul S. 1962. *Primitive Art: Its Traditions and Styles*. New York:
     Oxford University Press.

4

The African Art Historian as Conceptual Analyst

Barry Hallen[*]

Introduction

One of the enduring characterizations of indigenous African cultures is that they were insignificantly critical or reflective in character. Therefore, although they may have produced interesting works of art or religious world-views, it is presumed that if one were to have enquired of the people *why* they styled a piece of sculpture in a certain way or *why* they maintained a certain belief, ultimately their articulated response would have amounted to nothing more than a "because we've always done it this way" or "because this is the way the forefathers did it." It is at least partially for this reason that some Africanists argue these cultures expressed their abstract ideas in symbolic, poetic, or literary forms. By this they mean that reasons given or explanations made for *why* something was done or believed were in the form of appeals to historical traditions (via oral history, stories, or proverbs, etc.) rather than discursive arguments.

However, academics who make these cultures their professional concern do prefer to use discursive arguments and other analytic techniques (rather than proverbs) when explaining them in lectures and publications. The result has come to be an increasingly distinct and

---

[*] Barry Hallen joined Great Ifẹ as Lecturer in Philosophy in 1975. He received the PhD in philosophy in 1970 from Boston University with a thesis entitled *Boldness and Caution in the Methodology and Social Philosophy of Karl Popper.*

unfortunate polarity between: (1) the *poetic–symbolic* level of expression assumed appropriate to indigenous peoples; (2) a second, *meta-explanatory* level on which Africanists and other scholars, using their own discursive, analytic techniques (e.g., structural-functionalism), try to provide more satisfactory reasons for why such people believe what they can only say they do.

In the study of African arts this second, meta-explanatory level has produced theories such as William Fagg's principle of dynamism, which explains sculptural forms as potent symbols of growth and increase (Fagg 1963, 122–4), and led to the adaptation of Eurocentric-derived classificatory terms such as "pre-classical," "classical," and "post-classical" to group certain African plastic traditions (Fagg (on Benin) 1965; Willett 1967). No doubt these have been of value in organizing the material and suggesting certain important relationships. However, the point remains that ultimately the operative categories are not generally significant or meaningful to the people to whose work they are being applied.[1]

This polarity has been challenged by Professor Robert Farris Thompson in a stimulating and provocative series of papers and monographs (1971a, 1971b, 1973a, 1973b, 1974, 1984). He has argued that at least one "traditional" people, the Yorùbá of southwestern Nigeria, do articulate and defend a group of concepts or terms that are central to the *critical* value judgments they make about art in their own society. This means, then, that rather than having to rely solely upon the external, somewhat intuitive, hypotheses of the academic art historian, it may also be possible to study the critical concepts applied by traditional peoples themselves—to "view" their art as they do and thereby learn to appreciate the indigenous standards that apply during its conception and use.

The primary concern of this chapter is to examine critically Professor Thompson's interpretation of Yorùbá aesthetic thought, primarily in terms of the kinds of evidence he presents and the arguments he makes from it. For the onus is upon him to convince us, first, that the Yorùbá do think critically in such terms, and second, that his reporting/

interpretation of their thought on this plane is accurate. To this end Thompson's arguments will be considered on two different levels. The first, and in a sense most basic, level may be described as that of *Explicit References* (to the Yorùbá-language aesthetic criteria) or *Direct Quotations* (from Yorùbá informants making aesthetic judgments); the second as that of the *Aesthetic of the Cool* (the most fundamental Yorùbá aesthetic and philosophical principle) as expressed by Yorùbá *Art* and, finally, *Philosophy*.

Though this chapter will limit itself to what Thompson says of the Yorùbá[2] at each of these stages, this is not to ignore the fact that he has gone on to expand and incorporate his Yorùbá material into a general African or Afro-American aesthetics and philosophy. Nevertheless, the more specific criticisms made here should apply, *mutatis mutandis*, to the more general as well.

Explicit References and Direct Quotations

If Thompson's claims regarding the existence of Yorùbá aesthetic concepts are to be substantiated, and if we are to be able (at least somewhat) to view their art "as they do," then one would expect to find the relevant words in the Yorùbá language identified and explained in his published works, as well as illustrations of critical judgments incorporating them. This Thompson does attempt to do, though his claims as to the *meanings* of these aesthetic concepts and judgments far exceed the evidence he presents.

"Yorùbá critics are experts of strong mind and articulate voice who measure in words the quality of works of art" (1973b, 19). Thompson names eighteen aesthetic criteria[3] which he says Yorùbá critics[4] display in ordinary discourse. "Eighteen *indigenous criteria* of sculptural excellence …. Each criterion, a *named abstraction*, defines the categories of excellence by which Yorùbá recognize the presence of art" (1973b, 29). But upon closer examination one comes to wonder, for at least seven of the eighteen,[5] who is doing the naming. For in terms of the data Thompson himself advances there is no conceptual equivalent in the Yorùbá language for these English-language terms. This means, then, that the Yorùbá themselves do not have names for certain of the "named abstractions" Thompson attributes to them. How can this be? Here is where we must distinguish between *articulate* and *inarticulate* concepts (or criteria).

Normally a concept is taken to be an abstract idea that can be named—that has a meaning in the language of which it is a part (e.g., "beauty"). But what if it can be determined that I react in a regular and predictable manner to something in my environment for which there is no name in my language? For example, I as a social person might respond cordially only to those whose speech evidences a certain kind of accent. I myself might not be aware of this behavioral idiosyncrasy, and the language I speak might have no special name for the accent to which I respond. Yet it still could be noticed and commented upon, either by myself or others. In other words, for an articulate concept to *be* a concept, there must be a name for it. But such is not the case with an inarticulate one (Overing 1987; Sallis 2002).

Thompson does not explicitly make this distinction, or necessarily observe it, but it seems to be the only way to make sense of certain of his passages. For when he refers to the criteria as "*collective* rationalizations" (1973b, 22) or as "canonical notions developed by the investigator [Thompson]" (1973b, 29), the implication clearly is that even though the Yorùbá may have no explicit abstract term with which they identify each criterion, they do make aesthetic judgments that make Thompson feel he is justified in extrapolating and postulating these inarticulate concepts.

However, again *based on the evidence presented*, one wonders whether the inference from the particular (judgment) to the abstract (criteria) is always justified, particularly in view of the disproportionate richness of meaning of the latter. For example, Thompson justifies the positing of a Yorùbá criterion of *proportion* with a number of interesting direct quotations in which the speakers are clearly concerned with comparing the relative proportions of one part of a piece of sculpture to those of another part. But when it comes to defining the underlying *general* principle of proportion in a precise manner, he claims that the Yorùbá are unable to do this and ultimately has recourse to the statement of a single informant who says, "We take our measurements from our heart" (1973b, 45). Thompson therefore suggests that this criterion is better described as one of *emotional proportion*.

The introduction of the word "emotional" is justified by the possibly anomalous rationalization of a single informant. A further point for concern is his imposition upon the Yorùbá conceptual scheme of a "loaded" English term like "emotional." Much of Eurocentric personality theory, as well as ordinary discourse, is based upon the assumption that the emotions may (even should) be rigidly distinguished from intellect or reason. Thompson's imposition of even one half of this dualism on the Yorùbá implies—without justification— that they think along the same (conceptual) lines.

Thompson's apparent justification is his informant's reference to the heart. But then he must in addition assume that when the man refers to his heart he is referring to his feelings or emotions in the same way a eurocentrist would. However, assuming that in his original statement the man used the standard word for heart, "*okan/okọn*," in fact the most important function of the heart for the Yorùbá *is* to act as the repository of mind or consciousness.[6] So the expression "heart," which Thompson took to refer to the emotions, was in fact being used to describe something much more like the Eurocentric concept of mind or reason.

Thompson's central criterion of *relative mimesis* (1971a, 3/1) is potentially troublesome also. The conclusion he wants to establish is that the Yorùbá ideal for the representation in sculpture of any specific person falls mid-way between the polar extremes of exact replica and something that barely manages to convey the human form. The most important evidence he submits in support of this claim are the single-statement critiques of twenty different Yorùbá who, upon viewing examples of Yorùbá carved representations of human beings, made assessments to the effect, "*Ó jọ ènìyàn*" ("It resembles/looks like a person.").[7]

Thompson finds this assessment to be of significance because, rather than identifying one of the carvings as being of a particular person with a proper name (e.g., "That looks like my cousin 'Tunde."), *the critics never seemed concerned to move beyond the level of general human representation*. From this he concludes that an important criterion informing Yorùbá carvings of human beings is that they be no more than *generally* or *relatively* representational of any real person, including the particular individual they are *meant* to portray.

In describing his techniques for soliciting such opinions in the field, Thompson tells us that his general approach was to place a selection of carvings on public view in a town or village, and then solicit critical evaluations of them from curious onlookers. In tabulating the identities of these informants, he comes to several interesting conclusions: (1) With only a single exception, *carvers* refused to comment on their own work (1973b, 28); (2) The *owners* of carvings were generally reluctant to contribute to critical discussions about the artistic merits of their possessions (1973b: 26); (3) In particular, no woman could be persuaded to comment upon her own *ibejì*, carvings of deceased twins she bore in the past and keeps as representatives of them (1973b, 27).

The combined force of these three qualifications is to make one wonder whether, in general, Thompson's informants had sufficiently detailed information about the carvings (since they were neither their carvers nor owners) to say anything more than *that* they looked like carvings of "people." The statement they made (*Ó jọ ènìyàn.*) is what might be expected of the curious but proud, and thereby guardedly cautious, Yorùbá male whose aesthetic opinion is solicited in an unorthodox manner (for money) and therefore in an unorthodox situation, by a foreigner of whom he has no intimate acquaintance.

If Thompson were to protest that this is a misrepresentation of the *meaning* of his informants' remarks, what evidence does he offer to convince us that his own is the better? Little that may be called concrete or convincing. For there is a step in his argument that is missing. At one extreme he is able to tell us that twenty individual Yorùbá made statements to the effect, "It resembles a person." At the other he *claims* to be able to tell us that what the speakers mean by this is that when they "see" a statue or carving, they do not see it as a particular person. They always see it as *ènìyàn*—as man, as human-being-in-general. But nowhere is Thompson able to provide us with an analysis or explanation of the "*Ó jọ ènìyàn*" statement *by a Yorùbá*[8] that supports his own extremely theoretically weighted interpretation.

Thompson's justification for not providing this sort of explanation appears to be that, in effect, the Yorùbá don't talk (or explain their remarks) in this way. For he has described their aesthetic judgments in the following terms: "Characteristically phrasing was lexically simple but conceptually rich" (1974, 3). In other words, simple statements of the "*Ó jọ ènìyàn*" form are deceptive in view of their "hidden" conceptual richness.

However, there do seem to be topics with reference to which the "lexically simple but conceptually rich" Yorùbá can extrapolate and elucidate their own meanings as well as concepts. For example, in a series of individual discussions with Yorùbá *oníṣègùn* revolving about the topic of *ènìyàn*, they repeatedly stressed that the bad things (or "evil") in the world were caused by and the responsibility of mankind rather than the gods. "They [bad things] are the work of *ènìyàn*," each said to me on at least one occasion. But, rather than leaving it at this, they were all willing to go on and discuss what they meant: namely, whether there were bad people who chose bad destinies before coming to the world [yes], what to look for in deciding whether any given individual is good or bad [behavior], whether there are different categories of bad people [accidental, deliberate, etc.] and hence bad actions, whether such people are conscious of themselves as bad [yes], etc.

In short, a remark like Thompson's "*Ó jọ ènìyàn*," like the *oníṣègùns'* "They are the work of *ènìyàn*," usually does (or certainly can) occur within the context of a fuller or more complete statement. And it would be of immense help in appreciating and agreeing with the meanings Thompson wishes to attribute to his critics' statements if he were to provide a fuller and more explicit rendering of that context. Otherwise the banal but alternative interpretation suggested above is no less compelling.

Thompson set out to help us understand Yorùbá art and aesthetics as they do. In fact it appears that a number of the aesthetic criteria he attributes to them are not named by them as their own. It is Thompson himself who reads the criteria into certain kinds of statements the Yorùbá make about their art. When we considered examples of these aesthetic statements or judgments we found that sometimes the meanings he attributes to them are not warranted or justified by the evidence he presents.

African scholars are by now accustomed to having recourse to the comparatively few "world" languages that can today be used for the popular dissemination of cross-cultural information. But Thompson would have to be much more explicit in his exposition before any of the above complaints could be excused as due to the ever-present problems of translation. Though it also appears that the liberties he sometimes takes with translations are excessive. Such specialized English-language terms as "proportion," "composition," and "symmetry" are too full of Eurocentric theoretical connotations to directly represent a Yorùbá point-of-view. Thompson does much better when he attempts to "work" upon English terms so they will better represent a Yorùbá viewpoint and so comes up with expressions such as "pleasing angularity," "sinister bulges," and "shining smoothness," but once again the Yorùbá-language originals one would expect him to provide are lacking or inappropriate. In addition, because many of the original Yorùbá expressions hinge upon a verb (to shine, to round, etc.), Thompson would have better conveyed the original meaning by translating them as gerunds, e.g., "smoothing," "proportioning," "rounding," etc.

Aesthetic of the Cool

For a civilization to persist through change and adversity, I assume there were organizing principles and philosophic insights which kept their world on course. What these values were, and continue to be, is implied in Yorùbá myth and stated forthrightly in aesthetic …

(1971a, 1/1)

Our original interest in Thompson was kindled as much by his methods as by the theories to be derived from them. For he set out to let Africans finally speak for themselves about the arts of their cultures, suggesting "that Yorùbá critics surpass all but the most professional of Western students of Yorùbá art in fluency of verbalization" (1973b, 25).

The euphonious *aesthetic of the cool* is the most celebrated remaining part of Thompson's overall theory, yet difficult to make clear. For the cool is said to be a fundamental principle of the whole of the Yorùbá philosophy or world-view as well as of Yorùbá art. "Myths and art extend a common heritage, but they are not merely illustrations. They seem joint bearers of Yorùbá sensibility" (1971a, 2/1).

Initially, purely for expository purposes, we shall distinguish between the cool in art and in the world-view, philosophy or myth. But as the two are so fundamentally interrelated in Thompson's own exposition, the artificiality of this division must inevitably become manifest, and the theory reconsidered as the coherent whole he obviously feels it is. The aesthetic of the cool thereby becomes an aesthetic of life, and the beautiful merges with the good.

In Art

Thompson describes the cool as "a matrix … the criterion of coolness seems to unite all the other canons" (1971a, 2/2). In terms of aesthetic canons or criteria, this would mean that the preceding eighteen in some sense derive from and are united by that of the cool. Exactly what Thompson means by this is not easy to determine.

As with the other aesthetic criteria, he offers several quotations in which Yorùbá seem to refer to their art as cool—statements such as "because its face is cool [one carving is better than another]" and, "If someone is beautiful, he has a cool face" (1971a, 2/2). Neither of these is supplemented by additional quotations in which the same speaker explains what he means by the word "cool" (*tútù*) itself. In Thompson's exposition, the first of the above quotations is immediately followed by the sentence, "The face of the image was rounded and the features were balanced and composed" (1971a, 2/2). But it appears that Thompson here is again immediately beginning to interpolate and thereby *himself* supplementing a speaker's remarks for us, rather than paraphrasing (and why paraphrase?) additional remarks made to him by the informant.

The same must be said for the argument that the cool underlies all other aesthetic criteria. Thompson tries to explain the meaning of this claim in the following:

> Seen as a unit, Yorùbá aesthetic criteria form an exciting mean, vividness cast into equilibrium. Mimesis, as Yorùbá understand it, strikes a balance between abstraction and literal likeness; artistic representations are neither faint nor conspicuous, lackluster nor blatant, too young nor too old. Compare the Yorùbá folk novelist, Tutuola, describing a beautiful woman: "She was not too tall and not too short, she was not too black and not too yellow." And when a young Yorùbá told Justine Cordwell that his favorite color was blue—"It is midway between red and black. It is not too conspicuous as red and it is not so dark as black. It is *cool* and bright to see"—he spoke with the full authority of his ancestors.
>
> (1971b, 378–9)

Elsewhere he describes the cool as "divine energy in juxtaposition with a composed human mask of equilibrium and control" (1971a, P/1); and as "the calm expression of energy, which in degree of control and restraint loomed far more impressive and intimidating than mere unleashed naked power" (1971a, 12/6).

We must temper our exposition here somewhat so as not to forsake the realm of art entirely for that of philosophy. However, the sense of "coolness" that begins to come through is of a mean between opposing forces that blends a stabilizing, attractive order and composure with the "hot" vitality and energy that animates (in excess, destructively) the whole of life. Thompson's Yorùbá aesthetic criteria apparently express this same sense of proportion, in that the aesthetically pleasing mimesis is midpoint—between hypermimesis and excessive abstraction. When just proportion is exceeded, the art object becomes unattractive and may be characterized by such negative criteria as "Nonpleasing Protrusions" and "Sinister Bulges."

Nevertheless, Thompson is still unable to back up his *generalized* principle of the cool in art with a parallel Yorùbá statement of the same magnitude. It is not enough for him simply to say the Yorùbá don't talk this way. There must be additional sources of evidence to warrant his feeling justified to extrapolate and posit a *Yorùbá* principle of such considerable theoretical intricacy. One of these other kinds of evidence is Yorùbá art itself. But here again, when we examine examples of his analyses of this art we will be forced to conclude that the balance, indeed preponderance, of his general theory on this level too is due primarily to his own amazingly syncretic (but non-Yorùbá) powers of artistic observation and interpretation:

> Notions of coolness, character, and force are interwoven in a thousand different ways in Yorùbá art. In a sense, each program of sculpture for each god is a dialect of the cool, a restorative of affirmation from a different point of view.

> (1971a, 20/2)

In different contexts Thompson assigns different meanings to the cool, in that it is sometimes referred to as the polar opposite of the hot ("The hot and the cool seem a metaphor of life's opposing forces" (1971a, 2/2)), and at others as the valued reconciliation of the hot and its opposite ("Balance is achieved by recognition of the elements of bad which complement the elements of good" (1971a, 2/2)). Nevertheless we may take it that for Thompson the second meaning is the dominant one.

Given this basic model of the hot and the cool, Thompson's primary concern in his analyses of the various forms of Yorùbá sculpture is to demonstrate how each reflects the tension between these extremes and their reconciliation—the latter being the "cool" keystone of his Yorùbá aesthetic. Èṣù (Bascom 1969, 79; Pemberton 1975) is one of the very few divinities whom the Yorùbá will allow to be represented in graven-image form. His primary task is to act as messenger to the gods, in that whenever a person consults a diviner he is in effect communicating with the *orisa* (divinities), and it is the *Èṣù*'s task to transmit messages between the two parties. In addition to this the *Èṣù* is well known as a kind of "trickster" or mischievous troublemaker for both gods and man. When one encounters unpredicted trouble or calamity (sometimes fortune) it may be attributed to his intervention. Since the outcome of any divination prescription is never absolutely assured—is always somewhat unpredictable—these two sides to his character may not be entirely unrelated.

In spite of this, the Yorùbá certainly do not regard him as an intrinsically evil or malicious character. His helpfulness and opposition, service and disservice, are inextricably and unpredictably combined. Even so, those who suffer his misfortunes often genuinely deserve them because of their own sins and omissions. In any case, many of his escapades are recounted with humor because the *Èṣù* is not one to be feared so much as placated and avoided.

Thompson's problem is that this popular image of an ambiguous and unpredictable *Èṣù* does not suit a model of polar extremes. He is therefore forced to construct a "deeper" level of analysis. "Although the common image of the deity elaborates his nature as trickster, catalyst, and mischief-maker, the visual and verbal arts combine *to suggest* further, positive dimensions. *Eshu-Elegba*, to use his famous double name, resembles *the dark side of the ideals* of the Yorùbá, a kind of fallen king whose dignity can be restored by devotion" (1971a, 4/1; my emphasis). Having hazarded this hypothesis (without explaining what he means by "dark side" or "ideals"), Thompson again has recourse to non-Yorùbá powers of observation and interpretation in order to develop the "positive and negative valences" (1971a, 4/1) necessary to justify the application of his model.

In doing so, his central reference is to an article on the interpretation of the art forms arising from the worship of *Èṣù* by Joan Wescott, which is of methodological interest in its own right. For Wescott admits that she was totally unsuccessful ("The Yorùbá inability or reluctance to explain these symbols" (Wescott 1962, 349–53)) in her attempts to get the Yorùbá to discuss the meaning or significance of the art forms of the *Èṣù* (336–7). The explanations she did receive ("This is how my father taught me to carve for Elegba" (340)) were along the lines of what anthropologists have told us to expect from the members of traditional cultures. Consequently *she was forced to rely upon her own powers of interpretation* as applied to "myths and praise songs," supplemented by *what she observed* "of the use of [the] sculpture in ritual" (336).

Thompson has affirmed, in the strongest terms, the existence of and his own predilection for indigenous artistic interpretation. Our surprise is therefore justifiable when we find him referring to Wescott's variety of meta-explanatory, non-Yorùbá, interpretative analysis as "definitive" (1971a, 4/2) and incorporating her conclusions into the body of his work. For it is Wescott, rather than her Yorùbá informants, who hypothesizes that *Èṣù* iconography expresses such themes as "phallic power and sexuality," "a world of extremes," and "provocation, aggression and anti-social behavior" (1971a, 4/2; Wescott 1962, 349). And it is Wescott who cautions us that because of her meta-explanatory approach these same analyses must inevitably contain "an element of the arbitrary—a certain degree of subjectivity" (337).

Let us follow the arguments through which Thompson attempts to merge his own model of the hot and cool with the above-mentioned dominant themes Wescott "identifies" in the *Èṣù* corpus. Since Thompson's model will only allow him to incorporate these particular themes as elements of the hot, as hot themes, he is forced to go beyond Wescott (whose analysis was supposedly definitive) and discover "other" cool *Èṣù* themes. "What remains is to limn aspects of *hidden* dignity and *latent* kingship within the art for the boy-elder who wreaks famous mischief on the world" (1971a, 4/2).

Somewhat paradoxically, two of his arguments in support of these cool, kingly themes are that iconographic elements which were previously interpreted as hot are also cool. He refers to the statement of an *Èṣù* worshipper in which the peculiarity of the deity's headdress (hair style plus pointed cap) is said to be designed to provoke ridicule from passersby, which then provides *Èṣù* with an opportunity to discipline: a "power" associated with kingliness (1971a, 4/2). Analogously, he refers to a Cuban-Yorùbá verse in which the *Èṣù*, whose headdress is said to make it physically difficult to bear a load on his head, is referred to as "Your Majesty" (1971a, 4/2). The point is that the freedom from bearing such loads (and therefore the headdress) is associated with the cool, controlled authority of kingliness.

To someone who is familiar with the kinds of explanations (and rationalizations) the Yorùbá do make, both of these arguments are suspect. For that the ordinary man would ridicule a peculiar headdress and thereby inadvertently be subjected to the deity's power is as likely to be a secondary, chance *consequence* as a primary *cause* for its design. It is like saying that traffic accidents were a cause for the creation of the automobile. As for the *Èṣù's* majesty, that must derive, intrinsically and immediately, from the simple fact that he is an *òrìsà*, a god. This is more likely the reason for "the burnishing with indigo of Eshu statuary" (1971a, 4/3) which Thompson again tries to convert into evidence of the kingly coolness of the *Èṣù*.

What remains significant is the basic color of the *Èṣù* statuary to which the indigo dye is applied—black.[9] This is symbolic of his ever mischievous, potentially dangerous nature (Wescott 1962, 346). True, the blackness is complemented by the white cowries also worn by the *Èṣù*. However, what strikes Wescott as significant about these colors, and other opposing qualities displayed by this peculiar deity, is not that they are hot and cool (opposing forces which can be reconciled) but that they are *contradictory*. She therefore concludes that the key to the character of the *Èṣù* is ambiguity, inexplicability, rather than the balance of opposites required by the aesthetic of the cool. "The ambiguous nature of the Yorùbá trickster who contains many contradictions, who belongs nowhere and is involved with everyone, who destroys for the sake of recreating ..." (352, 346 fn. 1).

Statements made by Yorùbá *oníṣègùn* describing human behavior that is said to emulate or reflect the character of the *Èṣù* support Wescott's interpretation, for the phrase, "*ẹmí* [spirit] of *Èṣù*" is used to characterize abnormal behavior in normal situations; behavior that, given the person and his or her problem, doesn't make sense or is inexplicable and therefore ambiguous.

> It is the *Èṣù* which makes a person become annoyed. You know, a person can just become annoyed without anyone offending him or her. When that *èmí* of *Èṣù* gets away from his or her heart/mind (*okan*), he or she will say that he or she doesn't know what happened to him or her.

In general, the *èmí* of the *Èṣù* is said to be opposed by the *èmí* of *sùúrù* (patience), i.e., to be the polar opposite of the cool.

In order to demonstrate the relevance of his hot–cool model, Thompson is forced to have recourse to what he describes as "hidden" or "latent" or "suggested" levels of meaning contained in Yorùbá iconography and myth. As these levels are repeatedly revealed and explained primarily by Thompson, one is justified again in worrying about the distinction between how much he is allowing the Yorùbá to speak for themselves and how much he is speaking "for" them.

If one does have recourse, again following Thompson's own method, to the kinds of statements Yorùbá *oníṣẹ̀gùn* actually do make about, for example, the *Èṣù*, they do not evidence the polarity and reconciliation principle requisite to "proving" the relevance of the aesthetic of the cool. This again argues that this kind of model, rather than being an articulated, fundamental artistic or philosophic insight of Yorùbá culture, is in fact of the discursive, meta-explanatory variety traditionally used by Africanists as hypothetical tools of exposition and analysis.

In Philosophy

> The Yorùbá accomplished a monumental synthesis, guided by a rich and complex series of values. To learn more of these Yorùbá accomplishments, and learn well, it is necessary to consider Yorùbá philosophy and world-view, indissolubly blended with their life and art …
>
> (1971a, 1/5)

This final section is concerned with Thompson's contention that in order to view things as the Yorùbá do one must relate their art to their philosophy. For the art is expressive of certain philosophical principles and the reverse. "Carvers seek to express generalized principles of humanity" (1973b, 35). These generalized principles prove to be essentially moral values (1971a, 1/1, 2/1),[10] and serve as the basis for Thompson's account of the relationship between the beautiful and the good.

Briefly, his hypothesis is that certain values contribute to the form of Yorùbá religious, figural[11] sculpture (1971a, 19/1). These values are both moral and aesthetic. Their observance by a person may be indicated by his adopting certain behavioral forms, which are considered (by society) both good and attractive. Correspondingly, in figural carving these same values may be indicated by certain sculptural forms, which are therefore beautiful and good (1974, 1).

The most prominent of these values are command, composure, and character (1971a, 20/1). "Yorùbá, in brief, assume that someone who embodies command, coolness, and character is someone extremely beautiful and like unto a god" (1971a, P/5). As individual values they are said to reflect the reconciliation and balance of the underlying cool in that, for example, the form of composure ("coolness" in the last quote) that is valued is vitality (hot) tempered by balance (cool). It is in this way that the aesthetic of the cool underlies and structures the morality of the cool, the beautiful and the good.

That it may be possible to identify and relate the important moral values of the Yorùbá in such neat form is certainly intriguing. But when one examines Thompson's writings for evidence in support of the hypothesis, very little is forthcoming. There are no quotations from informants ("It is not that traditional Yorùbá respond directly to the moral implications of their sculpture " (1971a, 20/3)), evidently because the Yorùbá don't make such statements. When Thompson turns to the myths to, in a sense, make them speak *for* the Yorùbá ("The values of the Yorùbá appear in art and myths" (1971a, 2/1)) his exegesis of the cool as a moral principle is even less convincing than it was as an aesthetic.

He draws his conclusions from brief summaries of two Yorùbá myths which refer to potentially opposing forces, such as heaven and earth and the hot and the cool. The exegesis of myth—reducing poetic literature to discursive form—is a controversial and complex process. For, in effect, it is to determine what a piece of literature means. However, it apparently presents Thompson with no problems. In the paragraph of interpretation immediately following the two summaries (1971a, 2/2), without mention or apparent use of any sort of method, he simply asserts (rather than proves) that they say everything about the cool that his argument requires. In effect, then, he begins the difficult process of exegesis by assuming that his texts mean what he needs to find in them. All of this in two pages (1971a, 2/1–2/2)!

What is perplexing is why it must be primarily Thompson who is doing the assuming. Since he introduced the heading "Yorùbá philosophy," where are the Yorùbá philoso*phers*? Why not let them speak and explain what their myths mean? That Thompson chooses to use the term "philosophy" at all is interesting in view of the numbers of scholars who have argued that traditional thought is essentially non-philosophical. This is a claim that is being challenged repeatedly throughout this text. It was summarized in the opening paragraphs of this chapter: because traditional peoples generally were said to be unable to provide discursive arguments when justifying their beliefs, they were said to be non-reflective or non-critical in nature, and therefore non-philosophical. Academic (Eurocentric-derived) philosophy, on the other hand, *is* said to be critical because one of its primary aims is to analyze, evaluate, and, if possible, improve upon the various kinds of explanatory systems man has developed over the course of history.

A further question, then, is whether Thompson uses the title "Yorùbá philosophy" with a critical or non-critical connotation. His response to this is ambivalent, but interesting nevertheless. He acknowledges that a characteristic of Yorùbá thought is "an overpowering sense of reality where everyday facts have religious and ritual meaning" (1973b, 24). With this he seems to be agreeing that the linkage of a specific belief in Yorùbá thought to a specific type of event in Yorùbá life is fixed and absolute—rarely questioned and therefore relatively non-critical. Shortly thereafter, however, he goes on to note that: "If some traditional Yorùbá are endowed with an overpowering sense of reality, it is difficult to see where their attitude differs from that of clergymen or philosophers in the West" (1973b, 25).

It may be that the academy must suffer the burden of some philosophy instructors who "preach" certain species of criticism as a kind of dogmatic credo and therefore in an essentially non-reflective manner. But resisting (with some difficulty) the temptation to be sidetracked by the sociology of philosophy, let us return to our original question of what it is that Thompson sees as the *philosophical* content of Yorùbá thought, given its "overpowering sense of reality." He claims to have identified important critical elements on the aesthetic level. He claims that the aesthetic should not be divorced from the philosophical. May we then take it that Yorùbá philosophy is critical as well?

Though there is no passage in which Thompson explicitly replies to this question, judging from his practice the answer must be "no." In spite of the fact that he does eventually identify the diviner or *babaláwo* as a kind of Yorùbá philosopher:

> Yorùbá qualitative criteria are consensual. This means that they are matters of opinion, widely shared, but perhaps only fully comprehended by *the guardians of philosophic thought*. The best examples of the latter are the priests of the divination cult.
>
> (1973b, 22; my italics)

For that which the *babaláwo* act as guarantors is that most important echelon of oral tradition—divination literature, which includes numerous "myths." But from Thompson's account of his own relationship with the oral literature, it is clear that the "philosophical" principles he extrapolates from it are products of *his own* insight and imagination rather than the teachings of Yorùbá *babaláwo*:

> Before *I began to examine Yorùbá myth*, I had been exposed to Yorùbá artistic criticism. When I later began reading translations of vernacular collections of *myth* embedded in hunters' ballads and other sources, *I began to see philosophic points*, about composure and reconciliation, parallel to the collective testimony of the critics. *The people of Yorùbáland evaluating their art and their dance taught me to regard the following myths as essential statements of their view of the nature of things.*

> (1971a, 2/1; my emphasis)

One is therefore forced to conclude that it is Thompson who was the initiator of what he terms Yorùbá philosophy, for it was Thompson who "began to see philosophic points." Although he acknowledges a certain indebtedness to the aesthetic "critics" for making him aware of their cultural standards on that level, it was then *his* own genius that enabled *him* to see conceptual parallels and extensions of the aesthetics in Yorùbá oral literature generally.

It is now possible to appreciate the significance of the word "myth" that Thompson uses to describe Yorùbá oral tradition—for him the locus of Yorùbá philosophy. Myths, as a form of expression, belong to the poetic–symbolic level of non-discursive thought. The role of the *babaláwo* or the *oníṣẹ̀gùn*, of the Yorùbá "philosopher," is to act as the reciter and repositor ("guardian") of the myths, proverbs, verses, etc., into which Thompson then proceeds to read meanings. As a result Thompson's own position with reference to the intellectual character of Yorùbá culture appears much more traditional than it at first seemed. The "philosophic" points he attributes to their culture are developed by *him* out of their "poetic" oral literature. He is, in the end, performing another piece of *meta-explanatory* analysis of a *poetic–symbolic* culture; though his conclusions—indeed entire analyses—are often stated in such strong language that one is misled into believing that "traditional" Yorùbá think in the same terms.

Notes

1   "The Western scholar may assign value to a work which would elicit equal praise in the compound of a traditional king, assuming the work and critics were from the same African society, but he cannot assume that the reasons for his choice are present in the mind of the native critic" (Thompson 1973b, 19).

2   The African group Thompson has apparently studied in greatest detail and about whom he has published some of his most original work. In effect, then, his Yorùbá aesthetics serves as the most important cornerstone of his African/Afro-American aesthetics (1984).

3   (1) Midpoint Mimesis; (2) Hypermimesis; (3) Excessive Abstraction; (4) Visibility; (5) Shining Smoothness; (6) Emotional Proportion; (7) Positioning; (8) Composition; (9) Delicacy; (10) Roundness; (11) Protrusions; (12) Nonpleasing Protrusions; (13) Sinister Bulges; (14) Pleasing Angularity; (15) Straightness; (16) Symmetry; (17) Skill; (18) Ephebism (1973b, 31–58).

4   Thompson says these may be kings, priests, or commoners, which would seem to include just about everyone in Yorùbá society (1973b).

5   (1), (2), (3), (6), (7), (8) and (16).

6   For example, a Yorùbá *oníṣègùn* (alternative medical doctor) gave the following explanation of learning: "You know that the hearing is in the *okan* (heart/mind). When you use the ear to hear what they teach you, it goes into the *okan*. If your *okan* 'goes there' [pays attention], you must know that thing. If your *okan* does not 'go there' [pay attention], you cannot know it. It means that you are just 'looking' (*wò*) [i.e., not really concentrating]."

7   Out of 88 interviewed (1973b, 26).

8   Compare with the following explanation given by an informant of something akin to relative mimesis found in Fang culture: "The figure represents no ancestor. There are many skulls in the reliquary. Who should we choose to represent? And who would be satisfied with the choice if his own grandfather should be ignored? The figures were made to warn others that this was 'the box of skulls' and they were made to represent all the ancestors within" (Fernandez 1973, 205).

9   The 1975 article by Pemberton contains some excellent photographs.

10 Thompson also makes reference to a kind of Yorùbá ontology of the cool, according to which everything that "is" exists as the outcome of balanced but opposing cosmic forces.

11 "In Yorùbáland as, I suspect, in most of tropical Africa, people, not objects, are the essence of art"(1971a, P/4).

References

Bascom, William. 1969. *The Yorùbá of Southwestern Nigeria*. New York: Holt, Rinehart and Winston.

Fagg, William. 1963. *Nigerian Images*. New York: Praeger.

Fagg, William. 1965. *Tribes and Forms in African Art*. New York: Tudor Publishing Company.

Fernandez, James. 1973. "The Exposition and Imposition of Order: Artistic Expression in Fang Culture." In *The traditional Artist in African Societies*, edited by Warren d'Azevedo, 194–220. Bloomington: Indiana University Press.

Overing, J. 1987. "Translation as a Creative Process: the Power of the Name." In *Comparative Anthropology*, edited by L. Holy, 70–87. Oxford: Basil Blackwell.

Pemberton, John. 1975. "*Èshù-Ẹ̀lẹ́gbá*: The Yorùbá Trickster God." *African Arts* 9, no. 4: 20–27; 66–70.

Sallis, John. 2002. *On Translation*. Bloomington and Indianapolis: Indiana University Press.

Thompson, Robert Farris. 1971a. *Black Gods and Kings: Yorùbá Art at UCLA*. Los Angeles: Museum and Laboratories of Ethnic Arts and Technology, University of California.

Thompson, Robert Farris. 1971b. "Aesthetics in Traditional Africa." In *Art and Aesthetics in Primitive Societies*, edited by Carol Jopling, 374–81. New York: E. P. Dutton (Reprinted from 1968 *Art News* 66, no. 9 (January): 44–5; 63–6).

Thompson, Robert Farris. 1973a. "Aesthetic of the Cool." *African Arts* VII, no. 1 (Autumn): 40–43; 64–7; 89-91.

Thompson, Robert Farris. 1973b. "Yorùbá Artistic Criticism." In *The Traditional Artist in African Societies*, edited by Warren d'Azevedo, 19–61. Bloomington: Indiana University Press.

Thompson, Robert Farris. 1974. *African Art in Motion*. Los Angeles: University of California Press.

Thompson, Robert Farris. 1984. *Flash of the Spirit: African & Afro-American Art & Philosophy*. New York: Vintage Books.

Wescott, Joan. 1962. "The Sculpture and Myths of Èshù-Ẹlẹ́gbá." *Africa* XXXII, no. 4: 337–554.

Willett, Frank. 1967. *Ifẹ in the History of West African Sculpture*. New York: McGraw Hill.

5

Yorùbá Aesthetic Criteria

Rowland Abiodun and Babatunde Lawal*

Some might assume this should be the most important chapter in this text. That would be the case if one treats the Eurocentric "art for art's sake" orientation and the singular emphasis that places on aesthetic criteria and values as a paradigm that non-Eurocentric cultures are obliged to imitate. It is important to remember that one aim of the present volume is to argue there are a number of topics that are relevant to appreciating the Yorùbá overview of so-called art objects. That can involve learning about the culture's social concerns, cosmos, language, literature, metaphysics, and the methodologies underlying and interconnecting them all. Each chapter in the present volume therefore constitutes a same-sized slice of a pie that must be consumed in its entirety to begin to appreciate the place of art in Yorùbá culture.

Hallen's methodological critique of Thompson does nothing to provide information about the criteria the Yorùbá actually do apply to the creation and valuation of art objects. It would appear that the best people to provide this kind of information, what some have characterized as an "insider's view," would be insiders—Yorùbá—who themselves are art historians. They are fluent in the language and have no need of intermediaries (translators, etc.) to connect with the culture. They know how to undertake fieldwork, participant observation, and other research practices. They are able to have direct access to the

* Rowland Abiodun was appointed Research Fellow in Art and Art History at Great Ifẹ̀ in 1966. He was awarded a Commonwealth Fellowship to attend the University of Toronto, Canada, where he was awarded the MA in Art History in 1969. The title of his thesis was *The Origin of Ifẹ̀ Naturalism*. He returned to Great Ifẹ̀ in 1970.

literature and artistic personalities that enable and enhance superior understanding of these things. They can be resident in the culture in a manner that enables them to exercise these skills while undertaking sustained research projects.

> The fact that the study of African art is relatively recent compared with its counterpart in the West means that it will take some time to identify and articulate all its artistic and aesthetic terms and indigenously derived terms for our immediate use.
>
> (Abiodun 2014, 4)

many indigenous terms that embody important artistic and aesthetic concepts should be given prominence in our studies. To leave out these African names and terms, for whatever reasons, is to make future research in African art difficult if not impossible. But, perhaps, a much worse repercussion would be the creation of an African art field in which African thought and language no longer are considered relevant in understanding African art. By then, we would have unwittingly removed the "African" from "African art," which I believe is the very opposite of our goal.

> (Abiodun 1990, 85–6)

Babatunde Lawal's multifaceted research methodology was outlined in Chapter 2. He also devoted years of fieldwork to identifying the most important artistic criteria which will be summarized later in this chapter. Art historian Rowland Abiodun is another Great Ifẹ̀ scholar who has important things to say about the place of art in Yorùbá culture. In this chapter the primary focus will be on the methodologies he employs. Discussion of applications or the results of his methodologies will for the most part be deferred to Chapter 6, where elements of his findings appear to complement the thinking of another celebrated Great Ifẹ̀ scholar, Wole Soyinka.

> one of my arguments will be that the methodological problems in the study of African art have been created, partially if not wholly, by the conventional divisions among academic disciplines in the humanities in general, which has had the effect of concealing and even eliminating the social and religio-aesthetic foundation of the visual arts.
>
> (Abiodun 2014, 4; passages elided)

Presumably this is another reason why African art objects end up being treated as "art for art's sake." In the academy or the museum the objects tend to be isolated from their wider and deeper cultural foundations. The first task of the African art historian, therefore, is one of restoration: "to identify and articulate all its [African art] artistic and aesthetic terms and indigenously derived paradigms" (2014, 4).

Meanings and paradigms derived from the Yorùbá language will therefore be a key component of Abiodun's methodology. He acknowledges the positive contributions of the numerous Eurocentric scholars who have studied and written about the art of the culture. But when it comes to the appreciation and expression of Yorùbá meanings in foreign languages, serious problems can arise: "I believe that negotiating artistic meaning and aesthetic concepts between two linguistically different cultures cannot be done only from an outsider's language and point of view" (2014, 8).

In this and the next chapter Abiodun's methodology will be treated as operating on two tracks. One involves accessing the highest forms of understanding in the culture, what he describes as "*walking with the elders' (bá àwọn àgbà rìn)*" (1983, 21; Abiodun 2014, 247). Abiodun also renders the meaning of the phrase in English as "taking an interest in traditional procedures and studying them" (Abiodun 1990, 65). One group that serves as exemplars of such sophisticated understanding are the priests who are responsible for Ifá divination. "Ifá priests are intellectuals—knowledgeable of just about everything in the Yorùbá world and beyond it" (Abiodun 2014, 131). It is by associating with such people in a serious manner that a capable individual can achieve the level of cognitive refinement that enables superior understanding. Arising from his own fieldwork, Abiodun is able to specify the faculties that distinguish such individuals generally, as well as the supplementary cognitive refinements that are particular to the artistic and aesthetic consciousness.

The other methodological track involves his use of the culture's literature to understand its art and aesthetics. As an insider and by widening his definition of linguistic, of what expresses meaning, to encompass much more than language/words he arrives at his methodological trademark—"the interrelationship of the *visual and verbal* arts among the Yorùbá of West Africa" (2014, 5; my emphasis). This linkage, between the verbal and visual, is exemplified by the role *oríkì* play in the metaphysics underlying the Yorùbá world. One particularly grievous mistranslation of Yorùbá meanings occurred when the word *oríkì* was rendered into English as "praise poetry." This gives the impression that they represent a lighter form of entertainment. In fact:

> *Oríkì* affirm the identity of almost everything in existence. Thus, *oríkì* extend beyond our traditional categories of two- and three-dimensional arts and color. They include architectural space, dress, music, dance, the performed word, mime, ritual, food, and smell, engaging virtually all the senses.
>
> (2014, 5)

An example of an *oríkì* will be provided in Chapter 6. The more important point here is that there can be *oríkì* that are verbal *and* non-verbal. Art objects are never just a material substance because, as *oríkì*, they are or have metaphysical content that makes them ontological invocations in their own right.

> Yorùbá art, like most African art forms, is more like an active "verb" than a static "noun." Irrespective of whether they are sculpture, shrine paintings, poetry, or performance, Yorùbá art forms are affective—they cause, they influence and transform. Many things happen, not just what one can see, hear, or comprehend at one time.
>
> (2014, 5)

How does this happen? For Abiodun the process of creating an art object is not just physical, involving things like smoothening, straightness, and symmetry. It is also a metaphysical process whereby an *oríkì* is quite literally being created. Artists who are able to do this are intellectually refined as well as exceptionally talented human beings.

Although Abiodun and Babatunde Lawal both have important things to say about Yorùbá aesthetic criteria and values, they have different priorities. Lawal's research prioritizes criteria and values that apply to art objects ("The assessment of outer beauty in artistic representations" (2022, 158)), while Abiodun's prioritizes those that apply to artists ("It is against this background that we can begin to know the artist" (1983, 19)). As a result their respective findings are treated here as complementary. In this chapter the primary focus will be on criteria that relate to art objects. There will be a bit of an overlap because Lawal also identifies some criteria that apply to artists. Those will be listed, but detailed consideration of Rowland Abiodun's criteria relating to artists will become the subject matter of Chapter 6.

Abiodun does have several important things to say about Thompson's method:

> Yorùbá artistic criticism emanates from the highest level of aesthetic consciousness. Not everyone can be an art critic or *amẹwà*, "expert on beauty." This is something that requires a significant and a conscious effort to acquire. The market woman, the *egúngún* audience, the art user, or even the artist will not necessarily be an art critic, even though each may have acquired some rudimentary appreciation of the Yorùbá concept of beauty through a random or accidental encounter with art. To say this is not to deny, of course, that their comments can be interesting, intelligent, and even insightful.
>
> (Abiodun 1990, 65)

The genuinely aesthetic consciousness is limited to the very capable few who have "walked with the elders" and are thereby able to appreciate and/or create the *oríkì* that are linked to the essential natures of art objects. This is in clear disagreement with Thompson's open-ended view of who can qualify as a critic in the culture, a view that seemed to involve potentially everyone on every level of the society.

Abiodun also singles out one of Thompson's eighteen criteria as in need of refinement. That criterion is *dídón* which was translated as "shining smoothness":

> Although other scholars [fn. ref. Thompson] have translated *dídán* as "shining smoothness," I have not done so since it may include rough surfaces, as in *ẹpa* masks, which emphasize color for their

"completeness," or rough-textured, handwoven cloth with attachments of ritual or decorative objects as is often the case in Yorùbá *egúngún* costumes.

(2014, 266)

These considerations cause Abiodun to redefine *DÍDÁN* as FINISHING TOUCH (2014, 266). As for the other seventeen, Abiodun references them only indirectly when he footnotes a later essay by Barry Hallen (1995) that discusses the possible errors arising from "the efforts of prominent Africanist scholars to invent some foreign descriptive terms or words to characterize the aesthetic experience in African art" (2014, 332 fn. 54). Without endorsing any specific consequences of Hallen's point, Abiodun makes it clear he is aware that it addresses a pertinent issue: "Hallen's concern, as I see it, is that African art historians could do more to fulfill all the criteria for a 'good'/'legitimate' cross-cultural description" (2014, 332 fn. 54).

What Abiodun does do is introduce a new criterion, *PÍPÉ*, which he defines as COMPLETENESS (2014, 266). He explains it as follows:

The criterion of *Pípé* requires that art works in a state of disrepair need to be mended and renovated before use, and those beyond repair or badly damaged … are sold to outsiders or thrown away …. In the case of ritual sculptures and objects however, *pípé* would refer more to their potency and efficient functioning in their respective rites or relevant religious contexts. This is achieved through proper care for the objects, which may involve appropriate offerings, ritual bathing, regular "feeding" and clothing, redecoration, and constant acknowledgement through the changing of praise names to keep them ritually potent.

(1983, 23)

How to Reconcile Different Accounts of the Criteria Relating to Art Objects in Yorùbá Culture

To facilitate these comparisons, let's begin with a condensed list of Thompson's original eighteen criteria:

1. *JÍJQRA* (English-language MIDPOINT MIMESIS).
2. [Yorùbá concept??] (English-language HYPERMIMESIS).
3. [Yorùbá concept??] (English-language EXCESSIVE ABSTRACTION).
4. *ÌFARAHÒN* paired with FÍNFÍN (*Ìfarahòn* as English-language VISIBILITY and *Fínfín* as CUTTING OF DETAILS AND FINE POINTS OF EMBELLISHMENT).
5. *IṢÉ DÍDÓN* (English-language SHINING SMOOTHNESS).
6. [Yorùbá concept??] (English-language EMOTIONAL PROPORTION).
7. [Yorùbá concept??] (English-language POSITIONING + PROPORTION).
8. [Yorùbá concept??] (English-language COMPOSITION).
9. *WẸ́/KÉKERÉ/KÉRÉ/TÍNRÍN* (English-language DELICACY).
10. *RÓBÓTÓ* (English-language ROUNDNESS).
11. *YQ* (English-language PROTRUSIONS).
12. *YQ* (English-language NONPLEASING PROTRUSIONS).
13. *WÚ* (English-language SINISTER BULGES).
14. *SÓNṢÓ* (English-language PLEASING ANGULARITY).
15. *GÍGÚN* (English-language STRAIGHTNESS).
16. [Yorùbá concept??] (English-language SYMMETRY).
17. [Yorùbá concept??] (English-language SKILL).
18. *JQ* (English-language EPHEBISM).

For seven of the eighteen Thompson does not indicate concepts in the Yorùbá language. That is odd. That means the seven are inductive generalizations made by Thompson arising from the remarks made by the bystanders, who occasionally are artists, that Thompson ranks as critics.

Based on his own fieldwork Lawal proposes five Yorùbá artistic criteria that are refinements of and/or additions to 6+ of Thompson's own:[1]

1. *ÌFARAHÀN* (which Lawal translates as CLARITY OF MASS (2022, 158), and Thompson translated as 4. VISIBILITY).

2.   *FÍNFÍN* (which Lawal treats as an independent criterion
     and translates as METICULOUS DELINEATION (2022,
     158), and Thompson subsumed under 4. VISIBILITY and
     translated as CUTTING OF DETAILS AND FINE POINTS OF
     EMBELLISHMENT).
3.   *DÍDÓN* (which Lawal translates as RELATIVE LUMINOSITY
     AND DELICACY (2022, 158), which would appear to combine
     Thompson's 5. SHINING SMOOTHNESS and 9. DELICACY;
     Abiodun translates as FINISHING TOUCH (2014, 266)).
4.   *DÍDÓGBA* (In this case Lawal supplies a Yorùbá-language
     equivalent for both COMPOSITION and SYMMETRY
     (2022, 158), while Thompson induces English-language 8.
     COMPOSITION and 16. SYMMETRY as Yorùbá criteria but does
     not provide a Yorùbá-language concept for either).
5.   *GÍGÚN* (which Lawal translates as RELATIVE STRAIGHTNESS
     OF POSTURE, and Thompson as 15. STRAIGHTNESS).
     Then there is the new criterion added by Abiodun:
6.   PÍPÉ (which Abiodun translates as COMPLETENESS).

The following summary observations are relevant:

a.   Lawal is silent about eleven of Thompson's criteria. No further
     inference from this is warranted.
b.   It is noteworthy that the five Yorùbá-language names on which
     Thompson and Lawal agree were provided to Thompson by actual
     Yorùbá artists/carvers rather than casual bystanders.
c.   Thompson's criterion 5, which rules out EXCESSIVE
     ABSTRACTION, would appear to be challenged by Lawal's
     principle of SELECTIVE REALISM. The principle does allow for
     things like highly stylized portrayals of the dearly departed on
     family altars and extremely stylized depictions of ancestors by
     Egúngún masques.
d.   Reviewing Thompson's eleven remaining criteria, the emphasis
     placed on descriptive forms could be said to represent a mild
     variety of *formalism*, even if as criteria they become more than

descriptive and express normative values: 1. Midpoint Mimesis; 2. Hypermimesis; 3. Excessive Abstraction; 6. Emotional Proportion; 7. Positioning; 10. Roundness; 11. Protrusions; 12. Nonpleasing Protrusions; 13. Sinister Bulges; 14. Pleasing Angularity; 18. Ephebism.

e. Thompson's criterion 17. SKILL is too vague to be of value for providing information about what distinguishes the talented artist in the culture. Lawal's and Abiodun's research on this is much more detailed.

Criteria Relating to Artists[2]

Arising from his fieldwork Lawal proposes the following as essential to the artistic consciousness:

ÌMỌ̀ (defined as "mastery of time-honored conventions");
ÌMỌ̀Ọ́ṢE (defined as "technical proficiency");
OJÚ ỌNÀ (defined as "design consciousness");[3]
ÀWÒ (defined as "artist's preliminary contemplation of the raw material");
ÌRÁNTÍ (defined as "pictorial memory necessary for visualizing and objectifying the subject.")

(2001, 501)

The most important point arising from the above is that this material provides reliable evidence the Yorùbá do have at least six specific criteria they honor for the creation and valuation of art objects. As presented here in the abstract they are admittedly of limited informative value. SYMMETRY is a complicated concept in Eurocentric aesthetics. Presumably the same can be said for *DÍDỌ́GBA* in Yorùbá aesthetics. One wonders whether, when those complications are compared, they will prove to be symmetrical or only approximate. The criteria need to be linked to actual art objects to bring them to life. Those sorts of applications can be found in the publications of Rowland Abiodun and Babatunde Lawal.

Notes

1   6+ because Thompson make's *fínfín* a sub-criterion under 4. Visibility.

2   Lawal also provides terminology for a number of steps in the carving process: (1) SÍSÁ ("blocking out"); (2) ONÀLÍLÉ ("tracking forms"); (3) ÀLÉTÚNLÉ ("consolidation"); (4) DÍDÁN ("smoothening"); (5) FÍNFÍN ("incising") (2001, 501). DÍDÁN and FÍNFÍN occur here as things an artist is obliged to do to art objects rather than as attributes of those objects.

3   Lawal in a footnote attributes the identification of this criterion to Abiodun 1990.

References

Abiodun, Rowland. 1983. "Identity and the Artistic Process in Yorùbá Aesthetic Concept of *Iwa*." *Journal of Culture and Ideas* 1, no. 1: 13–30.

Abiodun, Rowland. 1990. "The Future of African Art Studies: An African Perspective." In *African Art Studies: The State of the Discipline*, 63–89. Washington, DC: Smithsonian Institution Press.

Abiodun, Rowland. 2014. *Yorùbá Art and Language: Seeking the African in African Art*. Cambridge: Cambridge University Press.

Hallen, Barry. 1995. "Some Observations about Philosophy, Postmodernism and Art in African Studies." *African Studies Review* 38: 69–80.

Lawal, Babatunde. 2001. "*Àwòrán*: Representing the Self and Its Metaphysical Other in Yorùbá Art." *Art Bulletin* 83, no. 3: 498–526.

Lawal, Babatunde. 2022. "*Ìwàlẹ̀wà*: The Dialectics of Inner and Outer Beauty among the Yorùbá." in *The Language of Beauty in African Art*, edited by Constantine Petridis, 154–61. Chicago: The Art Institute of Chicago.

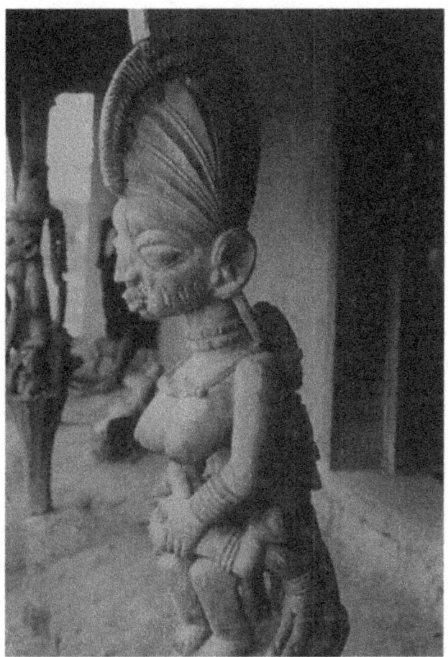

Figure 16 Obo Aiyegunle, Nigeria, Veranda Post by Areogun (Photo: John Picton, 1964)

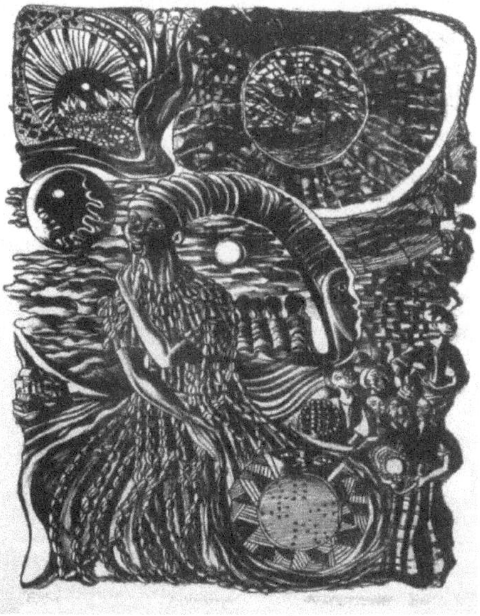

Figure 17 Eṣù by Agbo Folarin (Great Ifẹ̀!) (Photo: John Picton)

6

The Verbal, the Visual, and the Fourth Stage

Rowland Abiodun and Wole Soyinka*

Introduction

The art historians of Great Ifẹ̀ argue that Yorùbá culture has always articulated aesthetic values. For a variety of reasons these values have been underappreciated. This chapter will draw, first, upon the writings of Wole Soyinka, the Nigerian playwright, poet, essayist, and author who was awarded the Nobel Prize for Literature. It will then experiment with synchronizing his views of Yorùbá metaphysics and aesthetics with those of Rowland Abiodun, author of *Yorùbá Art and Language: Seeking the African in African Art*. Finally, epistemological criteria arising from Barry Hallen's *The Good, the Bad and the Beautiful: Discourse about Values in Yorùbá Culture* will also be interrelated.

According to Soyinka there is serious work to be done by Yorùbá scholars if the culture is to recover from the damage done by colonialism and contemporary Eurocentric cultural imperialism. Europeans have failed to understand the true nature of Yorùbá culture. The accounts that one finds in the monographs of anthropologists tend toward the superficial and simplistic. The sometimes implicit but foundational assumption that African people operate on the basis of a different kind of or less developed form of intellect has essentially falsified the

---

* Nobel laureate Wole Soyinka joined Great Ifẹ̀ as Professor of Comparative Literature in 1975.

findings of this supposedly social "science."[1] When discussing the work of a Malian colleague, Yambo Oulouguem, Soyinka puts it this way:

> The quest for and the consequent assertion of the black cultural psyche began as a result of the deliberate propagation of untruths by others, both for racist motives and to disguise their incapacity to penetrate the complex verities of black existence.
>
> (1976, 107)

Yorùbá culture was denigrated by the colonial experience. This is not something that should be consigned to the past, as something that is no longer current. The Yorùbá are still engaged in a process of cultural liberation, and Soyinka aims to make his own contributions to that process. But it will be left to the Yorùbá more generally to disown alien misrepresentations and continue indigenous processes of cultural reflection and repossession: "the right of any community or people to determine what constitutes the progressive or retrogressive aspects of its culture" (1988b, 131).

Soyinka begins by outlining what he describes as the Yorùbá "world-view," and he asks that we not interpret it as some form of "religion." The term "religion" has come to be associated with rather narrowly conceived beliefs and practices in cultures generally. For the Yorùbá, the "world" is better understood as a cosmos, and the principles on the basis of which it is governed or operates constitute an African metaphysical system (1976, 121–2). When discussing the culture generally, as well as "metaphysics" he will also refer to the prominence in it of "philosophy" and "reasoning." Another consequence of the colonial hangover is that Africa's indigenous cultures have been denied entitlement to this kind of terminology. The African intellect has been misrepresented as "intuitive" rather than "rational," and African cultures as "traditional," in the sense that beliefs and practices are said to be resistant to reflection and change. Artists and their audiences in Yorùbá culture are no longer to be denied intellects that reason and think critically:

> a culture whose ... oral history of art records most faithfully the achievements of carvers and griots, whose art criticism, alive till today, distinguishes between the technique and refinements of one

smelter and another, between one father and a son in the same line of profession.

(1975, 43)

One consequence of the reassessment of Yorùbá culture's intellectual character will be that it is no longer assigned to categories that are reserved for cultures that are rated intellectually different and somehow inferior. To be sure the culture may have its intellectual issues—as do Eurocentric cultures—but it must be approached with a supposition of shared rationality and common intellectual integrity firmly in place. This means that Yorùbá and Eurocentric cultures are intellectually on the same level playing field. Soyinka is, in effect, *re*introducing Yorùbá culture to Eurocentric scholarship while also making the noteworthy claim that the culture's insights into life and creativity may privilege certain forms of expression and understanding.

The Yorùbá cosmos is inhabited, most importantly, by deities and human beings. But the deities are not transcendent, as is the case with the Muslim Allah or the Christian God. The Yorùbá deities, in a sense, have their own humanity. They have tried and failed to live with human beings. They can experience the same agonies and uncertainties as human beings. They are subject to the same fundamental principles that govern the cosmos as a whole: "finally, it is the innate humanity of the gods themselves, their bond with man through a common animist relation with nature and phenomena" (Soyinka 1988a, 30). Nature is not something independent, apart from human beings and the deities. All of these principles are essentially interrelated, so that the natural order, and disturbances of that order, can also be moral. All of these principles are elements of Yorùbá metaphysics.

In the Yorùbá cosmos there are powerful forces at work that are difficult, sometimes seemingly impossible, to understand, much less predict and, therefore, that are deeply disturbing. Yet, such forces are also intrinsic to the cosmos and its natural order: "offenses even against nature may be part of the exaction of deeper nature" (1988a, 36). Soyinka names this dimension to experience and/or existence the

"Fourth Stage." There is a deeper level of metaphysical analysis in his writings in which the Fourth Stage represents articulated speculations that represent profound insights by the Yorùbá into the nature of existence and/or experience:

> I shall begin by commemorating the gods for their self-sacrifice on the altar of literature, and in so doing press them into further service on behalf of human society, and its quest for the explication of being.
>
> (1976: 1)

These insights are most importantly expressed by myth and ritual involving both the gods and humanity.[2] This has been underappreciated in accounts of the culture, in part because this kind of subtle insight into and appreciation of existence was not thought to be characteristic of an African world-view. Understanding this about Yorùbá culture by scholars requires an in-depth firsthand experience that has all too often been lacking.

A variety of descriptive terms are associated with the Fourth Stage: tragic, abyss, transition, abnormal, unnatural, disasters, annihilation, dissolution, and so forth. They apply to tragic situations and experiences that can overwhelm the individual or community or deity in any culture. This means there are attributes to the tragic that are universal, but how the tragic is caused, received, interpreted, and responded to can be culturally relative. The experience of acute depression may be a human universal. But the circumstances that occasion it may not be. On a somewhat cross-cultural scale, the abyss Oedipus falls into when he realizes he has murdered his father and fornicated with his mother exemplifies the tragedy of the Fourth Stage:

> The deities stand in the same situation to the living as do the ancestors and the unborn, obeying the same laws, suffering the same agonies and uncertainties, employing the same masonic intelligence of rituals for the perilous plunge into the fourth area of experience, the immeasurable gulf of transition.
>
> (1988a, 32)

In the metaphysics underlying the cosmos, in the natural and moral orders that deities and human beings discover and create, diverse kinds of situations and events can involve the Fourth Stage. An example Soyinka provides involves the deity, Ògún:

> Ògún in his wanderings came to the town of Ire where he was well received, later returning its hospitality when he came to its aid against an enemy. In gratitude he was offered the crown of Ire. He declined and retired into the mountains where he lived in solitude, hunting and farming. Again and again he was importuned by the elders of Ire until he finally consented.
>
> When he first descended among them, the people took to their heels. Ògún presented a face of himself which he hoped would put an end to their persistence. He came down in his leather war-kit, smeared in blood from head to foot. When they had fled he returned to his mountain-lair, satisfied that the lesson had been implanted. Alas, back they came again. They implored him, if he would only come in less terrifying attire, they would welcome him as king and leader. Ògún finally consented. He came down decked in palm fronds and was crowned king. In war after war he led his men to victory. Then, finally, came the day when, during a lull in the battle, our old friend Èṣù the trickster god left a gourd of palm wine for the thirsty deity. Ògún found it exceptionally delicious and drained the gourd to the dregs. In that battle the enemy was routed even faster than usual, the carnage was greater than ever before. But by now, to the drunken god, friend and foe had become confused; he turned on his men and slaughtered them. This was the possibility that had haunted him from the beginning and made him shrink from the role of king over men.

(1976, 29)

One point of this narrative is that even gods can fail, in fact fail disastrously. "It is because of the reality of this gulf, this abyss, so crucial to Yorùbá cosmic ordering, that Ògún becomes a key figure in understanding the Yorùbá metaphysical world" (1976, 31). But that is not the end of the matter. For the gods, as well as human beings, can survive rather than be destroyed by such tragic experiences. That too is a lesson to be learned from the Yorùbá cosmos.

The Fourth Stage is deeply involved with myth and ritual, in their capacities as essential components of Yorùbá metaphysics.[3] Myths and rituals[4] are not the petrified remains of beliefs and practices inherited from ages past:

> the protean [changeable] nature of the symbols of African metaphysics, whether expressed in the idiom of deities, nature events, matter or artifacts, are an obvious boon to the full flow of the imagination.
>
> (1976, 121–2)

This is again that deeper level of understanding to which reference was made. Myths and rituals express reflections of the Yorùbá on a variety of life experiences: "let it always be recalled that myths arise from man's attempt to externalise and communicate his inner intuitions" (1976, 3). One of Soyinka's concerns via his writings is "to transmit through analysis of myth and ritual the self-apprehension of the African world" (1976, ix).

Rituals can be used to relive insights arising from and relevant to the Fourth Stage. They can be viewed as forms of drama, but drama in which the so-called "audience" is as meaningfully involved as the so-called "protagonists." This means there is, in effect, no audience, since everyone involved becomes a protagonist, a participant *in* the drama which is, after all, enacting the drama of life. As with life itself, the form of drama that Soyinka finds particularly insightful, perhaps in any culture, is tragedy. Tragedy in the sense that those involved experience some form of disaster (the abyss) over which, it seems, they have no control:

> Tragedy dares to thrust it [dramatist's lens] beyond [conventional life], suggesting areas of unplumbable mysteries in its passage. It is possible to experience or to penetrate the framework of a world perception from tragedy.
>
> (1976, 55)

There are, it seems, two views of experience here. One can involve deities, individuals, or communities firsthand in real-life situations that relate to experiencing the abyss. The other involves ritual expressions and experiences of the abyss. But given the immediacy of all the participants' involvement it cannot be said to be secondhand experience.

According to Soyinka, the lesson to be learned from the Yorùbá world-view about how to deal with and survive transitioning the abyss is to rely upon the exercise of one's *will*:

> This is the fourth stage, the vortex of archetypes and home of the tragic spirit … nothing rescues man (ancestral, living or unborn) from loss of self within this abyss but a titanic resolution of the *will* … when disasters and conflicts (the material of drama) have crushed and robbed him of self-consciousness and pretensions, he stands in present reality at the spiritual edge of this gulf …. It is at such moments that transitional memory takes over … his struggle and triumph over subsumation through the agency of *will*.
>
> (1988a, 32; my italics)

Exercising one's will in the sense of deliberate choices of attitudes and actions that represent "man's penetrating insight into the final resolution of things and the constant evidence of harmony" (1988a, 33). Such resolve enables those involved to return from the abyss and resume a life of "normalcy," even if now on a bed of tragedy. And it is that bed of tragedy that provides important creative inspiration for the artist:

> Ògún is the embodiment of *Will*, and the *Will* is the paradoxical truth of destructiveness and creativeness in acting man. Only one who has himself undergone the experience of disintegration … can understand and be the force of fusion between the two contradictions.[5] The resulting sensibility is also the sensibility of the artist, and he is a profound artist only to the degree to which he comprehends and expresses this principle of destruction and re-creation.
>
> (1988a, 32–3; my italics)

There is something existential about this. The deity, human being, artist, or community involved has no choice but to become self-determining in order to create as well as survive. There is no external savior. Those involved must face the fact that they have responsibility for themselves and their creations, and muster the resolve to endure and fashion choices that also restore a positive balance to the cosmos. The alternative would be to surrender to negativity, to disaster and annihilation, an absence of creative will that would amount to self-destruction.

The more explicit consequences of all of this for sculpture in the Yorùbá cosmos are profound.[6] One must first dispense with the false portrayal of African, more specifically Yorùbá, artists and sculptors as functioning on the basis of intuition and conservative traditions that dictate the aesthetic. To dismiss this stereotype, Soyinka quotes Leon Damas' caustic portrayal of the consciousness of the "primitive" African sculptor who is lamenting the disappearance of his work into the museums of the Eurocentric world:

> Give my black dolls back to me so that I can play with them.
>
> (1988c, 175)

For a better appreciation of Yorùbá sculpture, he directs our attention to the deity, Ọbàtálá, who is prominently associated with it:

> Ọbàtálá the sculptural god is not the artist of Apollonian illusion but of inner essence … It [Apollonian illusion] is alien to the Ọbàtálá spirit of "*essential*" art …. when we are faced with Yorùbá art … much of it has a similarity in its aesthetic *serenity* to the plastic arts of the Hellenic. Yorùbá traditional art is not ideational however, but "*essential*". It is not the [Apollonian] idea (in religious arts) that is transmitted into wood or interpreted in music or movement, but a quintessence of *inner being*.
>
> (1988a, 27–8; passages conflated; my italics)

When Soyinka refers to "Apollonian illusion," it appears that he is referring to the lifelike appearance of ancient Greek sculpture. What Yorùbá sculpture does share in common with this sculpture is the guise of serenity, by which he appears to mean its external appearance. For the most part there is no obvious evidence of the discord and annihilation symptomatic of the abyss: "Yorùbá 'classical' [his preferred alternative to "traditional"] art is mostly an expression of the Ọbàtálá resolution and human beneficence, utterly devoid, on the surface, of conflict and irruption" (1988a, 35). But the key to such sculptures' appreciation is not its outward plastic form. It is the part it plays in whatever is the appropriate myth and ritual. Then it is in the context that provides the reason it exists:

> What is transmitted in ritual is *essence* and response, the residual energies from the protagonist's excursions into the realm of cosmic *will* which ... charges the community with new strength for action.
>
> (1976, 34; my italics)

The deeper aesthetics associated with the deity Ògún relates to the Fourth Stage. There is another aesthetic dimension that is associated with the deity Ọ̀bàtálá:

> Yorùbá "classical" [preferred alternative to the pejorative "traditional"] is mostly an expression of the Ọ̀bàtálá resolution and human beneficence, utterly devoid, on the surface, of conflict and irruption.
>
> (1988a, 35)

Soyinka refers to this dimension of the aesthetic as involving "the enigmatic wisdom of spiritual *serenity* (1988a, 35; my italics)." By this I take him to mean that Yorùbá classical sculpture is deceptive if its appearance is taken at face value. Presumably there is an aesthetics in Yorùbá culture that governs the formal aspects of this sculpture Soyinka describes as "serene."

As does Soyinka, Rowland Abiodun sees much of Yorùbá sculpture prioritizing inner essence rather than external form. To explain what this involves, he also has recourse to Yorùbá metaphysics. He begins by identifying three elements that are foundational to the world-view and the place of sculpture within it: *iwà*, and *ẹwà*, and *oríkì*. Abiodun tells us that what is truly essential about art objects in the culture is expressed by the Yorùbá phrase *iwà l'ẹwà*. In standard bi-lingual dictionaries one finds *iwà* translated as *nature* or *character*, and *ẹwà* as *beauty*. Abiodun acknowledges that the phrase, *iwà l'ẹwà*, can be used in ordinary discourse with moral intent to compliment a person's character as beautiful/good. But there is a whole other dimension to its use involving art objects with a meaning that is profound, metaphysical.

Since every object as well as person or deity that exists in the Yorùbá cosmos, metaphysically or empirically, is said to have *ìwà*, Abiodun argues it is much more meaningfully translated as "essential nature" (2014, 62). Rather than "beauty," Abiodun argues that the attribution of *ẹwà* indicates that something's essential nature is being truly and successfully expressed or conveyed by it. Art objects are invested with this deeper identity and meaning by the artists who create them. It is this deeper identity that is responsible for and critical to their *non-decorative* roles in the culture. A mask is not able to play a vital role in a masquerade simply because of the way it looks. It is able to *be* the masquerade because of the more special *ìwà* (*nature* now as *essential nature*) that provides its inner *meaning* as *that* mask in *that* masquerade. It is the artist's creative responsibility to ensure that identity and meaning are instilled in and expressed by the form of the created mask or piece, and is what it should be. This then becomes its *ẹwà*.

If a person's or deity's true nature is not being expressed by their representation or behavior, they cannot be said to "have" *ẹwà*. It is when *ìwà* and *ẹwà*, the inner and the outer, are successfully combined, as is again the deeper significance of the *ìwà l'ẹwà* expression, that a person or sculpture succeeds in communicating their/its essential nature. What happens if a piece of sculpture fails to do this? Presumably it should be regarded as inferior or unacceptable, since it fails both metaphysically and aesthetically. What about the person who deliberately conceals and thereby fails to express their *ìwà*? Liars and hypocrites come to mind.

This essence or deeper identity also finds subtle expression via a remarkable genre of chanted oral literature known as *oríkì*. Abiodun's work on the relationship(s) between the visual and the verbal in Yorùbá culture is one of his most important contributions to aesthetics.

> It is said that everything in existence has its own *oríkì* …. for *oríkì* are felt to encapsulate the essential qualities of entities …. They evoke a subject's qualities, go to the heart of it and elicit its inner potency. They are a highly charged form of utterance. Composed to single out and arrest in concentrated language … their utterance energises

and enlivens the hearer. They are "heavy" words, fused together into formulations that have an exceptional density and weight …. All … are felt to evoke the essence of their subjects.

(Barber 1991, 12–13)

At some point *oríkì* came to be misleadingly characterized in the English language as "praise poetry." Abiodun argues that this translation trivializes their status as metaphysical statements and sets out to prove *oríkì* are verbal "keys" that open the portal to, among many other things, the essence of a piece of sculpture.

Oríkì generally play a role in Yorùbá culture that involves far more than sculpture or art. Appreciating this requires those whose intellects have been conditioned by the literacy arising from writing that so dominates Eurocentric cultures to appreciate the entirely different character of metaphysics when expressed by literature in a culture that is significantly oral:

> Above all, for an *oríkì*-text to be apprehended as a text, it must be heard and seen in action. In a sense, as "performance theory" has demonstrated, all oral texts should be thought of as action rather than object, as process rather than pattern. They are fully realised only in the moment of performance. *Oríkì* chants demand this approach more insistently than most forms of oral literature, however. There is a sense in which they are simply not accessible at all viewed as words on a page. They are not texts that "speak for themselves." Their obscurity goes beyond the opacity of particular verbal formulations or references. They are "obscure" because it is what they are *doing* that animates them and gives them their form and significance. Detached from the scene of social action, laid out on the page they may appear to the untutored eye as little more than a jumble of fragments.

(Barber 1991, 7)

In Eurocentric cultures today the performance arts have achieved new prominence. But when a poet is asked to read their work out loud, or a dramatic performance is remarkably impassioned, that remains a form of aesthetic rather than metaphysical experience. When an *oríkì* is expressed, it can be a metaphysical event with powers and consequences that go far beyond the realm of the so-called "empirical." This is perhaps unlikely to be felt by the literate eurocentrist so fortunate as to witness an actual expression (not "performance") of *oríkì*. They may be unable to receive it as anything more than the experience of poetry or song. Hence perhaps the origin of that misleading English-language translation.

Are there occasions in Eurocentric culture that might compare?[7] What about the effects of Hail Mary's in the confessional? What does *saying* them *do*? What takes place when a priest *speaks the words* of Eucharistic consecration over the then transubstantiated bread and wine at Mass? Or *special prayers* meant to affect the growth of vegetation? If these suggested parallels are inadequate or inappropriate, that is further evidence of how difficult it can be to convey this aspect of the Yorùbá metaphysical and aesthetic worlds to an outsider. Furthermore, according to Abiodun, in the Yorùbá cosmos *oríkì* can be more than verbal. An object itself may *be*, may constitute an *oríkì* in its own right. Abiodun uses the phrase "visual invocation" to characterize this:

> In Yorùbá sculpture, the visualization of *oríkì* might take the form of a prescribed body posture like raising one leg or … [a] woman kneeling and holding or lifting up her breasts; the representation of a head with an usually elaborate coiffure; the donning of special dress, colored beads or objects of adornment …
>
> (Abiodun 2014, 65)

At this point a concrete example would be helpful. What follows should be taken with a grain of salt, since it involves the writing down and reading of a piece of literature whose metaphysical power derives most importantly from context and oral presentation. The explanation about to be attempted, relative to the deity Èṣù, is a mélange of Barry Hallen's ideas on the subject from Chapter 4 with those of Abiodun. Èṣù is one of the very few divinities whom the Yorùbá allow to be represented in graven-image form. One of his tasks is to act as communicator between the gods and mankind. Èṣù, the divine mediator between gods, ancestors, spirits, and humankind, is the bearer of the demands of the gods and spirits and the petitions and offerings of humans. In addition to this the Èṣù is well-known as a kind of "trickster" or mischievous troublemaker because of his failures to accurately convey messages between both gods and human beings: "his largely seemingly unpredictable behavior" (Abiodun 2014, 73). Many of his escapades are recounted with humor because the Èṣù is not one to be feared so much as placated. When one encounters unpredicted trouble or calamity, or sometimes good fortune, it may be attributed to his influence. Here is an *oríkì* that addresses the ambivalent and ambiguous dimensions to Èṣù's character:

> *Èshù* turns right into wrong, wrong into right. When he is angry, he hits a stone until it bleeds. When he is angry, he sits on the skin of an ant. When he is angry, he weeps tears of blood. *Èshù* slept in the house— but the house was too small for him. *Èshù* slept on the verandah—but the verandah was too small for him. *Èshù* slept in a nut—at last he could stretch himself. *Èshù* walked through the groundnut farm, the tuft of his hair was just visible. If it had not been for his huge size, he would not be visible at all. Lying down, his head hits the roof. Standing up, he cannot look into the cooking pot. He throws a stone today and kills the bird yesterday.
>
> (2014, 261–2)

One problem with correctly portraying the Èṣù is that he was adopted and altered by Christian missionaries who needed a source of spiritual evil for their Yorùbá converts. To do so they refashioned the Èṣù to take on the identity of the Christian Satan. Correctly identifying his pre-Christian nature, therefore, requires care. This is possible because believers in the indigenous Èṣù remain current.

This concern about his identity is evident in Abiodun's writing. He argues that an important role of the indigenous Èṣù also is to act as the arbiter or reconciler of opposing parties or forces: "true to the *iwà* of Èṣù, unrelated and opposite materials are brought together" (2014: 288).[8] Acknowledging this confirms that the Èṣù is a character who is involved firsthand with contraries and contradictions that may be resolved but sometimes may not because, as his *oríkì* says, he can be involved with a situation where right turns to wrong. It is a fact of life that positive consensus is not always the predictable outcome of disagreement. This would accord with Soyinka's argument that Yorùbá myth is used to represent insights into life itself, in this case that there is always an inescapable element of the indeterminate and the unpredictable.

Visual, sculptural representations of the Èṣù suggest this. He is often colored black, perhaps because things become more obscure in a world that is without light. This is also representative of a character that can be hard to predict—his ever mischievous, potentially deviant nature: "the supra-normal and unusual child who fails to conform to the Yorùbá norm" (2014, 288).[9]

As is the case with Soyinka, the deity Ọbàtálá features prominently in Abiodun's Yorùbá metaphysics and aesthetics. Soyinka argues that the aesthetic values associated with the deity enunciate *serenity*. Abiodun seems to agree: "An *oríkì* describes this [deity] … as patient, silent and without anger, that is, *imperturbable*" (2014, 280; my italics). This should be conjoined with "In most Yorùbá figurative sculpture, the emphasis on a strong, vertical movement, an arresting frontal presence, and a *serene* facial expression" (2014, 267; my italics). Soyinka argues that the aesthetic values associated with this deity emphasize *form*. Abiodun agrees: "[Ọbàtálá] is the supreme expert on identity and the character of *form*" (2014, 281). When Soyinka and Abiodun appear to agree, that perhaps provides added confirmation of their separate findings. But Yorùbá culture is not some easily observed monolith that encourages unanimity of interpretation. One should therefore be prepared for scholars to differ. As Abiodun says, scholarship involving indigenous Yorùbá aesthetics is a work in progress.

An aesthetic that emphasizes the formal character of sculpture while also placing emphasis upon its essential nature might appear inconsistent. Formal, implying the external, and essential nature, the internal. Following both Soyinka and Abiodun, the more important point is that Yorùbá sculpture can be deceptive. The casual or uninformed observer is likely to miss its deeper significance, especially when isolated from its cultural context. This deeper aesthetic is revealed when the superficially serene plays its part in the appropriate deeper ritual. A conclusion that follows is that Yorùbá aesthetics is not something that can be understood on the basis of straightforward empirical observation. Accessing the "true" nature of the culture involves subtlety and sophistication.

Eurocentric cultures have invented categories for different artistic styles or traditions, such as classical, naturalistic, modern, etc. Abiodun argues that these Eurocentric categories are not suitable for the classification of Yorùbá sculpture. He therefore proposes original categories that are more suited to its aesthetics:

Àkó-graphic: a sculptural style that "concerns the idealized and reconstructed [likeness] in the most positive and flattering light; the features are very stylized but their placement and combination look normal" (2014, 226–7). This category would accommodate the famous Ifẹ̀ bronze heads.[10]

Àṣẹ-graphic: this category accommodates most of the sculpture one finds in museums and publications today, the sculpture that Soyinka and Abiodun relate to *serenity*, *form*, *essence*, and the deity Ọ̀bàtálá.

Èpè-graphic: sculpture that represents "destruction … injury … blemishes … imperfections … diseases … unwholesomeness … sickness" (2014: 241). This is the aesthetic that involves Ògún and the tragic and turbulent experiences in a lifetime. Abiodun recognizes this when he writes: "art is not just about beauty that is pleasing or 'good' but about things that move us deeply, whether with awe, fear, dismay, disgust, or joy" (2014, 253). This should be conjoined with: "This would explain the Yorùbá respect for divinities like … Ògún [and] Èṣù … whose appearance or behavior may be perceived as unattractive, immoral, or detrimental in human terms" (2014, 288). This is a category Thompson's criteria would exclude from being art. Abiodun would seem to agree that there is an aesthetic that arises from and relates to this kind of experience. Soyinka may be more explicit about its metaphysical status and consequences.[11] But here Abiodun clearly acknowledges its importance. In any case, the analysis of the verbal and the visual is ongoing.

Abiodun identifies a number of attributes that should characterize the essence of someone who is a superior artist or sculptor. Point of order—their English-language translations may not do them justice: calmness (*ìfarabalè*), teachableness (*ìlutí*), sensitivity (*ìmọjú-mọra*), and steadfastness (*títọ́*). They are therefore attributes of the *ìwà* of a person who is thereby suited to be an artist or sculptor. They must then be conjoined with two other attributes that are the consequences of professional training: insight (*ojú-inú*) and design consciousness (*ojú-ọnà*). Finally, the successful acquisition and demonstration of all of these qualities is said to be the consequence of the even more fundamental essential attributes of patience (*sùúrù*) and gentle character or imperturbability (*ìwàpèlé*).

For those who wish to pursue the matter, Abiodun discusses all of this at greater length (2014, 245–83). What is of primary interest here is that in Yorùbá aesthetics it appears that there is as much emphasis on the *ìwà* or essential nature of the artist or sculptor as there is upon the *ìwà* or essential nature of their sculpture.[12] This is perhaps a consequence of the remarkable emphasis the culture overall places upon the importance of *knowledge* (*ìmọ̀*). The ensuing discussion about this and its consequences for Yorùbá epistemology arises from Barry Hallen's and J. Olubi Sodipo's research involving ordinary language analysis and Yorùbá discourse (Hallen 2000; Hallen and Sodipo 1997).

In Eurocentric epistemological theory the most problematic and controversial subcategory of information is what has come to be known as propositional knowledge. Generally, this is associated with information in written or oral propositional (declarative sentences) form that is supposed to be knowledge and therefore true, but which the individual recipient is in no position to test or to verify. When one reflects upon what a member of Eurocentric society may "learn" in the course of a lifetime, it becomes clear that most people's "knowledge" consists of information they will never ever be in a position to confirm in a firsthand or direct manner. What they "find out" from a history book, "see" via the evening news on television, or "confirm" about a natural law on the basis of one elementary experiment in a high school physics laboratory—all could be (and sometimes are) subject to error, distortion, or outright fabrication.

Propositional *knowledge* is therefore generally characterized as *secondhand*, as information that cannot be tested or proved in a decisive manner by most people who have it and therefore has to be *accepted as true* because it "agrees" with common-sense or because it "corresponds" to or "coheres" with the very limited amount of information that people are able to test and confirm in a firsthand or direct manner. Exactly how this coherence or correspondence is to be defined and ascertained is still a subject of endless wrangling in (Eurocentric) epistemological theory. What is relevant to the present discussion is that this wrangling is evidence of the intellectual concern and discomfort (in academic parlance it becomes one of the "problems" of philosophy) on the part of (Eurocentric) philosophers about the weak evidential basis of so much of the information that people in that culture are conditioned to regard as *knowledge*, as true.

The distinction made in Yorùbá-language culture between putative "knowledge" and putative "belief" reflects a similar concern about the evidential status of firsthand versus secondhand information. Persons are said to "know" (*mọ̀*) or to have "knowledge" (*ìmọ̀*) only of experience they have witnessed in a firsthand or personal manner. The example most frequently cited by discussants, virtually as a paradigm, is visual perception of a scene or an event as it is taking place. "Knowledge" is said to apply to sensory perception generally, even if what may be experienced directly by touch is more limited than is the case with perception. "Knowledge" in a Yorùbá context implies a good deal more than mere sensation, of course. Perception implies cognition as well, meaning that persons concerned must comprehend that and what they are experiencing. The terms "*òótọ̀*"/"*òtítọ́*" are associated with "knowledge" in certain respects that parallel the manner in which "true"/"certain" and "truth"/"certainty" are paired with "know"/"knowledge" in the English language.[13] In the English language "truth" is principally a property of propositional knowledge, of statements human beings make about something. While in Yorùbá "òótǫ́" may be a property of both (oral) *propositions* and *certain forms of experience*. Therefore, in some contexts it is better rendered into English as being "certain" or "certainty."[14]

The Yorùbá noun form that is rendered as "belief," "ìgbàgbǫ́" (and its verb form "gbàgbǫ́"), arises from the conflation of "*gbà*" and "*gbǫ́*." The two components are themselves verbs, the former conventionally translated into English as "received" or "agreed to," and the latter as "heard" or "understood." Yorùbá linguistic conventions suggest that treating this complex term as a synthesis of the English language "understood" (in the sense of cognitive comprehension) and of "agreed to" (in the sense of affirming or accepting new information one now comprehends and accepts as part of one's own store of secondhand information) is perhaps the best way to render its core meaning. "*Ìgbàgbǫ́*" encompasses what one is *not* able "to see for oneself" or to experience in a direct, firsthand manner. For the most part this involves things we are told about or informed of—this is the most conventional sense of "information"—by others.

What makes it different from the English language "believe"/"belief" is that "*ìgbàgbǫ́*" can apply to *everything* that might be construed as *secondhand* information. This would apply to most of what in English-language culture is regarded as propositional knowledge: the things one is taught in the course of a formal education, what one learns from books, from other people and, of particular interest in the special case of the Yorùbá, in specific contexts about oral traditions. While English-language culture decrees that propositional or secondhand information, since classified as "knowledge," should be accepted as *true*, Yorùbá usage is equally insistent that, since classified as *ìgbàgbǫ́* (putative "belief"), it can only be treated as *possibly true (ó ṣe é ṣe)* or untrue *(kò ṣe é ṣe)*.[15]

The consequences of this epistemological framework for Yorùbá aesthetics are of interest. The disturbing experiences distinctive of the Fourth Stage do not seem to be primarily aesthetic even if their consequences can result in original creations on the part of those involved. What is essential to such experiences is that they be firsthand. Merely being told about them, as is the case with the discussion of the Fourth Stage in this text, is very pale by comparison. On the other hand, if the tragic sense indicative of the Fourth Stage is represented by ritual drama and its consequence is to draw the audience "in" so that they too experience (rather than merely witness) it, there would be a transition to firsthand experience. If that does not happen, if some participants are only witnessing a "story" about someone, their encounter would remain as secondhand. The most sensible conclusion, then, is that genuine aesthetic experience must be firsthand. What makes *oríkì* important as components of art and aesthetic experience is that they make the art "come alive" and generate a firsthand experience.

Knowledge of a piece of sculpture's or a person's essential nature (*ìwà*) is said to be obtained, most reliably, from observing (firsthand) their *behavior* (*ìṣesí*). And in Yorùbá discourse "behavior" conventionally extends to "what they say" and "what they do," which also pretty much corresponds to the standard Eurocentric notions of verbal and non-verbal behavior. But what is again in evidence here is the fact that *sculpture is most alive when experienced in the appropriate ritual context*, and that this must be witnessed in a firsthand manner by participants for it to amount to knowledge. The point being that sculptures' verbal and non-verbal behavior, in ritual contexts, is firsthand evidence (*ìmọ̀*) of its essential nature or character (*ìwà*).

The consequences of Rowland Abiodun's Yorùbá aesthetics for the sculptor become evident once one recognizes that the primary source of knowledge is firsthand experience. Firsthand acquaintance with a sculptor and their work becomes fundamental to going beyond secondhand information heard about or from them regarding such matters. In Abiodun's case this would involve behavior evidencing the various qualities he attributes to the superior Yorùbá artist and sculptor. Teachableness (*ìlutí*) implies that they can also articulate their knowledge to others as well as demonstrate it, most importantly, via their work.[16]

The epistemology also has consequences for the statements people make when recounting their aesthetic experiences. A person who makes what is a secondhand statement about aesthetic competence or an experience may be obliged to recount the precise firsthand circumstances thru which he or she came by it. Or did it arise from secondhand information? A person is expected to say whether there is any cause for uncertainty or imprecision about the information. Determining whether the information is derived from the speaker's own firsthand (*ìmọ̀*) or secondhand (*ìgbàgbọ́*) experience is obviously an important part of the epistemic process. A person's diligence in doing all of this could be considered evidence of their character (*ìwà*) generally. At least four behavioral values would seem to be involved: (1) being scrupulous about the epistemological basis for whatever aesthetic matters one claims to know, to believe, or to have no information about; (2) being a good observer, with the emphasis upon cognitive understanding rather than a polite and respectful demeanor; (3) being a good speaker, with the emphasis upon speaking in a positive, thoughtful, and perceptive manner rather than mere elocution; (4) having patience, with the emphasis upon being calm and self-controlled in judgment and intellect rather than merely in manner and demeanor.

It is noteworthy that these values cohere with those articulated by Abiodun above as essential to the *ìwà* of the superior artist or sculptor.[17] Calmness (*ìfarabalè*), teachableness (*ìlutí*), sensitivity (*ìmọjú-mọra*), steadfastness (*títọ́*), patience (*sùúrù*), and gentle character or imperturbability (*ìwàpẹ̀lẹ́*) are *epistemological virtues* as well as *aesthetic criteria* because of their *instrumental* value for promoting the *knowledge* requisite for superior artistry.

That sculpture in the Yorùbá context is so importantly integrated with myth and ritual explains why scholars like Soyinka and Abiodun are unhappy with its being severed from those contexts and hung on the walls of museums. Soyinka refers to a piece he encounters in a museum in Dresden, Germany as in and an "exile" and imaginatively recreates its meaning in a ritual context:

The Nimba mask of the Baga peoples, true to its function, which brings it out at night in massed procession with its companions, rising eight to twelve feet tall in a clearing in the woods, the Nimba is a pure expression of organic dominance. It threatens and encroaches on the viewer's sense of adequate being, leaving no route for the individual except to weld his ego into the security of that community of being, of which these metaphysical symbols are both part and completion.

(1988c, 163)[18]

It is in part to circumvent the fact that African sculpture is being severed from its ritual contexts that it has been revalued by art historians on the basis of what Abiodun refers to as "essentially formalist and self-referential" criteria (2014, 278). It is worth repeating part of the quotation from Chapter 3:

Yorùbá figure carving shows certain very distinctive characteristics. The figures are lively [what happened to serenity?] and show great variety, every posture is attempted, and the trunk and body no longer remain on one axis. Forms are rounded, but are kept clear-cut and decisive; there is the usual African tendency towards enlarged heads and great reduction in the size of the legs. The form of the head is usually unmistakable; the general shape of the face is naturalistic, with pointed chin and large brow; the features are strongly marked ... [and on and on it goes].

(Trowell 1970, 72)[19]

To conclude, Soyinka and Abiodun argue that the effects of European colonialism and Eurocentric cultural imperialism continue to hamper the development, recognition, and appreciation of indigenous Yorùbá aesthetics. Combined, their arguments underline how badly Africa was victimized by outside forces. This helps to explain why they place so much emphasis on the importance of reviving processes of indigenous cultural creation and appreciation.

Philosophy plays a role in the aesthetics of both of these scholars. It is noteworthy they agree that the best way to approach Yorùbá sculpture and aesthetics is via the exegesis of the literature of that culture. For

Soyinka this relates to the substance of myth and ritual. For Abiodun it is the conceptual networks in the language and literature that involve meanings relevant to the creation and appreciation of sculpture. What is clear from their argumentation is that the way Yorùbá sculpture has come to be appreciated in the international community is very different from the way it is appreciated in the culture that is responsible for its creation.

Notes

1 "the traditional one-dimensional conception of African reality, a largely anthropological creation" (Soyinka 1976, 124–5).

2 To promote continuity with previous chapters, Soyinka sees myth as a form of literature and ritual as a form of drama.

3 "Recourse to an indigenous *metaphysics*, a 'cosmological religiosity' or 'inner landscape' has become impossible, because it is deprived of identity by the intellectual conmanship of Europe's anthropologists …. the long heresy of Eurocentric belittlement of black Africa" (Soyinka 1976, 102, my italics; while discussing work of Oulouguem).

4 Bear in mind these are English-language terms that are being journeyed into Yorùbá. In English-language culture "myth" and "ritual" may now have diminished epistemic significance.

5 In a private communication Rowland Abiodun said that he could see similarities between Soyinka's view of will and his views on the Yorùbá concept of the individual's *àṣẹ*.

6 One way to view examples of Yorùbá sculpture is to do a Google search for that topic.

7 Karin Barber rightly regards such verbal efficacy in Yorùbá culture as relevant to the work of philosophers J. L. Austin (1962), H. P. Grice (1075), and John Searle (1969) on English-language usage involving speech *acts* (Barber 1991, 304–5, fn. 6).

8 Here Abiodun is referring to objects attached to a sculpture of the Èṣù.

9 Here Abiodun is referring to a particular manifestation of the Èṣù.

10 Internationally the most famous examples of Yorùbá sculpture are the lifelike, life-size bronze Ifẹ heads. They are few in number by comparison

with the thousands of pieces that fall under Soyinka's Ọbàtálá and Abiodun's *Àṣẹ-graphic* headings. Abiodun is being caustic when he remarks on the tendency to treat these sculptures as anomalies in African art. Soyinka says the following: "The idealist bronze and terra-cotta of Ifẹ̀ which may tempt the comparison implicit in 'Apollonian' [lifelike] died at some now forgotten period, evidence only of the universal surface culture of [royal] courts, never again resurrected. It is alien to the Ọbàtálá Ọbàtálá spirit of 'essential' art" (1988a, 27).

11 "Yorùbá religious art blinds us therefore to the darker powers of the tragic art into which only the participant can truly enter. The grotesquerie of the terror cults misleads the unwary into equating fabricated fears with the exploration of the Yorùbá mind into the mystery of his individual *will* and the intimations of divine suffering to which artistic man is prone" (1988a, 35; my italics).

12 See also Abiodun's discussions of qualities like completeness (*pípé*) and finishing touch (*dídán*) as criteria of sculpture in Chapter 4 and in (2014, 266).

13 The *Dictionary of Modern Yorùbá* compiled by R. C. Abraham (1958) often serves as the standard reference for Yorùbá–English translations of this variety. Abraham treats "òótọ́" as a straightforward equivalent of the English-language "truth," and the same is the case with "ìgbàgbọ́"/"gbàgbọ́" (233) and the English-language "belief"/"believe." Both are examples of the understandably "loose" translation equivalences that are a necessary evil for the conventional, cross-cultural translation of everyday matters, and which cannot afford to take account of all semantic differences, even if they happen to be more than nuances.

14 The author is grateful to W. V. O. Quine for this suggestion.

15 The Yorùbá alternatives would also suggest the novel thesis that what philosophers conventionally refer to as universal propositional attitudes are in fact culturally relative. Such attitudes are represented by the various verbs used to indicate a speaker's predisposition with respect to a particular statement they make. In English-language discourse such attitudes are expressed by: "I *know* that …"; "I *believe* that …"; "I *hope* that …"; "I *doubt* that …"; "I *fear* that …," and so forth. The point being that, if the criteria intrinsic to a natural language (English) that govern such expressions as "I know" or "I believe" can be very different from those of another natural language (Yorùbá)—most obviously as indicated

by the very different status of firsthand versus secondhand experience—
the possibility should be raised that perhaps other words taken to refer
to universal "mental" states or verbal dispositions may be unique and
culturally relatively defined as well.

16 "*Ìlutí* … Used idiomatically it refers to qualities such as teachableness,
obedience, and understanding, all of which are highly esteemed in the
traditional, educational, and apprenticeship systems of the Yorùbá"
(Abiodun 2014, 271). This may prioritize the attitudes of the student, but
that also implies the expertise of the teacher.

17 Reiterating Abiodun's specifications of patience (*sùúrù*) and
imperturbability (*ìfarabalè*) on 15 above.

18 By which he apparently means the sculpture is identified and defined by
aesthetic assessments arising from its physical (formal) characteristics, as
in the Trowell quotation, and does not go beyond comparing it to others
said to be of the same type.

19 Presumably the return of the objects to their cultures of origin would
not involve replication of the "formal" aesthetic status they are accorded
in Eurocentric cultures. That was introduced, in part, to facilitate the
assimilation of objects that were not products of Western culture.

References

Abiodun, Rowland. 2014. *Yorùbá Art and Language: Seeking the African in African Art*. Cambridge: Cambridge University Press.

Abraham, R. C., ed. 1958. *Dictionary of Modern Yorùbá*. London: University of London Press.

Austin, J. L. 1962. *How to Do Things with Words*. Cambridge, MA: Harvard University Press.

Barber, Karin. 1991. *I Could Speak Until Tomorrow: Oríkì, Women, and the Past in a Yoruba Town*. Washington, DC: Smithsonian Institution Press.

Grice, H. P. 1975. 1975. "Logic and Conversation." In *The Logic of Grammar*, edited by Donald Davidson, 64–75. Encino, CA: Dickenson Publishing Co.

Hallen, Barry. 2000. *The Good, the Bad and the Beautiful: Discourse about Values in* Yorùbá *Culture*. Bloomington: Indiana University Press.

Hallen, Barry and J. Olubi Sodipo. 1997. *Knowledge, Belief, and Witchcraft: Analytic Experiments in Africa Philosophy*, rev. ed. Stanford: Stanford University Press.

Searle, John. R. 1969. *Speech Acts: An Essay in the Philosophy of Language.* Cambridge: Cambridge University Press.

Soyinka, Wole. 1975. "Neo-Tarzanism: The Poetics of Pseudo-Tradition." *Transition* 48: 38–44.

Soyinka, Wole. 1976. *Myth, Literature and the African World.* Cambridge: Cambridge University Press.

Soyinka, Wole. 1988a. "The Fourth Stage: Through the Mysteries of Ògún to the Origin of Yorùbá Tragedy." In *Art, Dialogue, and Outrage: Essays on Literature and Culture*, 27–39. New York: Pantheon Books.

Soyinka, Wole. 1988b. "Cross-Currents: The 'New African' After Cultural Encounters." Also in *Art, Dialogue, and Outrage: Essays on Literature and Culture*, 124–33.

Soyinka, Wole. 1988c. "The External Encounter: Ambivalence in African Arts and Literature." Also in *Art, Dialogue, and Outrage: Essays on Literature and Culture*, 163–85.

Trowell, Margaret. 1970. *Classical African Sculpture*, rev. ed. London: Faber and Faber.

Afterword

The glaring misinterpretations in much of the previous scholarship on African art has led a number of Africanist scholars to call for a new approach that emphasizes methodologies derived "from within" the African culture being studied. This is what Rowland Abiodun has done in his landmark book: Yorùbá Art and Language: Seeking the African in African Art, *which sheds light not only on form and meaning but also on the interconnectedness of word and image in Yorùbá culture.*

(Lawal 2020, 188)

In Chapter 5 the contents of this text were compared to pieces of a pie that needed to be consumed and digested before there could be a proper appreciation of art in Yorùbá culture. Here the operative metaphor is that they be regarded as pieces of a puzzle. When pieced together they enable an "insider's view" of art in that culture. J. R. O. Ojo infuses the methodological tools of social anthropology with his linguistic and cultural fluency to highlight the articulated reasoning that is foundational to ceremonies and their component "art" objects. Babatunde Lawal uses the corpus of oral literature to transform ordinary fieldwork into an enterprise that provides metaphysical insights into events mistakenly typed as beyond the realm of reasoned argumentation. Robert Farris Thompson, in search of an "insider's" view, errs when he finds methodological inspiration in a conjecture made about a different African culture by the anthropologist, Paul Bohannan: "And in Tiv-land, almost everyman is a critic" (1961, 94). Barry Hallen and others demonstrate that the methodology Thompson crafts on that basis is flawed and inappropriate for Yorùbá culture. Rowland Abiodun and Babatunde Lawal do succeed in detailing criteria and categories of the artistic that are truly representative of how the Yorùbá value and create art in their culture. Wole Soyinka's penetrating gaze illumines the art of the tragic in a cosmos that is as distinctively Yorùbá as it is human.

There is also an historical dimension to this text. It illustrates how long it is taking for the West to communicate successfully with the Yorùbá in order to understand their art and aesthetics. Initially, the West entertained the possibility that the Yorùbá might be incapable of saying anything of value about these things. Robert Farris Thompson certainly deserves credit for his pioneering effort to open new lines of communication. But those he chose to recognize as critics in too many cases were not competent to act in that capacity. The culture only begins to speak for itself when "insiders" like J. R. O. Ojo, Babatunde Lawal, Rowland Abiodun, and Wole Soyinka mine its deeper resources and put masques in their place, breathe life into its cosmos, relate the visual to the verbal, and reveal the creative force of the tragic.

What this process of communication also evidences is how uncomfortable African scholars can be when compelled to use Eurocentric languages to express African meanings. The convoluted phrasing, sometimes reluctantly and regretfully chosen to render technical Yorùbá meanings, is in too many cases, an approximation, a last recourse, a "lesser of evils." The West has no reason to be complacent about successfully capturing African meanings in its efforts to communicate with the cultures of Africa, since it is responsible for creating a special vocabulary suitable for the description of primitives, traditional peoples, or "others," that proved to be both false (no "there" there) and pejorative in nature.

> The Yorùbá term *ojú inú* (the inner eye) ... refers to the analytical attitude that enables an individual to go beyond surface appearances to the essence of a given subject. As Rowland Abiodun has aptly put it, *ojú inú* connotes a special kind of understanding of a person, thing or situation, and is not usually derived from a common source (1990, 75). In other words, it is an insight gained from both deductive and inductive reasoning. The quality of one's *ojú inú* depends on knowledge (*ìmọ̀*), intellect (*òye*), experience (*ìr íri*), wisdom (*ọgbọ́n*), and power of reasoning (*làákàyè*). The very existence of these terms in the language shows that the Yorùbá are aware that any subject or event is open to critical analysis with a view to revealing concealed meanings or truths.
>
> (Lawal 1996, 255)

Of the attributes associated with being primitive, traditional, or the "Other," it is being less than rational, more than any "other," that causes these scholars to become antagonized when used to define their culture. That is why Ojo is concerned when the culture is typed as essentially *ritualistic* or *mystical* or *magical*. There is a similar reaction to those who say the culture's paramount forms of expression are the *poetic, emotional,* or *symbolic*. That is why Lawal, Abiodun, and Soyinka opt for foundational vocabulary that favors the philosophical: *cosmos, ontology, metaphysics,* and the word *criteria*. Even so, none of these are concepts in the Yorùbá language. They are words Yorùbá scholars writing in English have recourse to, once again, when trying to convey Yorùbá meanings.

References

Abiodun, Rowland. 1990. "The Future of African Art Studies: An African Perspective." In *African Art Studies: The State of the Discipline*, 63–90. Washington D.C.: Smithsonian Institution Press.

Bohanan, Paul. 1961. "Artist and Critic in an African Society." In *The Artist in Tribal Society*, edited by Marian W. Smith, 85–94. New York: Free Press of Glencoe.

Lawal, Babatunde. 1996. *The Gelede Spectacle*. Seattle and London: University of Washington Press.

Lawal, Babatunde. 2020. "One's Head Is One's Creator: The Interconnectedness of Word and Image in Yoruba Art." In *Speaking of Objects: African Art at the Chicago Art Institute*, edited by C. Petridis, 188–95. New Haven, CT and London: Yale University Press

Addendum

The text reproduced here appears to represent the first recorded occasion (1964) when a famous Yorùbá carver was asked to explain some of the criteria applied when creating and evaluating sculpture. It first appeared as original remarks by George Bandele* and comments thereon by John Picton** in the latter's essay, "Art, Identity, and Identification: A Commentary on Yorùbá Art Historical Studies." Robert Farris Thompson had access to it and makes several references to it in the course of his essay in Chapter 3. Picton includes it as a Postscript to his essay and introduces it as follows:

Another document in my possession, worth publishing as a rich source of documentation with regard to discourse about art, is an account of conversations between Father Kevin Carroll[†] and George Bandele, son of Areogun of Osi-Ilọrin and pupil of Oṣamuka. At this time Carroll and Bandele were living and working at Ijẹbu-Igbo. Note: tone accents are not given in this transcription.

a. Who said his work is like a box? Here is a summary of my
conversation on this point with Bandele last week (February 1964):

CARROLL: Do you remember one day in Ilọrọ you and Lamidi were
looking at a post by Ayamola and you made a remark and laughed.
Can you remember now what you said?

---

* George Bandele Areogun (*c.*1910–95) was a Yorùbá master carver who became well known for his work involving Christian themes as well as more traditional pieces.

** John Picton was employed by the Department of Antiquities, Federal Government of Nigeria, 1961–70; the British Museum, 1970–9; and the School of Oriental and Asian Studies of London University, 1979–2003. His research and publication interests include Yorùbá and Edo (Benin) sculpture; Ebira masquerade; textile history; developments in sub-Saharan visual practice since the mid-nineteenth century.

† Kevin Carroll (1920–93) was a Christian missionary with a special interest in and talent for African art. During his years in Nigeria he fostered a number of Yorùbá carvers who produced art focusing on Christian themes.

BANDELE: I said his work was like *otita*?

CARROLL: But you said then "It is like *apoti*."

BANDELE: A ha! In Ekiti we call *otita* also *apoti*. (*otita* is a small stool carved out of a log of wood and keeping its cylindrival shape.)

CARROLL: Do you remember in Ọyẹ you and Lamidi used to stand back from your work to look at it from a distance? Why was that?

BANDELE: *gigun iṣẹ l'a nwo*—we were looking at the straightness of the work; *ki o ma wo*—so it would not be crooked.

CARROLL: But you told me once you wanted to see whether it shone—*dan*.

BANDELE: No. I did not look at the *didan* but the *gigun*. If you remember I was not as good then as I am now. Then I did not know *ọna bibu* as I do now (*ọna bibu = ọna lile*).

b. Here are some points from tape-recorded conversations with Bandele. We were discussing photographs of carvings. Remember the four divisions of work which Bandele insists are common to all carvers everywhere.

> *ọna lile*, which I interpreted as the first blocking out; the verb *le*, or *bu*, the noun *ọna* (which is used for pattern, in a slightly different sense though related); therefore, *le ọna, ọna lile, ọna bibu, bu ọna, ọna lile ti wọn le, lena, buna*, are all phrases from these verbs and nouns, their use depending on grammatical structure.

> *a le tunle*, repeating the *iṣẹ lile*—breaking up the masses into smaller forms and masses; this is my interpretation, the new element being *tun*.

> *didan*: *dan* means smooth, polish, shine (verbs). Technically *iṣẹ didan* means smoothing the forms with knife and chisel (the old tool in Ekiti was *unkan*—the handle and cutting edge formed from one iron bar). But as the phrase used later suggests, *dan* does not refer to the mere physical smoothness—I extended it to the meaning "shine," which, however, I cannot define exactly. *igi didan, dan igi*, depending on grammatical construction.

> *fifin*: this covers various types of knife work; *finfin* is *iṣẹ abẹ fin* (whereas *didan* is *abẹ* and *unkan/siseli*); *iṣẹ fifin, ọna fifin*. Much of the work

under *fifin* (*ara iṣẹ fifin*) cannot be used with the verb *fin*; e.g.—*wọn la oju* (*oju lila*), *ẹnu, ika ọwọ, ika ẹsẹ, ẹti*.

la, usually to "split," here to cut narrow, sharp lines [i.e. to divide eyes from eyelids, mouth and lips, fingers, toes, ears]

wọn lo ike ọwọ—they groove the *ike* (brass anklelts) on the wrists.

wọn ge ibẹbe—they cut the waist beads, and other beads.

won fin irun, ọja ọna—they incise hair, fringe of scarf, patterns.

Various comments of Bandele's using the above terms:

> BANDELE: we know a carver's work is good if he had blocked it out well, *ti o ba ti bu ọna, ti o ba ti lena ibi ọna lile dara*; and by the smoothing-shining, *nipa igi didan*. This one was not well blocked out, *wọn lena rẹ ko dara, o le ona lile ko dara*. They have not smoothed it well, *wọn on dan daru, ko dan dara*.

Discussing the *ọpọn ogun* made by his father (now in his house and in which his tools are still kept) and which his father did not finish (deliberately):

> BANDELE: the mouth remains [i.e., to be done], they have not lined, *la*, it; they have not lined, *la*, the fingers; they have not incised the *ọja wọn o fin ọja*; they have not grooved it, *lilọ ni wọn lọ*; smoothing, he has not smoothed it well, *didan o dan dara*.

[A note of explanation is required here. The *ọ̀pọ́n Ogun* referred to is a figure of a kneeling woman with a bowl carried on her head, sometimes also known as *arugba*, she who carries the calabash of sacred emblems. In this particular case, it was made by Areogun as a receptacle for worn carving tools, and as his personal shrine to Ògún at which he would offer sacrifice. I did not see the *ọ̀pọ́n* in Areogun's house, however, as Bandele had sold it to traders from Ìbàdàn. Fortunately, and quite by chance, it was purchased for the Lagos Museum by Tim Chappel, who by then was its curator. I recognized it from Carroll's account and photographs. The *ọ̀pọ́n* also once contained a brass pectoral mask that had been given by Rotimi Baba Ọlọja of Isare to his daughter at the time of her marriage. These were, of course, Areogun's parents. The mask, and the tools also once kept in it, were not present at the time of its sale to the Lagos Museum and are now missing. There is no known photograph of this mask either.—J. Picton]

Other revealing comments:

> BANDELE: I cannot say which work is better, that of Bamgboye
> or that of my father. Both are good. You know each man's work
> is different. The *ipoju* of one man's work is different from that
> of another, *ipoju lagbaja yatọ fun eyiti alagbabja*; *ipoju* = style,
> manner, *pipa oju*.

Regarding ẹpa masks: [and Carroll noted that] the whole mask can be called *igi*, stick, or *ẹpa*, but if we wish to distinguish the top [i.e., superstructure] from the mask proper, we can call the top *igi*, or *epa*, and the bottom *ikoko*, pot:

> BANDELE: The *ipoju* of the face of the stick is different from the
> *ipoju* of the pot, *ipoju oju igi yatọ fun ipoju ikoko*.

[It should be noted that in the Ọpin area the generic term for masks with a figurative superstructure carved upon a helmet mask is *àgúrù*. The term *ẹpa* is known as the generic term and used of this form elsewhere, but in Ọpin is usually restricted to the name of a particular cult of these masks—J. Picton]

Regarding *ọrun ọwọ*, the neck of the hand, ie. wrist, and *ọrun ori*, the neck of the head, ie., neck:

> BANDELE: if the hand of the stick [ie., sculpture] is good, and the
> neck of the stick upwards, his work will appear, *yọ, han*, good.
> Don't we look at the face of the stick, *oju igi*, first, and then the
> hand, *ọwọ*. Those two places we first take notice of. The body is
> not so difficult.

Supplementary Bibliography

This bibliography is meant to contain a representative sampling of the various methodologies that have been applied to Yorùbá art and aesthetics. It is left to readers to determine which among them would find favor with the four Yorùbá scholars whose work features in this text.

Abimbola, Wande. "Ìwàpèlé: The Concept of Good Character in Ifá Literary Corpus." In *Yorùbá Oral Tradition: Poetry in Music, Dance and Drama*, edited by Wande Abimbola, Ilé-Ifè, Nigeria: Department of African Languages and Literatures, University of Ifè, 1975.

Abimbola, Wande. *Ifá: An Exposition of the Ifá Divination Corpus*. Ibadan, Nigeria: Oxford University Press, 1976.

Abiodun, Rowland. "Ifá Art Objects: An Interpretation Based on Oral Tradition." In *Yorùbá Oral Tradition: Poetry in Music, Dance and Drama*, edited by Wande Abimbola, 421–68. Ilé-Ifè, Nigeria: Department of African Languages and Literatures, University of Ifè, 1975.

Abiodun, Rowland. "Naturalism in 'Primitive' Art: A Survey of Attitudes." *Odù* 11, no. 1 (1975): 129–36.

Abiodun, Rowland. "A Reconsideration of the Function of Àkó, Second Burial Effigy in Òwò." *AFRICA: Journal of the International African Institute* 46, no. 1 (1976): 4–20.

Abiodun, Rowland. "*Orí* Divinity: Its Worship, Symbolism and Artistic Manifestation." In *Proceedings of the World Conference on Òrìsà Tradition*, 484–515. Ifè: Department of African Languages and Literatures, University of Ifè, 1981.

Abiodun, Rowland. "Identity and the Artistic Process in Yorùbá Aesthetic Concept of *Ìwà*." *Journal of Cultures and Ideas* 1, no. 1 (1983): 13–30.

Abiodun, Rowland. "Verbal and Visual Metaphors: Mythical Allusions in Yorùbá Ritualistic Art of *Orí*." *Word and Image* 3, no. 3 (1987): 252–70.

Abiodun, Rowland. "Woman in Yorùbá Religious Images." *African Languages and Cultures* 2, no. 1 (1989): 1–18.

Abiodun, Rowland. "The Future of African Art Studies: An African Perspective." In *African Art Studies: The State of the Discipline*, 63–90. Washington, D.C.: Smithsonian Institution Press, 1990.

Abiodun, Rowland. *Conversations on Yorùbá Culture*: "A Young Man Can Have the Embroidered Gown of an Elder, but He Can't Have the Rags of an Elder," with Ulli Beier. Bayreuth, Germany: Iwalewa Haus, University of Bayreuth, 1991.

Abiodun, Rowland. "Introduction: An African(?) Art History: Promising Theoretical Approaches in Yorùbá Art Studies." In *The Yorùbá Artist*, edited by R. Abiodun, H. J. Drewal, and J. Pemberton, 37–47. Washington, D.C.: Smithsonian Institution Press, 1994.

Abiodun, Rowland. "Understanding Yorùbá Art and Aesthetics: The Concept of Àṣẹ." *African Arts* XXVII, no. 3 (1994): 68–78; 102–3.

Abiodun, Rowland. *What Follows Six Is More than Seven: Understanding African Art*. London: British Museum Press, 1995.

Abiodun, Rowland. "Preface." In *A History of Art in Africa*. New York: Prentice Hall, and Harry Abrams, 2000.

Abiodun, Rowland. "Riding the Horse of Praise: The Mounted Motif Figure in Ifá Divination Sculpture." In *Insight and Artistry in African Divination*, edited by John Pemberton III, 182–92. Washington, D.C.: Smithsonian Institution Press, 2000.

Abiodun, Rowland. "Hidden Power: Ọ̀ṣun, the Seventeenth *Odù*." In *Ọ̀ṣun across the Waters*, edited by J. M. Murphy and Meimei Sanford, 10–33. Bloomington: Indiana University Press, 2001.

Abiodun, Rowland. "African Aesthetics." *The Journal of Aesthetic Education* 35, no. 4 (2002): 15–24.

Abiodun, Rowland. "Who Was the First to Speak? Insights from Ifá Orature and Sculptural Repertoire." In *Òrìṣà Devotion as World Religion*, edited by J. K. Olupona and Terry Rey, 51–69. Madison, WI: University of Wisconsin Press, 2008.

Abiodun, Rowland. "On the Imperative of Language for Understanding African Art." *Yorùbá Studies Review* (2018): 271–96.

Abiodun, Rowland. "Ògún, the Òrìṣà Whose Fame Is Worldwide." In *Striking Iron: The Art of the African Blacksmiths*. Los Angeles: Fowler Museum, University of California, 2018.

Abiodun, Rowland, H. J. Drewal, and John Pemberton. *Yorùbá Art and Aesthetics*, edited by Lorenz Homberger. Zurich: Center for African Art and the Rietberg Museum, 1991.

Abiodun, Rowland, H. J. Drewal and John Pemberton, eds. *The Yorùbá Artist*. Washington, D.C.: Smithsonian Institution Press, 1994.

Abiodun, Rowland and J. K. Olupona, eds. *Ifá Divination: Knowledge, Power and Performance*. Bloomington and Indianapolis: Indiana University Press, 2016.

Adesanya, A. "Yorùbá Metaphysical Thinking." *Odù* 5 (1958): 36–41.

Akinjogbin, I. A. "The Òyó Empire in the Nineteenth Century—A Reassessment." *Journal of Historical Society of Nigeria* 3, no. 3 (1966): 449–60.

Akiwowo, A. A. "Understanding Interpretative Sociology in the Light of the *Oríkì* of Orunmila." *Journal of Culture and Ideas* 1, no. 1 (1983): 139–57.

Asiwaju, I. "*Gèlèdé* Songs as Sources of Western Yorùbá History." In *Yorùbá Oral Tradition: Poetry in Music, Dance and Drama*, edited by Wande Abimbola. Ifè, Nigeria: University of Ifè Press, 1975.

Asiwaju, I. "*Èfè* Poetry as a Source for Western Yorùbá." Also in *Yorùbá Oral Tradition: Poetry in Music, Dance and Drama*, edited by Wande Abimbola. Ifè, Nigeria: University of Ifè Press, 1975.

Babatunde, E. D. "The *Gèlèdé* Masked Dance and Kétu Society: The Role of the Transvestite Masquerade in Placating Powerful Women while Maintaining the Patrilineal Ideology." In *West African Masks and Cultural Systems*, Vol. 126, edited by S. L. Kasfir. Tervuren, Belgium: Musée Royal de L'Afrique Centrale, 1988.

Babayemi, S. O. *Egúngún among the Òyó Yorùbá*. Ibadan, Nigeria: Ibadan Board Publications, Ltd, 1980.

Barber, Karin. "The Secretion of Oríkì in the Material World." *Passages: A Chronicle of Humanities*, no. 7 (1994): 10–13.

Bascom, W. R. *The Yorùbá of Southwestern Nigeria*. New York: Holt, Rinehart and Winston, 1969.

Bascom, W. R. "A Yorùbá Master Carver: Duga of Meko." In *The Traditional Artist in African Societies*, edited by W. d'Azevedo. Bloomington: Indiana University Press, 1973.

Beier, U. *A Year of Sacred Festivals in One Small Yorùbá Town*. Lagos, Nigeria: Nigeria Magazine Publications, 1959.

Beyioku, A. F. "Historical and Moral Facts about the *Gèlèdé* Cult." A letter dated January 16. Archives, Nigerian Museum, Lagos, Nigeria, 1946.

Blier, Suzanne. *Art and Risk in Ancient Yorùbá*. Cambridge: Cambridge University Press, 2015.

Bowen, T. J. *Grammar and Dictionary of the Yorùbá Language*. (Smithsonian Contributions to Knowledge 98.) Washington, D.C.: Smithsonian Institution, 1858.

Carroll, L. K. "Yorùbá Masks." *Odù* 3 (1956): 3–15.

Carroll, L. K. "Èkìtí Yorùbá Woodcarving." *Odù* 4 (1956): 3–10.

Carroll, L. K. *Yorùbá Religious Carving.* London: Geoffrey Chapman, 1967.

Carroll, L. K. "Art in Wood." In *Sources of Yorùbá History*, edited by S. O. Biobaku, 165–75. Oxford: Clarendon Press, 1973.

Chappel, T. J. H. "Critical Carvers: A Case Study." *Man* 72 (1972): 296–307.

Cole, H. M. and R. F. Thompson. *Bibliography of Yorùbá Sculpture.* Primitive Art Bibliography No. 3. New York: Museum of Primitive Art, 1964.

Cordwell, Justine M. "Naturalism and Stylization in Yorùbá Art." *Magazine of Art* 46, no. 5 (1952): 220–5.

Cordwell, Justine M. "The Art and Aesthetics of the Yorùbá." *African Arts* 16, no. 2 (1983): 56–100.

Crowder, Michael. *The Story of Nigeria.* London: Faber and Faber, 1978.

Drewal, H. J. *African Artistry: Techniques and Aesthetics in* Yorùbá *Culture.* Atlanta, GA: High Museum of Art, 1979.

Drewal, M. T. *Yorùbá Ritual: Performers, Play, Agency.* Bloomington: Indiana University Press, 1992.

Drewal, H. J. and M. T. Drewal. *Gèlèdé: Art and Female Power Among the Yorùbá.* Bloomington: Indiana University Press, 1983.

Drewal, H. J., J. Pemberton, and R. Abiodun. *Yorùbá: Nine Centuries of African Art and Thought.* New York: Center for African Art, 1989.

Fakeye, Lamidi, Bruce Haight, and David H. Curl. *Lamidi Olonade Fakeye: A Retrospective Exhibition and Autobiography.* Holland, MI: DePree Art Center and Gallery, Hope College, 1996.

Hallen, Barry. "Indeterminacy, Ethnophilosophy, Linguistic Philosophy, African Philosophy." *Philosophy* 70, no. 273 (1995): 377–93.

Hallen, Barry. "'My Mercedes Has Four Legs!' 'Traditional' as an Attribute of African Equestrian 'Culture,'" (Illustrations by Carla de Benedetti). In *Horsemen of Africa: History, Iconography, Symbolism*, edited by G. Pezzoli, 49–64. Milan, Italy: Centro Studi Archeologia Africana, 1995 (revised and republished in Hallen, Barry. *African Philosophy: The Analytic Approach*, 275–98. Trenton, NJ: Africa World Press, 2006).

Hallen, Barry. "African Meanings, Western Words." *African Studies Review* 40, no. 1 (1997): 1–11 (revised and republished in *African Philosophy: The Analytic Approach*, 263–74. Trenton, NJ: Africa World Press, 2006).

Hallen, Barry. "Moral Epistemology: When Propositions Come Out of Mouths." *International Philosophical Quarterly* 38, no. 2 (1998): 187–204 (revised and republished as "Moral Values and Epistemological Virtues in an African Philosophy," in 2006 *African Philosophy: The Analytic Approach*, 173–86).

Hallen, Barry. "Aesthetics, African." In *Encyclopedia of Philosophy*, edited by E. Craig and K. A. Appiah. London: Routledge, 1998.

Hallen, Barry. "Yorùbá Epistemology." In *Encyclopedia of Philosophy*, edited by E. Craig and K. A. Appiah. London: Routledge, 1998.

Hallen, Barry. "'Handsome Is as Handsome Does': Interrelations of the Epistemic, the Moral, and the Aesthetic in an African Culture." Invited Panel on Intercultural Perspectives in Aesthetics, *The Proceedings of the 20th World Congress of Philosophy*, Vol. IV, "Philosophies of Religion, Art, and Creativity," edited by Kevin Stoehr, 187–96. Bowling Green State University, KY: Philosophical Documentation Center, 1999 (revised and republished in 2006 *African Philosophy: The Analytic Approach*, 237–48).

Hallen, Barry. *The Good, the Bad, and the Beautiful: Discourse About Values in Yorùbá Culture*. Bloomington: Indiana University Press, 2000.

Hallen, Barry. "Variations on a Theme: Ritual, Performance, Intellect." In *Insight and Artistry: A Cross-Cultural Study of Art and Divination in Central and West Africa*, edited by John Pemberton, 168–74. Washington, D.C.: Smithsonian Institution Press, 2000 (revised and republished in 2006 *African Philosophy: The Analytic Approach*, 187–200).

Hallen, Barry. "Cosmology: African Cosmologies." In *Encyclopedia of Religion*, 2nd edn, edited by Lindsay Jones. New York: Macmillan Reference, 2004.

Hallen, Barry. "Yorùbá Moral Epistemology." Chapter 21 in *A Companion to African Philosophy*, edited by Kwasi Wiredu, 296–303. Malden, MA and Oxford: Blackwell Publishing, 2004.

Hallen, Barry. "Yorùbá Moral Epistemology as the Basis for a Cross-Cultural Ethics." In *Òrìṣà Devotion as World Religion: The Globalization of Yorùbá Religious Culture*, edited by Jacob K. Olupona and Terry Rey, 222–9. Madison: University of Wisconsin Press, 2008.

Hallen, Barry. "African Aesthetics" rev. entry. In *Encyclopedia of Aesthetics*, 2nd edn, edited by Michael Kelly, 37–42. Oxford: Oxford University Press, 2014.

Hallen, Barry. "African Sculpture: Interrelating the Verbal and Visual in Yorùbá Aesthetics." In *Philosophy of Sculpture: Historical Problems, Contemporary Approaches*, edited by Kristin Gjesdal, Fred Rush, and Ingvild Torsen, 93–110. New York: Routledge, 2020.

Hallen, Barry. "The Knowledge that Joins Ethics to Art in Yorùbá Culture." In *Oxford Handbook of Ethics and Art*, edited by James Harold. Oxford: Oxford University Press, 2023.

Hallen, Barry and J. Olubi Sodipo. *Knowledge, Belief, and Witchcraft: Analytic Experiments in African Philosophy*. Stanford, CA: Stanford University Press, 1997.

Harper, Peggy. "The Role of Dance in the *Gèlèdé* Ceremonies of the Village of Ìjió." *Odù* 4 (1976): 67–94.

Harper, Peggy. Combined Peggy Harper [African dance] and Francis Speed [Nigerian photos] Archive, British Library, London, 2003–23.

Horton, Robin. *The Gods as Guests*. Lagos, Nigeria: Nigeria Magazine Publications, 1960.

Ibitokun, B. M. "Ritual and Entertainment: The Case of *Gèlèdé* in Ègbádò-Kétu." *Nigeria Magazine* 36 (1981): 55–63.

Ibitokun, B. M. "The Praise-Names of 'Our Mothers' in Èfè Performances: Classifications and Analysis." *Nigeria Magazine* 55 (1987): 11–13.

Kerchache, J. *Masques Yorùbá, Afrique*. Paris: Galerie Jacques Kerchache, 1973.

Kerchache, J. *Dance as Ritual Drama and Entertainment in the Gèlèdé of the Kétu-Yorùbá Subgroup in West Africa*. Ilé-Ifè, Nigeria: Obafemi Awolowo University Press, 1993.

Lawal, Babatunde. "Some Aspects of Yorùbá Aesthetics." *British Journal of Aesthetics* 15, no. 3 (1974): 239–49 (reprinted in *Art in Small-Scale Societies: A Contemporary Reader*, edited by R. L. Anderson and K. Field. Englewood Cliffs: Prentice Hall, 1993).

Lawal, Babatunde. *Òyìbó: Representations of the Colonialist Other in Yorùbá Art, 1826–1960*. Discussion Papers in African Humanities Series, No. 24. Boston, MA: African Studies Center, Boston University, 1993.

Lawal, Babatunde. *Yorùbá Art Past and Present*, Greensboro, NC: Mattye Reed African Heritage Center, 1995.

Lawal, Babatunde. "Art and Life in Yorùbá Culture." In *Nigerian Art: The Meneghelli Collection*, edited by Anitra Nettleton, 111–14. Johannesburg, South Africa: Totem Galleries, 2002.

Lawal, Babatunde. *Embodying the Sacred in Yorùbá Art: Featuring the Bernard and Pat Wagner Collection*. Atlanta, GA: The High Museum of Art, 2007.

Lawal, Babatunde. "Sustaining the Oneness in their Twoness: Poetics of Twin Figures (*Èrè Ìbejì*) among the Yorùbá." In *Twins in African and Diaspora Cultures: Double Trouble, Twice Blessed*, edited by Philip Peek, 81–98. Bloomington and Indianapolis: Indiana University Press, 2011.

Lawal, Babatunde. "Strong Like Iron; Durable Like Brass: Form, Meaning, and Material Metaphor in the Art of the Yorùbá Ògbóni Society." In *Peace,*

Power and Prestige: African Metalwork, edited by Susan Cooksey, 156–79. Gainesville, FL: University Press of Florida, 2020.

Lawal, Babatunde. "*Ìwàlẹwà*: The Dialectics of Inner and Outer Beauty in Yorùbá Aesthetics." In *Language of Beauty in African Art*, edited by Constantine Petridis, 154–61. Chicago, IL: Art Institute of Chicago and New Haven and London: Yale University Press, 2022.

Mudimbe, V. Y. "African Art as a Question Mark." *African Studies Review* 29, no. 1 (1986): 3–4.

Murray, K. C. "The Artist in Nigerian Tribal Society: A Comment." In *The Artist in Tribal Society*, edited by M. W. Smith. New York: Free Press of Glencoe, 1961.

Ojo, G. J. Afolabi. *Yorùbá Culture: A Geographical Analysis*. London: University of London Press, 1966.

Ojo, J. R. O. "The Anthropological Study of Material Artefacts." Paper presented at the Conference of African Museums (Section VI: Museums and Research), Livingstone, Zambia, July 1972.

Ojo, J. R. O. "Semiological Prospects in *Yorùbá* Art and Ritual." Paper presented at *Seminar on Yorùbá Oral Tradition: Poetry in Music, Dance and Drama*, 112–20. Institute of African Studies, University of Ifẹ̀, 1974.

Ojo, J. R. O. "Folk Taxonomies and Analytical Models: The Classification of *Ẹpa* Type Masquerade Headpieces." Paper presented at the Research Seminar on "Art, Artisans and Societies," University of Leicester, January 1975.

Ojo, J. R. O. "*Amerun Yanyan*, an *Òsanyin* Festival in a Small Ekiti Town." *Nigeria Magazine* 121 (1976): 50–60.

Ojo, J. R. O. "The Hierarchy of Yorùbá Gods: An Aspect of Yorùbá Cosmology." Paper presented at Department of African Languages and Literature Seminar, University of Ifẹ̀, Nigeria, 1978.

Ojo, J. R. O. "The Position of Women in Yorùbá Traditional Society." In *Seminar Papers 1978–79*, 115–38. Department of History, University of Ifẹ̀, 1978/79.

Ojo, J. R. O. "A Note on Yorùbá Aesthetics: Based on Evidence from Oral Literature." Seminar paper presented to Department of Fine Arts, University of Ifẹ̀, 1980.

Ojo, J. R. O. "Headress Warrior (*Ẹpa Ologun*), Nigeria, Yorùbá." In *For Spirits and Kings: African Art from the Paul and Ruth Tishman Collection*, edited by Susan Mullin Vogel and Jerry L. Thompson, 117–18. New York: Metropolitan Museum of Art, 1981.

Ojo, J. R. O. "Traditional African Art and the Anthropologist." In *Yorùbá Images: Essays in Honour of Lamidi Fakeye*, edited by M. Okediji, 1–33. Ifẹ̀, Nigeria: Ifẹ̀ Humanities Society Monograph No. 3, 1988.

Ojo, J. R. O. "A Cross-Cultural Study of Some African Masquerades." In *African Unity: the Cultural Foundations*, edited by Anthony Ijaola Asiwaju and B. O. Oloruntimehin, 119–32. Lagos, Nigeria: Centre for Black and African Arts and Civilization, 1988.

Ojo, J. R. O. "Reflections of War in an Èkítí Ritual." In *War and Peace in Yorùbáland: Selections from Papers Presented on the Centenary of the 1886 Kiriji/Èkítí Parapo Peace Treaty*, edited by A. Akinjogbin, B. Adeniran, O. Adbayo, and I. Olomola, 925–36. Ifẹ̀, Nigeria: University of Ifẹ̀, 1988.

Ojo, J. R. O. "The Origin and Significance of Yorùbá Beaded Crowns." Paper delivered at a public lecture at the National Museum of African Art, June 3, 1990, 14 pp., 1990.

Ojo, J. R. O. "Cultural Variety as a Factor of Creative Diversity in Nigeria, 1823–1892." In *Diversity of Creativity in Nigeria: a Critical Selection from the Proceedings of the 1st International Conference on the Diversity of Creativity in Nigeria*, edited by Bolaji Campbell with R. I. Ibigbami, F. S. O. Aremu, and Agbo Folarin, 211–24. Ifẹ̀, Nigeria: Department of Fine Arts, Obafemi Awolowo University, 1992.

Ojo, J. R. O. "Some Objects Used in Òrìshà Worship." In *Technicians of the Sacred*, edited by Jerome Rothenberg, 145–8. Burbank, CA: University of California Press, 1993.

Ojo, J. R. O. "Humanism in Èkítí Yorùbá Wood Carving: an Appraisal of the Application of European Art Historical Methodology to Indigenous African Art." In *Proceedings of the Kevin Carroll Seminar*, edited by B. Campbell and O. I. Ibigbami. Ifẹ̀: Department of Fine Arts, Obafemi Awolowo University, 1994.

Ojo, J. R. O. "Oral Literature and the Ọ̀yọ́ Yorùbá Cosmos." In *Cultural Studies in Ifẹ̀*, edited by B. Adediran, 127–56. Ilé-Ifẹ̀, Nigeria: Obafemi Awolowo University Centre for Cultural Studies, 1995.

Owerka, Carolyn. *A Bibliography of Yorùbá Art*. New York: Pace Editions, Inc., 1981.

Pemberton, J. and W. B. Fagg. *Yorùbá Sculpture of West Africa*, edited by Bryce Holcombe. New York: Afred A. Knopf, 1982.

Picton, John "On the Invention of 'Traditional' Art." In *Oritameta: Proceedings 1990*, edited by M. Okediji, 9–15. Obafemi Awolowo University,

Ilé-Ifẹ̀: Dept of Fine Arts, 1991 (republished 1992 in *Principles of "Traditional" African Art*, 1–10. Ilé-Ifẹ̀: Bard Books).

Picton, John. "Art, Identity and Identification: A Commentary on Yorùbá Art Historical Studies." In *The Yorùbá Artist: New Theoretical Perspectives on African Art*, edited by Rowland Abiodun, Henry Drewal, and John Pemberton, 1–34. Washington: Smithsonian Institution Press, 1994.

Picton, John. "The Horse and Rider in Yorùbá Art: Images of Conquest and Possession." *The Nigerian Field* 67 (2002): 111–38.

Soyinka, Wole. "Ògún is the Metaphor of My Actual Existence." *River Prawn: Journal of the Literatures* 1 (ca.1975): 26–32.

Soyinka, Wole. "Theatre in African Traditional Culture: Survival Patterns." In *African History and Culture*, edited by Richard Olaniyan, 237–48. Lagos, Nigeria: Longman, 1982.

Soyinka, Wole. "The Crisis of Yorùbá Culture: a Conversation Between Wole Soyinka and Ulli Beier." In *Character Is Beauty: Redefining* Yorùbá *Culture and Identity*, edited by Wole Ogundele, 3–25. Trenton, NJ: Africa World Press, 2001.

Soyinka, Wole. "Òrìshà Liberates the Mind: Wole Soyinka in Conversation with Ulli Beier on Yorùbá Religion." Also in *Character Is Beauty: Redefining Yorùbá Culture and Identity*, edited by Wole Ogundele, 151–62. Trenton, NJ: Africa World Press, 2001.

Soyinka, Wole. *Beyond Aesthetics: Use, Abuse, and Dissonance in African Art Traditions*. New Haven, CT and London: Yale University Press, 2019.

Speed, Francis. *Gẹ̀lẹ̀dẹ́: A* Yorùbá *Masquerade* (color film). Produced for the Institute of African Studies, University of Ifẹ̀, Ilé-Ifẹ̀, Nigeria, 1968 [also see listing under Peggy Harper].

Stevens, P. "Òrìṣà-Nlá Festival." *Nigeria Magazine* 90 (1966): 184–99.

Thompson, Robert Farris. "Abatan: A Master Potter of the Ẹgbádò Yorùbá." In *Tradition and Creativity in Tribal Art*, edited by D. Biebuyck, 120–82. Berkeley, CA: University of California Press, 1969.

Thompson, Robert Farris. "The Sign of the Divine King: An Essay on Yorùbá Bead-Embroidered Crowns with Veil and Bird Decorations." *African Arts* 3, no. 3 (1970): 8–17, 74–80.

Thompson, Robert Farris. *Black Gods and Kings: Yorùbá Art at UCLA*. Los Angeles: Museum and Laboratories of Ethnic Arts and Technology, University of California, 1971.

Thompson, Robert Farris. "Sons of Thunder: Twin Images among the Ọ̀yọ́ and Other Yorùbá Groups." *African Arts* 4, no. 3 (1971): 77–80.

Thompson, Robert Farris. "Aesthetic of the Cool." *African Arts* VII, no. 1 (1973): 40–43; 64–7; 89–91.

van Damme, Wilfried. *Beauty in Context: Towards an Anthropological Approach to Aesthetics.* Leiden: E. J. Brill, 1996.

van Damme, Wilfried. "Do Non-Western Cultures Have Words for Art? Epistemological Prolegomenon to the Comparative Study of Philosophies of Art." In *Proceedings of the Pacific Rim Conference in Transcultural Aesthetics*, edited by Rick Benitez, 96–112. Sydney, Australia: University of Sydney, 1997.

van Damme, Wilfried. "African Verbal Arts and the Study of African Visual Aesthetics." *Research in African Literatures* 31, no. 4 (2000): 8–20.

van Damme, Wilfried. "Western Philosophy and the Study of Aesthetics in African Cultures." In *Africa and Its Significant Others*, edited by I. Hoving, F-W Korsten, and E. van Alphen, 95–106. Leiden: Brill, 2003.

van Damme, Wilfried. "Appendix 1: A Brief History of Research into African Aesthetics." In *The Language of Beauty in African Art*, edited by C. Petridis, 310–12. Chicago: The Art Institute of Chicago, 2022.

van Damme, Wilfried. "Appendix 2: Methods in the Study of African Aesthetics." In *The Language of Beauty in African Art*, edited by C. Petridis, 313–14. Chicago: The Art Institute of Chicago, 2022.

Verger, Pierre Fátúmbí. *Notes Sur le Culte des Òrìṣà et Vodun.* Dakar, Senegal: Institut Francais d'Afrique Noire (I.F.A.N.), 1957.

Willett, F. *Ifẹ̀ in the History of West African Sculpture.* London: Thames and Hudson, 1967.

Willett, F. "An African Sculptor at Work." *African Arts* 11, no. 2 (1978): 28–33, 96.

Picture Credits

Map of Yorùbá Country: Courtesy of Cambridge University Press.

1. Speed Archive Pink M6821/11; copyright The British Library and with thanks to the Speed family.
2. Dallas Museum of Art, bequest of Dorace M. Fichtenbaum.
3. Copyright Louise Speed.
4. Copyright Louise Speed.
5. Copyright Louise Speed.
6. Speed Archive Pink M6812/06: The British Library and with thanks to the Speed family.
7. Speed Archive Green 6818/041: The British Library and with thanks to the Speed family.
8. Speed Archive Green 73002/0019: The British Library and with thanks to the Speed family.
9. Speed Archive Pink M69033/12: The British Library and with thanks to the Speed family.
10. Speed Archive Green 70020/0012: The British Library and with thanks to the Speed family.
11. Speed Archive Green 70020/0018: The British Library and with thanks to the Speed family.
12. Speed Archive Green 73025/0022: The British Library and with thanks to the Speed family.
13. Speed Archive Green 73004/0033: The British Library and with thanks to the Speed family.
14. Speed Archive Green 73004/0007: The British Library and with thanks to the Speed family.
15. Speed Archive Green 73006/0018: The British Library and with thanks to the Speed family.
16. John Picton.
17. John & Sue Picton Collection.

Colour Plates

1.   Dallas Museum of Art, Dallas, Texas.
2.   Speed Archive Pink 2 Colour Slides 2400/0021: The British Library and with thanks to the Speed family.
3.   Speed Archive Pink 1 Colour Slide 4800/0108: The British Library and with thanks to the Speed family.
4.   Speed Archive Pink 1 Colour Slide 4800/0061: The British Library and with thanks to the Speed family.
5.   Speed Archive Green 70020/0006: The British Library and with thanks to the Speed family.
6.   Speed Archive Green 70020/0005: The British Library and with thanks to the Speed family.
7.   John Picton.
8.   The Art Institute of Chicago, USA.